Born in London, Susie Kelly was five when she went to live in Kenya, where she spent the next twenty years, interrupted only by a three-year sentence at boarding school in Surrey.

She is happily married with two children. Home is a farmhouse in South-west France, where she tries, rather futilely, to lead a quiet and organized existence.

BEST FOOT FORWARD

Why would an unfit, fifty-something Englishwoman embark on a solo walk across France from La Rochelle on the west coast to Lake Geneva over the Swiss border? With no experience of hiking or camping, Susie Kelly found out the hard way that it is possible to be overloaded and ill-prepared at the same time. Scorching days, glacial nights, perpetual blisters, inaccurate maps, a leaking tent and an inappropriate sleeping bag were daily vexations, but as she hobbled eastwards, the glory of the French landscape revealed its magic and the kindness of strangers repaid her discomfort in spades.

SUSIE KELLY

BEST FOOT FORWARD

Complete and Unabridged

ULVERSCROFT
Leicester

First published in Great Britain in 2003 by
Transworld Publishers, a division of
The Random House Group Limited
London

First Large Print Edition
published 2004
by arrangement with
Transworld Publishers, a division of
The Random House Group Limited
London

British Library CIP Data

Kelly, Susie
    Best foot forward.—Large print ed.—
Ulverscroft large print series: non-fiction
1. Kelly, Susie—Travel—France
2. Hiking—France 3. Large type books
4. France—Description and travel
I. Title
914.4'0484

ISBN 1–84395–445–1

Published by
F. A. Thorpe (Publishing)
Anstey, Leicestershire
Set by Words & Graphics Ltd.
Anstey, Leicestershire
Printed and bound in Great Britain by
T. J. International Ltd., Padstow, Cornwall

This book is printed on acid-free paper

To all my family, with love

Acknowledgements

I would like to thank all the following who helped me in planning, surviving and writing about my journey:

The remarkable lady named Jennifer Shields — although no words can adequately thank her for all she did;

Terry for his moral and financial support;

The Tourist Offices of the regions of Poitou-Charentes, Limousin, Auvergne, Bourgogne, Rhône-Alpes, Franche-Comté, and the départements of Charente-Maritime, Deux-Sevres, Vienne, Haute-Vienne, Creuse, Allier, Puy de Dôme, Saône-et-Loire, Ain, Jura, and La Maison du Haut-Jura; Tourist Office of Charolles; Tourist Office of St Eloy-les-Mines; Mairie of Suin, all of whom gave me very useful information;

Bill and Gloria Hughes, Carol and Norrie Morrow, Carole Batch, Valérie Neveux and her parents; Frank and Agnes Welsh; Peter and Zoë Egerton-Gable; Janet and John

Nightingale; Ab and Berdien; Martin and Ine; Ron and Anne Turner; Mme Laurence Henrion; Michael Moore;

All the people whose names I never learned who gave me essential cups of water, encouragement and directions, and the restaurants who made me welcome despite my appearance.

Finally, in fairness to those places and campsites of which I may have painted a less than favourable picture, it is only fair to point out that the holiday season proper really starts at the beginning of July, and that it was still early in the year when I passed through. I am certain that all of them, in their season, would be delightful.

BEST FOOT FORWARD

Message posted to Internet, January 1998, 'Free use of French farmhouse in Poitou-Charentes in return for caring for animals (horses, dogs, cat, parrots, geese, fish) for six weeks while owner walks across France.'

Reply   'You must be joking!'

Reply   'My wife and I are prepared to care for your animals. Please give your exact location in Provence, details of local sights, shopping facilities, festivals, and whether transport is provided.'

Reply   'There is no mention of how much you are prepared to pay. I couldn't do it for nothing.'

Reply   'Hi. I saw your message. I am a 16-year-old student studying French, and would like to spend some time in France during the summer to improve the language. I like all animals. Would I be able to bring some friends who also like animals

	and want to improve their French?'
Reply	'I am very sorry. Please disregard my earlier response. You are not in Provence, and my wife doesn't want to do it anyway. Good luck.'
Reply	'I would be ready to look after the three dogs, but definitely no cats as I am allergic. What is the local nightlife like?'
Reply	'I am interested in your ad. I am an American lady from San Antonio, Texas, have kept horses and bred dogs and would very much like to visit France. Hope to hear from you, Jennifer.'

≪ Hi Jennifer. Thanks for your reply. I am an English woman, living in France, who is going to walk from la Rochelle on the Atlantic coast of France to Lake Geneva, just across the French/Swiss border. I anticipate that this will take six weeks; however, it could be longer. My start date is 1 May. My house is undergoing renovation, and is primitive but fairly comfortable. To be honest, I think making this kind of arrangement with someone as far away as Texas, USA, would be rather difficult. I anticipated it would be someone from England, who is already

4

familiar with France. But if you are still interested, let us talk some more. >>

Reply   'Ticket booked. Arriving Paris 10.00 a.m. Thursday 23 April. Jennifer.'

1

The Beginning

In an attempt to withstand the relentlessly penetrating cold of a French January, I had taken to marching briskly around the wintrous lanes and byways in my locality for several hours each day. It tended to be marginally warmer than staying in the house. But when you have started from and arrived at the same point for about the thirtieth time, you begin to feel that there may be more to life than going round in loops, and it was this realization that led me to decide to walk, instead, from one place to a completely different one. At first I thought I would walk round the whole perimeter of the country, but once I looked at the map I could see it would take me a year. On the other hand the nearest coastal point west of home was la

Rochelle, which, if you drew a straight line eastwards, lined up handily with Lake Geneva, only about four hundred miles away, a journey which I estimated should take about six weeks. It was not a project to undertake rashly, so I thought about it very carefully for twenty minutes before going to visit my friend and neighbour Gloria, to announce my intentions.

'Guess what? I'm going to walk across France.'

Gloria liked to get straight to the point. 'When?' she asked.

'May. The weather will be just right then.'

'Good for you,' she replied.

And that was it, really. I started planning. It couldn't require anything more than a bit of common sense, I thought.

There were a few potential snags — I'd never hiked anywhere further than a three-mile radius from my house before, or pitched a tent; I didn't and never would understand how to use a compass; and my level of physical fitness was somewhere on a par with that of Mother Teresa and the Pope. However, by far the largest obstacle to the venture were the animals: two elderly mares, six dogs, a cat, two parrots, some fish and a pair of killer geese, who were going to need someone to take care of them while I was away. Terry couldn't possibly leave his business unattended in England for several weeks; and, well, as a matter of fact, I hadn't actually mentioned the plan to him. I knew perfectly well that if he learnt about it in the early planning stages, it was absolutely certain that he would succeed in talking me out of going, and so all the arrangements had to be set in concrete before I told him what I was doing. Unless I could find someone crazy enough to come and caretake the menagerie, the whole project was not going to happen; so I posted a message to an Internet board and, to my astonishment, netted Jennifer. There was nothing to stop me now.

Over the next four months I rambled around with a backpack laden with dictionaries and encyclopedias masquerading as clothes and a tent. I tried to put in between twelve and twenty miles a day at a steady three miles per hour, and during daylight it all seemed simple. The boots and socks I had carefully chosen were supremely comfortable and I could walk effortlessly for several hours. But at night, in the dark, my sleepless mind wandered over all the potential problems ahead, and a little voice kept saying: 'You can't possibly do this thing, you silly woman. Swallow your pride and admit it,' while another voice assured me: 'There's nothing to it, just a question of putting one foot in front of the other. You said you were going to, now get on and do it.'

When I went to the station to collect Jennifer, the fact that she didn't arrive as scheduled came as no surprise. Seriously expecting a total stranger to travel from Texas into the French unknown was being rather optimistic, and I didn't know whether I was pleased to be off the hook, or disappointed. Another train was due in from Paris in a couple of hours, so I hung around for that, just in case. As the passengers disembarked I skinned my eyes for a lanky cowgirl, but there wasn't one. The human straggle tapered off, and as I turned with a resigned shrug to leave the platform the rattle of little wheels and some gasping drew my attention to the bottom of the stairs. The noises emanated from a short, wide figure clad in jeans and a checked shirt, topped by a huge stetson, with a backpack over her shoulders and a wheeled suitcase behind her. I waved. Her anxious expression converted itself into a brilliant ear-to-ear grin; she plucked off the stetson and jammed it on my head. 'Oh brother, am I glad to see you! I was real worried when I missed the train in Paris — the flight from the States was late getting in. And then when I didn't see a lady in a beret waiting on the platform, I thought I'd made a terrible mistake coming here!' I'd said I'd wear a beret when we met, and had forgotten to do so.

Over a couple of beers Jennifer took in the local scenery, and we started getting to know each other a little. You cannot meet this lady and not instantly adore her. She is necessarily built on generous lines, because she has an enormous heart that embraces every person, beast or plant she meets. Two devilishly blue eyes sparkle from an unlined face that gives no hint that she is a grandmother, or that she has survived numerous major health problems, including cancer involving radical surgery. She married at fifteen, and raised her three children single-handed. Amongst various jobs she had taken to earn her living, she had driven a giant bulldozer in a uranium mine. She radiates warmth and kindness, merriment and dependability. I was quite certain that my menagerie couldn't be in better hands than hers.

I introduced her to Tinkerbelle, my twenty-year-old Citroën 2CV, whose bodywork was mostly held together by patches of corrosion. Jennifer chuckled, 'Oh my, what a cute little car!' and laughed as we bumped and lurched along the roads towards home.

When we reached my slightly less than

half-restored farmhouse, I held my breath. Although I had written to give her a good idea of the state of the property, I wondered whether she would be prepared for the reality, and most particularly the archaic electrical supply, which was composed of numbers of extension leads plugged into each other and snaking their way from room to room, all emanating from a single ancient socket in one wall. 'Oh gee!' Jennifer breathed, gazing at the crumbly stone and flint walls with pieces missing, and the sagging floors. 'Just look at this. This is *real* history. We think the Alamo is old, but this is really something else.' She constantly delighted in everything French — the countryside, the kindness of the people, the food, and the buildings. Everything thrilled her.

To prepare her for her task, we'd agreed to spend a week together before my departure, to give her plenty of time to learn her way around the neighbourhood and the little eccentricities of Tinkerbelle, our animals and the neighbours. We visited the local stores and I introduced her to English friends, so that she wouldn't find herself completely alone once I'd left.

The animals, with the possible exception of the geese, fell instantly under the spell of her soft American voice and gentle, firm approach, and I had no qualms about entrusting them to her care. I wasn't at all sure how she was going to react when she learnt that Bill, my English next-door neighbour, was currently in a French prison, but she was quite unruffled when I told her, and had soon added Bill's wife, Gloria, to the large brood already under her expansive wing.

What made her decision to come to France particularly valiant was the fact that only a few weeks before her departure from the United States, her father had become seriously ill. Following much heart-searching, and with the unreserved encouragement of her family, she had decided to go ahead with the venture, and to stay here for as long as it took for me to cross the country to Lake Geneva. Her arrival in a country she knew nothing of, with a language she could not speak, undertaking to spend several weeks in primitive conditions taking responsibility for twenty assorted animals was breathtakingly heroic.

Once she was comfortably and confidently established, I let Terry in on the project, and despite his initial expostulations once he had met Jennifer he conceded graciously to my mad whim, whilst telling me I was absolutely crazy and he would be worried out of his mind while I was away.

'Don't be silly,' I said breezily. 'I've planned this thing quite meticulously and know exactly what I'm doing. Nothing can possibly go wrong.'

★ ★ ★

An essential factor in the enjoyment and successful outcome of my journey was the weather, which had to be not too cold, because I hate the cold, and not too hot because I keel over at anything much above 70°F. Having estimated the journey would take six weeks, I believed I would reach Lake Geneva before the blistering heat of summer if I departed on 1 May, when the weather would, I also believed, have settled to a pleasant dry mildness.

And so it came to pass that I stood damp and shivering on the cobblestoned quayside of la Rochelle in the Bay of Biscay, weighed down with a backpack I could hardly lift and looking at a journey of upwards of four hundred miles across terrain I knew almost nothing about, in a shroud of persistent drizzle driven by an Arctic wind, wishing that I was almost anywhere else. I wished too that I had kept my silly mouth closed back on that cold January day, and that someone would dissuade me, at this late stage, from my self-imposed madness; I would resist at first, protest a little, but gradually allow common sense to prevail, and with an outward reluctance hiding an internal whoop of relief would heft the backpack into the car and go home.

Nobody would be surprised — I knew that most people didn't believe I could or would do what I had said. And that was the main factor that drove me onwards — that, and the fact that nobody made any attempt to talk me out of it.

There weren't many people in la Rochelle that morning of 1 May, a public holiday marking the ancient pagan celebration of the start of the summer, and the modern-day recognition of the struggle for working-class rights. It is traditional in France, on this day, to offer friends posies of lily of the valley, and the flower vendors hunched over their loaded handcarts on the chilly street corners. The narrow lanes were bordered by splendid mansions, embellished with outlandish gargoyles of dolphins, lions and griffins, and the fifteenth-century timbered houses that were once the homes of wealthy merchants. La Rochelle had grown from a small fishing village in the eleventh century to become one of the premier ports on the Atlantic coast. It was a rebellious and independent town that minted its own coins and raised its own army, and when Protestantism was born in the early sixteenth century the people of la Rochelle embraced the new religion, which promoted a freedom of thought and deed quite different from the strict demands of the Roman Catholic Church. The town became a haven for the Huguenot Protestants, and an ally of France's great enemy, England. In the seventeenth century la Rochelle's power and independence was a thorn in the malevolent flesh of Catherine de' Medici, regent of France, and the town had to be brought to heel. Besieged by land and sea by Cardinal Richelieu and cut off from any outside aid, over a period of several months 23,000 of the original 28,000 inhabitants starved to death. The survivors surrendered.

A blend of history and high-tech, today la Rochelle is the Atlantic home of the super-yachts, with a harbour depth that can accommodate a draught of up to sixteen feet, and hosts major national and international nautical events throughout the year. The town has pioneered the use of electric vehicles; distinctive little yellow cars, and scooters, are available for daily hire; the urban dustcarts are electrically driven, as too are the ferries. The fishing industry thrives, as does heavy industry manufacturing amongst other things the high-speed TGV trains. It is one of France's largest tourist destinations and, with its dozens of theatres and music festivals, a cultural centre par excellence. Restaurants abound in the streets of the old town and around the harbour. It has several museums, a magnificent aquarium, and one of the sunniest climates in the country.

From this harbour, protected for more than six centuries by the great towers of la Chaine and St Nicolas, pirates and merchants have sailed away. Explorers ancient and modern have left from here to find Asia, Africa and the New World in their quests for adventure, wealth and knowledge. The seamen of la Rochelle were famed for their bravery and expertise; 'they brave the seas, control the storms and, despite all the anger that the winds can muster, they sail beyond the Sun' (Gaufreteau). Every one of them differed from me in one respect. They had all headed west. But then they had ships. If you don't, you've got to go east or drown, especially carrying a backpack and wearing heavy boots.

A few soggy tourists were braving the unspeakable weather in a spirited attempt to enjoy themselves, and behind a muffled loudhailer groups of chanting trades unionists, Communists and miscellaneous protesters trudged damply, half-heartedly waving droopy flags. My husband Terry, Jennifer and Gloria had come to see me off, and my friend Carole, who planned on meeting up with me five weeks later so we could cross the Jura mountain range together. They all transparently thought I was quite mad, but after two hours of coffee-drinking none of them had tried to change my mind and I knew there was no way out. We walked past the yachts that swayed and clinked amongst a flotilla of mysteriously dead fish, and I didn't push either of Carole's frightful little boys in. I'd have quite liked to; I was allergic to them — they made my hands itch every time I saw them. Now they were becoming increasingly, unhappily vocal. It was a good moment to leave. You just cannot imagine what those kids were capable of when they were upset.

We hugged and kissed. Terry tightened my bootlaces and hoisted the backpack into place and Jennifer pressed into my hand a small brass box containing her lucky tiger-eye, which I stowed in my fanny pack with the camera and tape recorder. You might think, with la Rochelle being such an important departure place for travellers to all corners of the globe, that there would have been some indication of where to start looking for Geneva, but there wasn't. You had to work it out for yourself. There was a small canal pointing in an easterly direction, so following Terry's advice I set off alongside it clenching a five-foot-long wooden hiking stick in my fist, with a nine-inch folding knife in my pocket so that I could kill someone if I had to. Actually I carried three knives — one with a very sharp stabbing point, one with sharp serrations, and a jungle-camouflaged flick knife that looked lethal and made a sinister hiss when opened, but was in fact little more than a glorified penknife.

After two hundred yards the canal disappeared, just disappeared into nowhere. Suddenly, it simply wasn't there. I should have recognized that this was prophetic. I scrambled down an embankment and up the other side, arriving on a major road, where a bicycle drew alongside and a beaming black man with shoulder-length dread-locks slowed his pace to mine.

'Where are you going?' he asked in French, in a flowing honey voice.

'Geneva.'

He wobbled slightly. 'Geneva where?'

'Geneva in Switzerland.'

'All alone? Like that? Walking all the way?'

'Yes, that's right.'

'English?'

'Yes.'

He shook his head and peeled away with a *'Bon courage'* and, rather disconcertingly, I could hear him laughing wildly as he vanished into the distance.

For the next couple of hours I wandered around in the immaculately clean and tidy industrial zone trying to work out where I was, with not a lot of success. It was by luck that eventually I found a place that was marked on the map, a neat residential area not too far off-track from where I was meant to be. There was an unfamiliar niggle on my right little toe that needed to be investigated, so I sat down on a convenient stone bench. Apart from reaching Lake Geneva, my other target was to transform my unsatisfactory physical shape into something more like Elle MacPherson, by dint of massive exercise coupled with spartan meals. In the backpack was an assortment of high-energy cereal bars and dried fruit — enough, I had planned, for six nutritious non-fattening breakfasts or midday meals. Many of the pre-packaged meals manufactured for hikers were meat-based. There wasn't a very exciting choice for someone like myself, a vegetarian who eats a little fish. The French still being a predominantly carnivorous race, shopping is never easy for a vegetarian on the move, and normally means bread, cheese, cakes and fruit, with which, in a tent and on a small single-burner stove, you are somewhat limited as to novel ideas.

After I had satisfied a deeply hollow feeling between my neck and my legs, there was just enough left for two meals if I ate sparingly. The niggly toe was bad news — it sported a raw red patch with peely skin over it, something it had never done before. Why today? Why now? I slapped a plaster on it and set off again for my first destination, Saint-Christophe.

Not long afterwards I found myself walking along a busy main road, instead of the quiet footpath which, despite being well marked on the map, didn't seem to exist. There was a very narrow strip of grass beside the road, prettily scattered with daisies, buttercups, dandelions already turned to fairy colonies, bluebells and cowslips, cow parsley still green, and purple vetch, all struggling to avoid being crushed on the tarmac. It was just their bad luck that I came along in my gigantic hiking boots, because I am pretty certain that very few people had ever been misguided enough to walk on the side of this particular road. Fast, heavy holiday traffic handled with what the drivers probably thought of as panache, but which anybody else would regard as homicidal mania, compelled me to leap sideways into the knee-high grass to avoid an accident every time a vehicle passed. It wasn't terribly easy jumping about with the load strapped to my back, especially when trying at the same time not to land on the poor flowers. Passing motorists watched me curiously.

Whether there is anything of historical or other importance about Saint-Christophe, I do not know — I hadn't been able to find a single fact about it in any guidebook or the entire worldwide web. It is a small and well-kept village of approximately nine hundred inhabitants, with a fine campsite that was my reason for being there. It was indeed the only village with a currently open campsite within a day's walk of la Rochelle, although walking was not what I was doing by the time I arrived. Both feet, the left one particularly, felt as if they had come fresh from a session with the world bastinado champion; the backpack weighed four times what it had when I set off, despite my having eaten most of the food it had held, and my right hip was emitting a rhythmic clicking-grating sound. Walk? I could barely stand. The last four miles had taken nearly three hours to cover, as I limped, clicked, shuffled, sat on tree stumps, and constantly adjusted the backpack straps in a hopeless bid to make it lighter.

The exquisite delight of unstrapping the pack, holding it for a moment longer than necessary, while savouring the anticipation of dropping it to the ground, and the supreme joy of unlacing and removing the boots is something that I will remember for the rest of my life. From the lake beside the campsite a couple of dozen men, women and children engaged in a fishing contest watched as I shook the tent from its cocoon. I slid the single telescopic fibreglass pole into the channel designed for the purpose and pushed the six metal pegs through the loops of the tent and into the soft mown lawn of the camping area as nonchalantly as if it were something I had done for years, and not just once before, on the living room floor. After admiring my new home I hobbled over the grass in my socks to the bar where a trio of knitting ladies sat clicking and chattering. They asked where I was heading for, and shook their collective heads in puzzlement when I said Lake Geneva.

'Where is that exactly?' asked one.

'It's in Switzerland,' I said.

'Geneva! You mean *Geneva*?'

I nodded.

'*Oh, là là!*' they cried. '*Oh, là là!*' and standing in unison they waved wildly to a large figure across the lake, who detached himself from his fishing line and, with a film-star smile of perfect white and gold teeth and an outstretched hand, introduced himself as the mayor of Saint-Christophe. Was the campsite to my liking, he was kind enough to ask. Looking at the velvet lawns, immaculately symmetrical hedges and spotless sanitary block, I couldn't fault it, other than that it was totally bereft of any other campers. During the planning stages of this safari I had imagined arriving at campsites and finding them full, and had devised contingency plans (bursting into tears, collapsing, throwing myself on the mercy of other campers). He asked about my plans and nodded solemnly as I explained I would be leaving in the morning en route to Geneva.

'Please enjoy your stay, and let me know if you need anything. There is no charge. My house is just there.' He pointed to a rooftop. 'I wish you a pleasant evening and a safe journey.'

I bought a couple of chilled beers from the knitting ladies and crawled into the tent, where I lay for half an hour, listening to the songs of the wild birds, occasional shouts from the fishing contestants, and the despairing wail of a peacock from the grounds of a nearby house. But mostly I was enjoying the relief from the weight of the backpack and the torture of walking, while idly wondering why today had been so unlike all the previous days of training, when the weight hadn't been a problem and my feet hadn't hurt.

When I tried to sit up, I found I had developed the flexibility of a railway sleeper. It was like rigor mortis — nothing would bend. I could neither sit, nor kneel, nor roll over. Nothing moved but my hands and eyes, and like a paralysed insect I lay on my back wondering what to do next. Maybe if I shouted loud enough the knitting ladies would hear and come to the rescue? But how damned stupid I would look. Finally, by grasping the legs of my jeans and heaving and writhing frantically, I managed to pull myself upright, and after a series of laborious and intricate manoeuvres like a metamorphosing pupa I emerged from the cocoon of my tent to take a blissful steamy shower that rinsed away the aches from my shoulders.

I wondered how Jennifer was adjusting to her new life-style. I gave her a call.

'How are you doing?' I asked.

'I'm doing just great. I have to tell you, when we watched you fading into the distance today we were all thinking the same thing: are you sure you want to do this?'

'I still want to do it. Today went really well,' I lied. 'Are the animals behaving?'

'Oh, they played around a bit. I went down the lane to bring the horses home. I had no trouble getting them back to the paddock but when I got there Leila spooked and scared Cindy, and she took off running with her halter and rope still attached. Every time I got close to Cindy, Leila would take off again and Cindy would be right behind her. I did finally get them both in a corner and Cindy stepped on her rope. I had just taken it off when the two geese came charging after me.'

'Well, it sounds as if they're testing you. I hope they don't give you too much grief. I'll call you tomorrow and see you again in a few days.' My route eastwards passed within a few kilometres of home, so I was going to make a brief stopover there to see how Jennifer and the animals were managing without me.

'Take care now.'

Dinner came out of a vacuum-packed aluminium envelope which promised that if you half filled it with boiling water it would transform itself into a delicious meal of pasta and vegetables. This was only partially true; it did transform itself into something, but delicious it was not. I certainly wouldn't ever want to have to eat it again. I reached for an open beer bottle and successfully sent it flying over sleeping bag, floor and scattered clothes, but by now I was too tired to care, so leaving it to disappear osmotically I slithered into my moist bedding and settled down with a torch and book.

When dusk arrived, the frosted creamy orbs of the campsite lights came on and glowed comfortingly through the night. There was no sound at all. Apart from the weather, my feet, the weight of the backpack and navigational difficulties, for the first day things could have been worse. Not much, though.

2

How Do You Say Merde in English?

The night was very cold and the ground was very hard and those conditions were not conducive to a good night's sleep. In the darkness the tent felt strangely clammy and wet, and as daylight arrived I could see a hundred rivulets of condensation racing each other in wiggly tracks down the walls, to join their predecessors and the remains of the beer in puddles on the floor, from where they seeped into my scattered belongings. My hair was wet. So were the too-thin mattress and far-too-thin sleeping bag. Outside it was a cold, damp and grey day exactly like the thirty-three that had gone before, so I swathed myself in a woolly vest, two T-shirts, sweatshirt and jeans, none of which were quite dry. While waiting for the water to boil for a cup of coffee, I draped my fragrant wet clothing and sleeping bag optimistically over the hedge in the hope that they would dry, and went to do some shopping.

In the centre of the village a sign on the corner of the building read *Bar/café/épicerie*[1]. Inside, a man polished glasses behind a bar.

'Good morning. Do you sell food?' I asked.

'No, not here. You must go to the *épicerie*, just round the corner.' He pointed to the door through which I had just come in.

I exited and went round the corner and in through another door which led to the area behind the bar. The same man was waiting there, still polishing glasses. There were tins of meat, jars of meat, frozen meat, fresh meat in slices, lumps and chunks, and not a lot else apart from some large heavy tins of beans. Confident that there would be somewhere en route where I could buy some bread and cheese for lunch, however, I wasn't too worried, so I bought a bag of peanuts and some stock cubes, out of politeness.

The clothing and sleeping bag were as dry as they were likely to get, so I pushed them into the backpack. They didn't want to fit, but I pushed them really hard. They had fitted yesterday. As I tugged the final zip closed, the tag came off in my hand.

---

[1] grocery

The sun displayed itself for microseconds between jagged cracks in the grey clouds, and emitted no warmth at all, and I set off with a slightly sour feeling towards the weather. It was now 2 May, the date when my next-door neighbour *always* puts her geraniums out, because it is safe to do so, she says; the fine weather has arrived. Well, it hadn't in Saint-Christophe.

I left Saint-Christophe at just after 11.00 a.m. and by midday gnawing hunger pangs had joined the miscellaneous discomforts that remanifested themselves once I began walking. There were no shops in the first two villages I passed, and in the third everything was closed for lunch by the time I arrived, so I sat on the stone steps of the post office, eating dried apricots and peanuts and watching, through a pair of tall wrought-iron gates leading to an elegant house, a handsome and substantial cockerel busily uprooting plants from a raised bed in the garden, under the disapproving eye of a peacock and a large pink rhododendron.

The gently undulating landscape of the Charente Maritime looks at its best in summer, when fields of gilded sunflowers stretch to the horizon, interrupted by bright green rows of vines. In today's overcast conditions the acres of oilseed rape and wheat didn't quite pull it off. My right hip and left foot had been joined in their misery by the second toe on the right foot, while both little toes felt as if at each step they were being vigorously caressed by a cheese grater. The diversity of pains was a benefit, because by concentrating on one at a time it was possible to overlook the others. I could thus choose between stabbing, biting, grating or throbbing, adding an interesting dimension to a journey that was otherwise quite unremarkable.

Briefly the sun came out, and coming upon a convenient strip of newly mown grass behind the stone wall of a farmhouse I pulled off my boots and socks, and lay relishing the temporary warmth. The farmer drove by on a tractor, waved a cheerful hand and came across to ask not why I was sprawled peculiarly on his lawn, but whether I thought it was going to rain. That was anybody's guess. It hadn't yet, but apart from a few blue smears, the skies were still grey and heavy. He lamented the fact that the continual rain of the previous month was threatening to ruin his wheat fields, and that unless he could spray within the next two days he would lose his entire crop to disease. To spray, he must have forty-eight dry hours. We discussed the unpredictability of weather the world over, and I thought it polite to apologize for being on his lawn. No, he said, he was pleased to see I had made myself comfortable there; my load looked heavy, and was I going far? I said I was heading for Surgères, the next campsite, as I didn't particularly want to be either laughed at or disbelieved when I announced my final destination. Besides, the way things were going so far, I was starting to have doubts about it myself. Well, he announced comfortingly, I didn't have far to go, only about another eight miles. He watched as I reshod myself, and helped me into the backpack. Could he offer me a cup of coffee? I declined politely, and wondered whether in England a farmer would have been so welcoming of a stranger on his land. The French do not seem, in general, to share the Englishman's territoriality, but maybe that's because there is a lot more land to go round in France. When they ask 'May I help you?' that's what they mean, and not 'What the hell are you doing on my land?'

Across a still barren, lumpy chocolate-coloured field a solitary hare sprinted, its long ears flicking, and two pairs of partridges blundered out from a thorny hedgerow right in front of me, then turned tail in noisy panic and scuttled back in again.

By 5.00 p.m. I had reached the outskirts of

Surgères, from where signs indicated the campsite. They took me on a two-mile detour along the main road, ending at the entrance to the site, just five hundred yards from where I had begun to follow them in the first place. Every part of my body hurt. I had had nothing to drink since the coffee six hours earlier, and was too weary to walk to the town a quarter of a mile away, so I gulped down two cups of tap water. Then I discovered that I had lost my tent pegs. I felt like bursting into tears.

The campsite was overrun with a large contingent of travellers in sumptuous caravans sprouting a forest of television aerials, with separate units housing fully fitted kitchens with electric rotisseries and microwave ovens. A row of washing machines swished rhythmically next to the sanitary block. Like a tangled mass of giant spaghetti, thick electric cables criss-crossed the ground from the vans to the power points, and through the lacy curtains of the caravan windows rows of glass and china gleamed on shelves. The men, all rather short of stature, wore smart sports jackets and tapered black trousers leading to neat little feet in pointed shiny black shoes; they stood talking and laughing around a collection of prestige cars polished to a mirror finish. The women were quieter, hard-faced and worn, and most of them wore short tight skirts and baggy sweaters.

I found a space between the caravans, and a supply of twigs to use as tent pegs; they sank easily into the damp earth. A small, brown and determined child wearing pink pyjamas and giant gold and ruby earrings, with a lustrous mane of gleaming chestnut curls and a top lip glistening from a runny nose, kept trying to uproot the twigs as I put them in. It wouldn't give up, and each time I prised a twig from its grubby stubborn fingers it would remove another one. I tried ineffectually to drive it away, hoping its mother wouldn't notice and take offence, because despite my selection of excellent knives I didn't feel fit or ready for a skirt-tucked-up fight around the campfire. Eventually a slightly larger child came and dragged it away by the seat of its pyjamas.

From the emergency rations I excavated and demolished another nasty meal of pasta and a strange chocolate and semolina dessert that was simultaneously gritty and mushy, and devoid of any taste. Instead of a cheese course I took four strong painkillers, and, hoping the twig-pulling child would hold off for the night, zipped myself, fully dressed, into the sleeping bag.

There were four mallards on the tiny river Gères bordering the campsite; through the night the three drakes relentlessly pursued the single duck, and her indignant protests rattled in the dark. The wind rustled the trees and spots of rain fell. It was not warm in the tent.

★　★　★

Next morning dawned even colder and greyer than the previous day. The pink-pyjama child wandered around in the drizzle, resolutely resisting all attempts by assorted adults to feed it into an anorak, expressing its resistance by sitting down with a fierce thump and rubbing the offending garment in the mud. The travelling ladies seemed to spend all their time washing clothes, washing dishes or washing their caravans; they were all out in their nightclothes in the early morning, washing and polishing their immaculate homes despite the gentle rain. I wondered whether they enjoyed their nomadic lifestyle quite as much as their little spouses.

A swirling wind kept tugging the flame from under my small gas stove, preventing the water from boiling. After a cup of lukewarm water with a brown scum floating on the surface, which I pretended was a cup of coffee, I decided to stay for the day and give my feet an opportunity to get their act together, and, having by now eaten nearly all my food supplies, hobbled into town to restock. On the way back I stopped at a wine cellar near the campsite, where they sold wine from giant stainless steel tanks, through long hoses ending in a petrol-pump type dispenser. An old man slouched against the counter, with the sad, blurry eyes of a committed drinker, a purple face and a moustache that needed mowing. He grunted into a glass of red wine and I thought it wasn't often one saw quite such a disreputable person about in broad daylight, let alone before 10.00 a.m. I bought a litre of Sauvignon for twelve francs, and was walking back to the campsite when muffled shouts issued from behind. The committed drinker was shuffling unsteadily towards me, both arms flailing in the air, and I waited for him to catch up. When he did so he pressed a fifty-franc note into my hand, stuttering through his moustache that I had dropped it in the cellar. As fifty francs represented exactly half of my total daily budget, I couldn't thank him sufficiently, and was humbled by my earlier judgement of him.

A large communal room at the campsite provided a comfortable and warm sanctuary from the hateful weather and would be a good place to write up my diary, so I installed myself, spread out my notes and map No. 2 (to see whether I could find a shorter route to where I wanted to go, which I couldn't), and settled down contentedly. About eight seconds later the door burst open and two little brown-skinned girls exploded into the room. The younger of the two, about nine years old, was very forward and either didn't know, or didn't care, about personal body space. She leant on the back of my chair, her bony brown elbow digging painfully into the side of my neck, while her companion watched her with admiration.

'What are you doing?' demanded the forward one.

'Writing.' I jolted my shoulder so that the bony elbow lost contact.

'What are you writing? What is it about? Are you English? What are you doing here? Why don't you have a car? Please can you spare a few francs?'

I tried to be patient, answering all her questions, giving a negative response to her request. She shrugged good-naturedly. A little brown hand closed over my map measurer — a small high-precision wheel that converted squiggles on maps into distances.

'What's this?'

I explained, and they insisted on being

shown how the device worked, selecting random points on the maps which I had to measure. When I announced the distance, they gasped and asked suspiciously: 'Are you *sure*?'

A small boy joined us.

'Go and get three pencils,' their chief commanded me imperiously. 'We are all going to play schools, and you can teach us how to write.'

I wished they would go away and leave me alone. 'No. I don't have three pencils, I'm too busy and I don't want to play schools. Why don't *you* be the teacher?' I suggested.

'OK.' She flitted out of the door and returned a few moments later with sheets of paper and pencils. Soon her two companions were bent over their work, obeying her barked orders.

I enjoyed ten minutes in peace, and then she was back.

'Teach us English,' she ordered.

'Look,' I said. 'I'm trying to do something important. Please leave me alone.'

She squinted at me for a moment, then offered peace terms. 'You teach us two English words, then you can do your writing.'

I agreed, and had a good idea what the words were going to be. The three clustered around me, giggling expectantly, eyes bright.

'Go on. What's the first word?'

'*Merde!*' shouted the leader. I was right.

'Shit,' I replied.

'Shit! Shit! Shit! Shit!' they chanted happily, clutching at each other in delight. I asked what the second word was, already knowing.

'*Pi pi!*' they yelled together. Right again.

Here lay a potential danger: in France Enid Blyton's famous children's character Noddy is know as Oui Oui (and Big Ears, his trusty companion, for some unfathomable reason, as Potiron, which means pumpkin). If we got into semantics about wee wee, explanations would become impossibly complicated and I would never escape.

'Pee pee,' I told them. 'It's the same in English.'

'Shit! Pee pee! Shit! Pee pee! Shit! Pee pee!' they trilled in unison, and rushed off to tell their friends.

Outside it drizzled with soft persistence. As an alternative to spending an afternoon being harassed by these merciless little people, it presented no contest. Enveloped in a capacious red nylon poncho which would have accommodated a hippopotamus and left room to spare, I dashed from the campsite before they could see me.

In a bakery on the main road in Surgères

the great wood ovens glowed and the proprietor shivered, remarking how cold it was. I wondered how he would feel in the tent. He announced comfortingly that the current weather would remain unchanged until 23 May. Why that date precisely he couldn't explain, or possibly I couldn't understand, but it seemed to be something to do with local lore and was a depressing prospect.

The Sunday-afternoon streets were quiet and almost empty, and I wandered about steaming damply inside the poncho, admiring gardens that enfolded clumps of sad white lilies, sweet-smelling roses, honeysuckle, vivid geraniums and pansies and impossibly beautiful jungles of wisteria. I walked around the public gardens, through the Renaissance gate, round the ramparts of the sixteenth-century château, which had been home to Hélène of Surgères, beautiful and gentle lady-in-waiting to the evil Catherine de' Medici, and the eleventh-century church of Notre Dame de Surgères, ornately carved both within and without, an impressive example of that style of architecture known as Romanesque, for which the Poitou-Charentes region is famous. Below the ramparts a fledgling blackbird was flopping around perilously close to the road, and I ushered it back into the shelter of the shrubbery, while both parents bounced around and screeched indignantly as it clumsily flapped and hopped its way to safety.

Back at the campsite, the determined little travelling folk lay in wait. Like cats, they seemed to have an unerring instinct that drew them to those people who would most prefer to be left alone by them.

'You look like Little Red Riding Hood,' said the bossy one.

Having seen my reflection in shop windows, I thought it was far more like Quasimodo playing Father Christmas, especially with my strange new gait. Not only was I festooned in the red poncho, which incorporated a shapeless baggy lump on its back to accommodate the backpack, but a completely rigid right hip was forcing me to walk stiff-legged, and to reduce the pressure on the ball of my left foot I was trying to walk on the heel, toes pointed upward. Not all the time, though. The little toes of both feet were so sore that sometimes I walked on the inside edges of my boots to give them a rest. There was no doubt about it, it looked odd.

The little girls watched as I lit the gas stove and boiled some water to make a hot drink. However, closer examination of the stock cubes that I had politely purchased in Saint-Christophe showed that they contained lard, so I gave them to the children, telling them to give them to their mother. Some time later they returned and stood around sheepishly. Bossy pushed the more timid older girl forward.

'Please, madame. How do you eat these?' She held out the mangled remains of a soggy cube.

I hid a smile and wished I had something nicer to give them. I asked whether they went to school.

'No,' said the younger one rather sadly. 'We're travellers, and we don't stay anywhere for long. Maybe one day . . . ' Her voice trailed off. She told me they were of Spanish origin. They were bright and inquisitive and left to amuse themselves, and I wondered what their future would be.

Behind us, voices rose. A girl of about eighteen stood red-faced and tearful, glaring at three of the small-footed men who were talking quietly to her. Suddenly she turned and ran sobbing and wailing into a caravan, slamming the door behind her. The men shrugged, smiled at each other and wandered off. I thought what an experience it would be to share their nomadic lifestyle with these people, and to learn and understand their ways.

To have a shower at the campsite, you had

to buy a token for ten francs. The *gardienne* recommended the second shower on the right.

'You get a full ten minutes of really hot water in that one,' she confided.

You did, too. It was absolute bliss.

I made a call to Jennifer. She'd been having fun getting used to driving my eccentric car, Tinkerbelle, whose peculiar gear lever made finding the correct gear something akin to solving a Rubik cube with your hands tied behind your back. She'd taken Gloria shopping; as she wrestled and wrenched, Gloria held on for dear life and they were both laughing tears. The gear lever wasn't Tinkerbelle's only idiosyncrasy. She had no key to start her, as it had jammed itself in the lock one day, most inconveniently in a supermarket car park, and had to be drilled out. It had been replaced with a starter switch taped to the steering column. The horn was on a stick that looked like a turn signal indicator, and to open the window for air you pushed the bottom half of the window out to flip up and connect with the top. Sometimes it stayed up and sometimes it didn't.

She told me: 'Your car is so much fun to drive, it's like being in 'Comedy Capers'. But what you call a two-way road here is about as wide as one lane of the streets we're accustomed to. When you meet an oncoming car there are only inches between you. The other cars don't flinch and they don't move over. I find it really scary.'

'Don't worry, you'll soon get used to it,' I assured her cheerily.

The Sauvignon, which was excellent, and of which I drank the lot, with a baguette, a chunk of rubbery cheese and four painkillers, made a simple supper, and I settled down for the third night under the clammy nylon roof.

Following another Arcticly cold night, I woke damp as usual, but my hip had stopped hurting. By misreading my watch, I gained an hour and after another cup of brown scum was on my way to Dampierre-sur-Boutonne by 7.15 a.m. The travellers were still sleeping.

Surgères seemed to be rather short on road signs, and I couldn't find any indication of which way I should be going. The compass wasn't any help — the needle kept spinning in a frantic, fruitless search for north, and even if it hadn't I didn't have much idea how to use it. If I didn't know where I was, what help would it be knowing where north was? I had decided to rely on the sun for navigational purposes, because, impervious to damp and shock and regardless of magnetic interference, it would still rise in the east and set in the west. As long as it was ahead during the first part of the morning, to my right for the middle part of the day and directly behind me in the early evening, I would be travelling in approximately the right direction, and when and if the thing ever came out again, it would be a great help. I'd been told that another way to work out direction was to see which side moss grows on a tree trunk, but the trees I examined had either no moss at all, or moss all round, so as far as direction went it was down to guesswork.

After circumnavigating an industrial area, the railway station and a sprawling housing estate (twice), I took a major road because it looked as if it should go where I wanted it to. One and a half hours later, I was four and a half miles off route in a northerly direction. The shortest distance between Surgères and the next staging post on my route, Dampierre-sur-Boutonne, was twenty-one miles, and additional mileage was the last thing I needed. If I turned back it would add another nine miles to the day's journey, making it impossible to reach Dampierre that night — and there was nowhere closer. A battered sign indicated a wine cellar and free tastings down a narrow lane, so that's where I headed for. Maybe 9.00 a.m. was early to start on the bottle, but when in Rome . . . and I really needed somewhere to sit while I worked out a solution to my new predicament.

I followed the sign into a small village, where the entrance to the wine cellar was blocked by a yellow van. A postman's van. It was no less than a gift from heaven, even better than a drink and certainly a lot more useful. Was it possible, I asked the friendly postman, to cut across country to get back on course again, and so avoid a long trek back to where I had started? I flapped the map at him and pointed to Dampierre. He pursed his lips and shook his head. The area was a network of farm tracks and footpaths and almost completely devoid of signs. He didn't advise risking it, because he was certain I would get lost. I was sure he was right.

As he was going towards Dampierre, he offered me a lift, which I refused on the grounds that I was meant to be walking, and taking a lift would be cheating.

'Well, if I only take you to the point you would have reached if you had been going in the right direction, would that be all right?'

I couldn't see why not, or think of any practical alternative, so we agreed on a point on the map and he handed me gallantly into the back of the comfortably carpeted van, where I settled back to watch my new friend and saviour going about his daily business, which he did with great dash and style. We sped around the village, the van drawing up with no more than the width of a coat of paint between the walls of the narrow passageways, dropping mail nimbly into letter boxes positioned at exactly the right height to enable him to reach them without getting out of his van, or even stretching his arm.

I remarked how convenient this was for him.

'Yes,' he replied. 'My customers are very kind. They have all put their letter boxes in the best possible position to make my job easy.'

How did they know how to do this?

'I told them,' he explained. 'And those people who couldn't put up the boxes themselves, I did it for them.'

Out of a round of several hundred houses, only two required him to get out of his van. He was a lively and friendly man, who, once he finished his post round, spent his time renovating old houses and renting them out. He dropped me at the agreed spot, a short distance from the small village of Saint-Félix, where in a loft above the corner shop, which smelt mustily of age and spices, a motherly lady served a warm buttery croissant and a perfect cup of coffee.

Fortified and relieved to be back on course,

I tottered along the road, no longer stiff-hipped, although the soles of my feet were raw and burning, and the backpack gouged furrows into my shoulders. I kept adjusting my grip, sometimes dragging down on the loops attached to the shoulder straps, and sometimes jamming my arms through the straps and locking my fingers together. It didn't make the thing feel any lighter, but did temporarily reallocate the pressure. The landscape was peaceful, mostly flat fields of young crops, for the area is almost entirely given to arable farming, and scenically not very exciting. The first high point of my journey came just a few yards past a tiny place named la Cavaterie, where I walked off the right-hand edge of the first of my six maps, and folded it up with a jubilant grunt, prodding it into a side pocket of the backpack. I did a mental celebratory jig, being quite unable to manage anything physical apart from remaining upright and continuing to put one foot gingerly in front of the other.

At midday I plopped down on a patch of grass beneath a feeble sun, and was munching a lump of cheese when a battered van drew up across the road, and three unshaven and unsavoury men sat watching me in a way I didn't much like. Since the lady

48

in Saint-Félix I hadn't seen another human being, and at that moment I felt distinctly alone. So I pulled the sharp stabbing knife from the pocket of my jeans, and, staring at the trio with what I hoped was a flinty expression, carved chunks of cheese and ate them from the knife-tip. They sat and watched as I wiped the blade slowly down my jeans, and stabbed it to the hilt in the ground beside me, still staring at them flintily. One said something, and they started the engine and drove away. Whew.

France had not yet awoken from her long winter hibernation, and there was almost no sign of life in the villages but for a few cats and dogs and chickens, and a reedy pond teeming with bellowing frogs. Most restaurants and bars were closed, and many were permanently closed down. I seemed to be the only person about, and the countryside had an oppressive air of desolation. The miles passed painfully but steadily and nothing occurred to break the quiet monotony, except when I came upon two blackbirds fighting savagely. They tumbled to the ground and lay in the road, locked in combat, screeching, pecking, and raking at each other with their claws. It took a fairly substantial prod with the hiking stick to break them apart.

From the west, you enter Dampierre-sur-Boutonne across a small bridge over the river Boutonne, from where a tall Frenchman and two women were admiring the remnants of the tiny, exquisite Renaissance château that nestles in the elbow of the river on a miniature island.

'Are you going to Compostela?' asked the man, referring to the great pilgrim route which leads to north-west Spain and the town of Compostela, reputedly the burial place of Saint James the Apostle, whose body is said to have arrived there in a boat bedecked with cockleshells. The cockleshell is the symbol of this pilgrim route, and can be seen etched into many buildings all over France that were and still are staging-posts for the pilgrims.

'No, to Geneva.'

'Ah yes, you must be English!' he roared. We all laughed at the crazy English.

They asked what route I was taking. I replied that it would be as near as possible to a straight line drawn between la Rochelle and Geneva, apart from a detour to visit some spectacular gorges in central France, but that as I was working my way from campsite to campsite, not wanting to camp alone in the wilds, the line was about as straight as a row of knitting.

One of the women walked behind me, and

patted the backpack.

'You look as if you are carrying too much weight. How much does this weigh?'

'Thirty-three pounds.'

'No! That's far too much. We do a lot of walking ourselves. The maximum anyone can carry is twenty-five pounds,' said the man. The women nodded in agreement, and one of them added: 'If you don't reduce the weight, you'll never finish your journey.'

I knew they were right, and promised to unload anything that wasn't vital.

Encouraged by their enthusiastic good wishes, and smiling at their exclamation of 'You English!' I continued to the campsite. There was no-one else there. As I searched for somewhere to pitch the tent, a man wearing the typical blue overalls of a French workman appeared and indicated a neat mown area bordered by a trim hedge.

'Here.' He smiled. 'The grass is cut and you will be sheltered by the hedges and the wall.'

It was a perfect spot, beside the river, with a backdrop of a small stone bridge and a copse of trees.

'You're very lucky. Last week the whole site was twelve inches under water.'

It was still pretty soggy.

The village restaurant was closed down,

and for sale, so I bought half a dozen eggs, a French stick, and a bottle of cider from the tiny, dusty grocery. I dined on two boiled eggs and a handful of dried apricots, washed down with the excellent cider, and cooked the remaining eggs into an omelette, which I jammed into the bread for the following day's lunch.

My phone call to Jennifer elicited the information that the weather at home was as cold and miserable as it was here, getting colder and wetter by the hour, and that the geese had chased her all over the place. As she couldn't get outside into the garden, she'd entertained herself dismantling and servicing the stove, after which she'd done the only sensible thing on a day like this, and settled down with a glass of champagne to read and listen to music. She sounded quite cheerful.

After a shower that was a few degrees below tepid, I climbed into the tissue-thin sleeping bag. A woodpecker rapped some-where close by, and the pigeons gurgled a throaty chorus to a blackbird's song. It was very peaceful, and bitterly cold. I didn't feel Dampierre-sur-Boutonne had anything to fear from global warming.

3

There are Châteaux and Châteaux, and Donkeys and Donkeys

Awakening (an inexactitude, as through the night I had shivered and rolled around trying not to freeze) to a hard frost and renewed aching in my back and shoulders, I came to a decision. Nicholas Crane would have to go. The only luxury I carried was his book, *Still Waters Rising*, the inspirational story of his six-thousand-mile tramp across Europe from Cape Finisterre to Istanbul. His smiling, bespectacled face peered good-naturedly from beneath the silly hat on the book's cover, and I felt a pang as I poked the end of his nose with my finger. He was a great guy, amusing, inspirational, and he had given me a lot of pleasure, but the time had come for us to part. The small and peaceful village was probably as good a place as any to say goodbye, so together with two pairs of socks, one pair of shorts and a T-shirt all smelling of beer, a large tube of Deep Heat, a roll-on deodorant and the first map, which I had finished with, I jammed him into a carrier bag and consigned him to the care of the smiling *gardienne*, promising to retrieve him in about eight weeks' time. He would understand. Being something of a walker himself, he knew that surplus weight simply wouldn't do.

Having dumped Nick, I set off to visit the little Château de Dampierre. There are châteaux and châteaux. Dampiere does not rank as one of the 'greats', whose vulgar opulence was such a poke in the eye to the poor that it was little wonder the latter ended up chopping off rich heads. It is simply gorgeous, set upon a tiny island in a bend on the river Boutonne. Designed as both a stronghold and a home it stands on three levels, the lower two bounded by a series of five arches. Originally built at the beginning of the sixteenth century in the Renaissance style just introduced to France from Italy, but still maintaining a little of the medieval, it served as a replacement for the original fortified castle that protected Dampierre. During its brief heyday it was an intellectual centre and a haunt of alchemists, as the many engravings in the stonework testify. The name Dampierre comes from Notre Dame la Pierre Philosophale — Our Lady of the Philosopher's Stone. During the wars of religion and the French Revolution the little château was sacked and ruined, although it really is difficult to imagine anybody being able to wantonly damage quite such a pretty place. Since 1851 it has been privately owned and restored, and I very much wanted to see inside it. However, it was closed, so with that idea knocked on the head I started on my way to the next stop, Brioux-sur-Boutonne.

It took an hour of pallid sunshine before the frost and ice had thawed and the tent had dried. I set off as briskly as the blisters would allow, hoping that the temperature would not slide below zero again during my expedition, because I had just noticed on the thin, light sleeping bag a label indicating that it was only suitable for use in temperatures of between +10°C and +26°C.

Despite having abandoned Nick and the other bits and pieces, the backpack didn't seem any lighter; in fact if anything it was worse than before. That was the case for the entire journey — however much I discarded the weight never became noticeably less. It was extraordinary that a handful of items individually weighing nothing could unite to form such a disproportionately heavy load. Never at any time in history could so few little things have weighed so much.

Just outside Dampierre, there was a sign to La Maison du Baudet du Poitou[1]. It was just too good an opportunity to miss, and worth however many extra miles it would add to the day's hike. A visit would compensate for missing a tour of the château.

There are donkeys and donkeys, and the *baudet* is really something else. The primary objective was originally to cross the stallions with huge Mulassière mares, in order to produce the prized Poitevin mules. As mechanization displaced the latter the *baudet* declined until, at the start of the 1980s, it was virtually extinct. Then a stud was set up to regenerate the breed at La Tillauderie, and it was thither that my path had so fortuitously led.

It was a good two miles' diversion to the stud, in, for the first time, warm sunshine. I was the only visitor this early in the day, and was able to roam at leisure amongst the docile and friendly Rastafarian equines. They reach up to sixty inches at the shoulder, with fifteen-inch ears, and the adults' coats grow into extremely long, shaggy rusty-brown

[1] Literally 'The house of the Poitou donkey'

dreadlocks that are their most distinguishing feature. The lengthy coat, matted with straw and dust, characterizes the breed and is not groomed. At La Tillauderie, together with mules and the enormous Mulassière horses, the magnificent *baudet* population is being rebuilt. These kindly giants of the donkey world produce teddy bear foals with dark chocolate, silky soft poodle-hair who jostle gently for attention with the equally friendly mules and the Mulassière mares and foals. I spent an enchanted hour with these creatures. The centre also houses a fascinating museum showing the history and development of the breed. There is a theatre where a video is shown, and one can take a guided tour of the stables to meet the stallions and newborn foals.

For the first time since leaving la Rochelle, I wasn't cold. The sun was blazing down. Rather than backtrack to the road, I opted for the forest route to Brioux-sur-Boutonne. The lady who directed me, who I am certain had never carried a backpack weighing about thirty pounds, or walked miles on feet that were held together with blisters, was determined I should enjoy the most scenic path, despite the fact that it would add nearly six miles to my journey. I really didn't care how beautiful the long way was; I would have traversed a barren wilderness or a disused coalmine, as long as it led to my destination by the shortest possible route. Withered by her scornful shrug, and armed with alarmingly complex directions that I felt were deliberately designed to confuse, I trudged around the woods following a network of narrow strips of dirt, tracks and ruts, trying to guess which was a path and which was not, and seeking with total lack of success the various features which I had been assured would be very apparent.

Eventually, after a very long and hot safari, which led out of the Charente Maritime and into the département of Deux Sèvres, I arrived in a village which should have been just one and a half miles from Brioux. Everything about the surroundings corresponded with the map, apart from the cemetery, which although very clearly marked on the map wasn't there in the village. The name on the village notice board was not the same as the name on the map. There were three merry ladies chatting like budgies nearby, and they waved me cheerily into their collective bosom.

'I *am* in le Pontioux, aren't I?' I asked, hoping that if I said it positively enough, it would be so.

'No, but it's not far away,' said one of the

ladies helpfully. 'This is Arsanges.' It certainly seemed well named. 'Le Pontioux is just three and a half miles in that direction.'

She pointed northwards. That meant nearly five miles to Brioux. Another two hours' agonizing walk.

'Come on, we'll put you on the right path.'

The cartel danced merrily beside me for a hundred yards, seemingly unaware of my discomfort as I shuffled and hobbled and thought dark thoughts. Or maybe they imagined I was a poor cripple. I just about was.

'There you are, turn right at the end and just follow the road. *Bon courage.*'

Well, three and a half miles may be no distance by car, bike or horses, or to someone who hasn't already walked over seventeen, but to me, then, it sounded unattainably far.

Based on the principle that a positive mental attitude can achieve anything, I kept telling myself that my feet were getting better, but it was a pointless exercise. They were fraying more and more with every step I took. After half an hour limping along the side of the road, I crumpled in a tearful heap next to a ditch and tugged off the backpack. I simply couldn't walk any further.

On the other hand, if I didn't, I would have to adjust to the idea of living here on the grass verge, because the chances of anybody stopping for a heavily laden character wielding a five-foot-long pole that looked like a martial arts weapon were non-existent. This wasn't the spirit that built an empire, and it wasn't going to get me to a hot shower and somewhere to take off my boots, so the only thing to do was to put my chin up, adopt a stiff upper lip, bite the bullet, and put my best foot forward, et cetera, et cetera, et cetera.

But I didn't have a best foot. So I sang instead. It's a Long Way to Tipperary. The White Cliffs of Dover. Land of Hope and Glory. Two Little Boys. Tie Me Kangaroo Down. Jerusalem (and did those feeeet). Tulips from Amsterdam. One Man Went to Mow. The Happy Wanderer. Until I got to Brioux I was not going to stop singing. If you had ever heard me sing, you would understand how motivated I was to reach my destination at the earliest possible moment. I was almost jogging by the time I completed the last of the twenty-two miles I'd walked since setting off that morning, and arrived at the deserted campsite. The pleasure of dropping the backpack and shedding the boots was secondary only to the joy of no longer having to listen to the horrible dirge.

A mixture of self-pity and triumph persuaded me that I was due for a reward, so I aimed at a pretty, rustic restaurant offering an excellent menu at an affordable price. Dressed in my cleanest dirty clothes, I enjoyed the luxury of a hot meal and a good bottle of wine. Only one other table was occupied, by a party of three — a man and woman who were obviously not married, and the woman's young daughter who was about ten years old. As the adults skirmished playfully, she alternately flirting and freezing while he plied her attentively with wine and meaningful looks, the child roamed around the room forgotten, looking at paintings, arrangements of flowers, me. I smiled at her and beckoned her over, but she responded by scowling suspiciously and returning to her table where she concentrated on pleating the cloth into a thousand wrinkles.

The restaurant owner's wife came over to chat, and, when she heard I was camping, asked whether it wasn't too cold at night. I agreed that it was, and she disappeared, returning a few moments later with a large fluffy blue blanket.

'You can bring it back when you leave,' she said.

* * *

I rang Jennifer to see how she was managing, and smiled as she recounted some of her experiences so far.

'Do you know,' she said, 'I've been noticing the old men around here are always hiding in the bushes. When I take the horses out and bring them back, I've seen them and acted like I didn't see them. Today I started waving to them. They smile and wave back and go on about their business.

'When I went to the store today I went to ask if Gloria needed anything. She invited me to sit in the garden and have coffee. Susie, this woman's garden is like the garden from hell. Have you seen all that junk her husband's left there? Old cars, rocks, construction equipment? The grass was so high you had to look to see the two Great Danes.'

I laughed. 'Anything else happened while I've been away?'

'Yeah. When I got home from the store, one of the dogs had jumped the fence around the pond, and gone for a swim. He was soaking wet and trapped inside the fence. He just stood there looking at me like, Who, me?'

I said I was pretty tired and didn't know if I'd walk tomorrow or stay where I was and rest. I'd been lost several times and walked farther than I'd planned, and although I should have been back home on the following day I didn't think I'd get there for another two or three.

'Well, you just take things easy and go at your own pace. Everything's just fine here.'

4

Dancing a Red Fandango

Had the mattress been inflatable, it would have been afloat next morning. Condensation was streaming down the inner walls of the tent and onto the waterlogged floor. I was accustomed to this by now and there wasn't much I could do about it, except to cram everything into the backpack at night, wrap it in the poncho and place it as far as possible from the tent walls to try to keep it dry. Thus only the bedding, tent and I would be wet. There was absolutely no prospect of anything drying on this dank and dreary morning.

After returning the rather soggy blanket to the kind lady in the restaurant, and paying the camp fees at the *mairie*[1], I turned towards Sauzé-Vaussais, seventeen miles away. I'd

[1] town hall

have to push hard to get there, with my ragged feet and the extra weight of wet tent and bedding.

The landscape was still predominantly flat and empty and there was nothing to catch the eye. Rain splattered onto the road. Trying to put on a lightweight poncho single-handed, over a backpack, is a challenge, especially on a windy day, but if you want to attract attention it's a surefire winner. The bright red poncho had long sleeves ending in elasticated cuffs, a full-length frontal zip and a hood. First I tried putting an arm in one sleeve — it was impossible to get the rest round my back to invade the second sleeve. Then I tried to put the hood on first — the whole thing billowed out behind me and I couldn't get at the sleeves at all. Doing up the zip and tugging it over my head didn't work either — it snagged on the backpack and I couldn't get my arms round behind to pull it down. At that point I started jumping and whirling like a mad dervish, arms flailing in a wild fandango, flapping the garment like a matador's cape. Cars slowed, mouths gaped, fingers pointed. Finally I got the thing on, just as the rain stopped and the blazing sun poked out again. You could try this yourself, if you like.

By the time I tottered into Chef-Boutonne

at 2.00 p.m., I was finished. My feet felt as if they were treading broken glass, and I had exhausted all my energy and resolve. Every step was agony, and I knew I couldn't walk any further. It was the end of the road, and I wept with rage and frustration. Why, after all the months of training, had I failed so pathetically? I could no more walk the remaining nine miles to Sauzé-Vaussais than sprout wings.

There was a campsite in Chef-Boutonne, but the weather had reverted again to cold and damp, and tent and bedding were soaking. I couldn't face it. I rang friends in Sauzé-Vaussais, begged a bed for the night, then went hunting transport. There was a bus that connected Chef-Boutonne with Sauzé-Vaussais once a day, which I had missed. It would have to be a taxi, as I had given a promise to everyone concerned for my welfare that I would not *faire du stop*[1] in any circumstances. I approached two old gentlemen who were standing in the road, eye to eye, murmuring conspiratorially and looking over their shoulders every few seconds, and asked if they knew where I could find a taxi. Nowhere in Chef-Boutonne, they replied; there were no taxis in the town. My eyes were

---

[1] hitch hike

starting to leak once again.

'Ah, wait a minute! What about the undertaker?' asked one of the other.

'Yes, I think you're right — he does run a taxi service.'

The prospect of arriving at my friends' house laid out in the back of a hearse, hands folded across my chest, the backpack at my feet, and still clutching the hiking stick, was just too much. I shook with laughter while tears raced each other down my cheeks in stinging salt trickles.

The old gentlemen looked rather perplexed and one said something rapidly to the other, who tentatively tapped my arm.

'I will take you to the undertaker. It's quite a long way,' he said, opening the door of his car, which looked as if it was about to fall to pieces. After a jerky and silent journey through the town, he deposited me outside the undertaker's establishment, a cheerful showroom which also served as flower shop and purveyor of headstones and photograph frames and solemn statuary of madonnas and cherubs, in fact of just about anything anyone could possibly need in a cemetery. The undertaker, a young and smiling man, was polishing the shop windows, and said he would be happy to drive me to Sauzé-Vaussais. He went off to collect the hearse, which I thought with rather bitter humour was an entirely appropriate vehicle for an adventure in its death throes.

Disappointingly, he reappeared driving a modern and mundane estate car, and ten minutes later unloaded myself and paraphernalia in the town square of Sauzé-Vaussais. The journey cost 127 francs, more than a whole day's subsistence, but as my expedition was finished it really didn't matter.

Dejectedly I tramped the remaining two miles to my friends' pretty farmhouse. The sun came back out just as I arrived. I had first met Carole and Norrie four years previously, since when they had rescued me from a number of predicaments, and in their company you were always certain of excellent food, liberal alcohol and lots of fun. A miserable wretch couldn't have turned up at a better place.

The dripping sleeping bag and tent hung in the sunshine to dry, while I soaked in a steaming bubble bath inhaling fragrant cooking smells. Later, by a blazing log fire, feeling properly clean for the first time in a week, well wined and dined, and with blisters shrouded in Second Skin and cotton wool, I accepted my failure philosophically. I had tried my best, and it simply hadn't been good enough. It had been a half-witted idea anyway, and I knew no-one would be surprised that it hadn't worked. Tomorrow I would go home.

Aided by the best part of a bottle of cognac, I enjoyed a brief, blissfully comfortable sleep, and woke the next day to dazzling sunshine. Fortified by several platefuls of hot buttered toast and mugs of coffee, I started tracking towards home twelve miles away, where Jennifer and the animals waited and my battered pride could repair itself in comfort and privacy.

Walking was almost a pleasure with my feet padded and bandaged. Second Skin is like a sheet of cold wet gelatine and gives total and immediate relief from blisters. Whoever invented it — thank you. I dawdled along under a blazing sun, crossing from the Deux Sèvres département into the Vienne at Les Maisons Blanches, extending my route to curve through small villages, chatting occasionally to people enjoying the long-awaited sunshine in their gardens.

Back on the main road traffic was heavy with motorists making an early start to the second long weekend in this month of May. The wake of huge trucks, passing very close, nearly dragged me under the wheels, and lifted my baseball cap off, so that I had to anchor it to my head with one hand. People often say, most unjustly in my opinion, that truck drivers show no concern for other motorists, cyclists or pedestrians. Having had considerable personal experience of their conduct, I can say truthfully that they accord other road users, and walkers in particular, every bit as much consideration as they extend to ants, beetles and paper bags.

On the outskirts of Civray stands the fifteenth-century Château de Leray, with its strange dog oven, used for drying hounds when they returned cold and wet from hunting, and a mile or so further on I stopped in a bar for a shandy. I was befriended by the proprietor's dog, Leo, who came to sit by me, and after socializing for a while he surreptitiously slid my hat off the seat and disappeared with it. A few moments later, still holding his prize, he headed for a door behind the bar, and opening it with a paw started to vanish through it. His owner captured him and made him relinquish his trophy. After that he lay relaxed by my side, until I stood up and assumed the backpack. He froze, raised his hackles slightly, and growled quietly. His owner said the dog thought it very unnatural for anyone to carry such a load. I couldn't have agreed more. I phoned home and asked Jennifer if she could meet me in town.

On a patch of grass beside the road, a brilliant crimson ladybird, glistening as if freshly lacquered, took off from a daisy launch pad, flew a few circuits, and returned. I stood watching it repeat this performance for several minutes before making for the town centre. Civray straddles a curve of the river Charente where it roams into the département of the Vienne. It is a peaceful and pretty market town, and in the centre is the celebrated twelfth-century Romanesque church of Saint Nicolas, with its extravagantly carved and well-preserved west wall decorated with wise and foolish virgins, virtues and vices, zodiac signs, and old men of the Apocalypse. The walls, columns and ceiling inside are wildly painted in exotic colours and patterns which would look more appropriate in a Turkish mosque, but which are part of the great charm of this little church.

Jennifer and Gloria were waiting for me in faithful Tinkerbelle, and we drove home to a rapturous welcome from the animals. That evening, in front of a crackling log fire, Jennifer and I sat until almost midnight, drinking, exchanging adventures and listening to music. I didn't mention my decision to abandon the journey. I'd walked just over eighty-four miles and it felt as if I'd been away for months, not just six days.

'Pleased to meet you, pleased to meet you,' called the chaffinches, in the brilliant early morning sunshine.

The animals were beginning their day, the horses munching methodically in the paddock, while in their straw beds inside the barn the dogs were stirring, yawning and grumbling at each other. Something had disturbed the geese, and they shrieked their rage. As daylight squeezed through the shutters, the two parrots shook their feathers and stretched their wings squeakily, and the cat hummed his Harley-Davidson purr as he kneaded my shoulder. How happy I was to be home, and lying in a warm, dry bed, never again having to hoist on a backpack or step into a pair of hiking boots. Jennifer was puttering about in the garden exchanging greetings with the animals. What a remarkable lady. She had flown from San Antonio, Texas to a country she didn't know, with a language she didn't speak, on the basis of nothing more than a few e-mail messages containing some scanty information, and my assurance that I would meet her at the local railway station and bring her here to look after thirteen assorted creatures for upwards of six weeks while I disappeared. It seemed too much to expect that everything would work out. But in no time at all she'd settled into the chaotic routine of life here and took everything placidly in her Texan stride. In fact she rather seemed to be enjoying herself.

I noticed that she had made a start on gardening, and little beds had been dug and planted with herbs and pansies, and she'd put up strong wire fencing around the newly weeded flowerbeds and the pond, to ward off the assaults of the dogs.

Today, 8 May, Carole and Norrie had invited her and Gloria to join them for the VE Day commemoration being held in Sauzé-Vaussais, an opportunity to participate in a truly French event, and so they set off at mid-morning, leaving me to my own lazy devices.

Sitting in the garden among the dogs sprawled in the sun, by using a mirror I was able to get a good look at the underside of my feet for the first time. It wasn't a very attractive sight. The ball of my left foot sported a great water-filled cushion nearly three inches in diameter. Both ankles were enormously swollen, and a bright red rash decorated my left leg from ankle to mid-calf. The undersides of my toes were a mess of calluses adorned with blisters. There was a large piece of something brown attached to one, and thinking it was an old piece of plaster I gave it a tug. It was not an old piece of plaster, but an old piece of me, and very reluctant to become detached. I had to cut it off.

It was quite obvious that these feet could not walk another three hundred and fifty miles, so I planned on a couple of hours sunbathing after which I'd unpack the backpack and resign from the project. Drowsiness floated around in delicious waves and every muscle crooned with pleasure. Then the phone rang.

'Are you the English lady with the horses?' It was one of my French neighbours.

Oh God, what now?

'They have escaped. They are by our garden.'

'How long have they been there?'

'Just a few minutes.'

'Thank you very much, I'll come straight away.'

There was no time to lose. From frequent past experience, I knew that they would head for the crossroads and make their way merrily through fields of crops across the road and over the hill beyond, nibbling contentedly as they continued on an itinerary which would lead them to a small vineyard nearly three miles away, where they would finally come to a hedge and have to stop.

I couldn't find any socks, and the swollen

feet wouldn't fit into my trainers. Sandals were out of the question, as if the chase went the way it usually did it would involve having to sprint over stony ploughed fields, so I jammed my bare feet into the only footwear I could find — my husband's Wellington boots, size 7½. I take a size 4½.

Lumbering to the back gate, I found Leila standing there patiently, looking slightly puzzled, and leading her by the mane I secured her in a stall. Of the other horse there was no sign. I hobbled at a run through the village. No horse. Neighbours joined in the hunt. In the stall, Leila whinnied hysterically. The other mare must have gone across the road. Snatching up a rope, I prepared for a long hike in the giant boots, which cut uncomfortably into the backs of my thighs at every step.

From the crest of the hill over the crossroads I stopped to catch my breath and looked back: there, unconcerned by the furore she had caused, Cindy grazed happily in her field, a dreamy, faraway expression on her hairy face. I plodded back.

'Did you find your horses?' called out the kindly lady who had telephoned.

'Yes, thank you very much.'

'We only saw the big one. Where did you find the other one?' she called.

'Not far away,' I answered.

Normality, or what passes for it here, returned. Ejecting five of the dogs who had installed themselves comfortably on the sun lounger, I settled down once more, and for a couple of blissful hours nothing much happened.

The arrival of unexpected visitors interrupted the deep hot bath I had just stepped into, and by the time they had left it was cold and not very enjoyable. I ran another one. The hot water ran out, and this bath too was tepid. I boiled a kettle of water and sat with my feet in a basin for an hour. They looked wrinkled and white, apart from the crimson rash that was flourishing and now reached well above my left knee. As I sat there contemplating my lower limbs, a small voice piped up inside my head. 'Gave up pretty easily, didn't you? Didn't take much to make you quit. Being a bit of a wimp really. Didn't have what it takes, after all. Ah well, there you are, you never really expected to do it, did you? Shame, after all the planning, and Jennifer coming so far, but if you haven't got the guts to carry on, then there's nothing else to say.'

A tiny ember of indignation lit itself. Of course I wasn't a wimp. I wasn't giving up easily. The ember grew into a small flame, and then flared into a roaring fire. How dare anybody call me a wimp. Another voice spoke: 'Get your act together. Sort yourself out, and get going again.'

To do that, there were two problems that needed addressing: the feet, and the weight of the backpack. After performing some gruesome surgery, I secured thick wads of cotton wool over the blisters and taped them up, which was fine, I could walk, but my feet wouldn't fit into my boots. The shock-absorbing insoles were very thick, so I cut away the fronts, allowing the injured and thickly padded toes to dangle in the space left. It felt OK. Then I attacked the backpack to see what could be weeded out from it.

There seemed to be nothing that wasn't absolutely indispensable, but if I was to have any chance at all of continuing something just had to go. The usefulness of the spare poncho, which doubled as a groundsheet, was surpassed by its weight, as was that of the inflatable pillow. It was unlikely that in the event of an attack I could wield more than one knife at a time, so two of those joined the surplus pile. That still left one small gas stove, two aluminium cooking pans, a pair of shorts, one pair of jeans, one jumper, the red fandango poncho, a nylon windcheater, optimistic swimming costume, two T-shirts, one of which bore a mysterious 'Kiwi Trikers' logo, two silk shirts, three pairs of pants, two thermal vests, two pairs of socks, a pair of foam flip-flops, a money-belt and a bra. Soap, toothpaste, toothbrush, hairbrush, mirror, small towel, packet of painkillers, plasters and cotton wool. One battery lamp. One drinking mug. Sleeping bag, mattress and tent, two lightweight survival blankets, a length of rope and a tent repair kit, boot wax, notebook and the five maps I needed. Neatly piled, it didn't look much for a six-week hike. But it was still too heavy, and I hadn't included the camera and the tape recorder, which rode separately in the fanny pack.

Although the lamp was heavy, it was essential, so the cooking facilities would have to go and I'd manage as best I could on picnics or bought meals. The stove was, after the tent, the heaviest item, so it joined the pile of rejects, and while the pans weighed almost nothing they wouldn't be the slightest use without the stove. Out they went too. The pack was still heavy, just over twenty-six pounds, without allowing for food or water. But that was as good as it was going to get, and I repacked it neatly and put it in the corner with my boots and stick.

Jennifer returned from Sauzé-Vaussais well fed and watered, slightly bemused by rural

French life but having thoroughly enjoyed her day out. She glanced at the backpack and freshly waxed boots, and raised one eyebrow.

'So you're going on, then?'

'Of course.'

'Are you sure that's a good idea?' she asked.

'Why not?'

'OK. But you just take care, you hear?'

'I will,' I promised. 'Tell me all about your day.'

While we talked I rebandaged the blisters and tried on the boots. The feet still weren't quite right, so I unwrapped them and bandaged them again. Jennifer tutted over my swollen ankles and the rash encompassing my lower legs.

'Are you really determined to continue on your trek tomorrow?' she asked.

I nodded.

5

Bring Me Some Figgy Pudding

The weather had finally changed for the better, and on this bright sunny morning, for the first time since I started out from la Rochelle, I really wanted to walk. As the next stop was only five miles along the way, there was plenty of time to go and buy some replacement tent pegs and supplies of food, and to enjoy a leisurely lunch with Jennifer by the river in Civray. My friend kept expressing concern about my feet and I was able to assure her, almost truthfully, that they felt fine as we said our au revoirs once again. Then I discovered I'd forgotten the hiking stick, so Jennifer obligingly drove back home, found it and caught up to deliver it to me.

The campsite was situated on a farm, down a narrow lane hedged by a tall purple wild flower that looked like a cross between an antirrhinum and an orchid, with a leaf like mint. A flock of sheep stared rudely as I hammered the tent pegs into ground that was as hard as concrete after two days of continuous sunshine. There were some geese and ducks on a nearby pond, and something invisible in it which plopped loudly and frequently. The mobile bakery/grocery rumbled down the dusty farm track, as it did several times a week to dispense fresh bread, cakes, tins of vegetables, biscuits, buttons, cheese, envelopes, string, matches and local gossip. I was well stocked up with most things I needed after my stay at home, but what the vehicle did have was large bottles of Coca-Cola. It was a funny thing. I used to really hate that drink, but since I started walking it had become the elixir of life, the only thing that quenched my thirst and gave me the energy I needed. (Note: this is an unsolicited testimonial. I have not been paid for it. But if you people at Coca-Cola read this, it is not too late. I am still open to offers.)

About fifteen feet from the baked patch of earth I was occupying, a group of French holidaymakers had rented a chalet for the long weekend, and incongruously, in the heat of the Poitou-Charentais sun, they were playing English Christmas carols on their tape player. Again and again and again. The same tape just kept on recycling. To the strains of 'The Holly and the Ivy' and 'God Rest You Merry, Gentlemen' I dined on bread and cheese, washed down with Coca-Cola, and then climbed into the little tent and lay down most uncomfortably on the thing laughingly called a mattress, just a narrow strip of very thin foam, which allowed every stone, clod and clump direct access to my person. The holidaymakers and their guests made merry loudly until the tiny hours, the Christmas carols cycling endlessly round and round. The frogs on the lake burped a loud chorus, and from every direction dogs were barking and howling. It really was a frightful cacophony, and despite jamming my fingers painfully into my ears I was still awake at 3.30 a.m. when the final carload of revellers accelerated away, showering the tent with dust and gravel. I'd been listening to the figgy pudding carol for so many hours that I could clearly visualize and smell the thing, and craved a taste of the fragrant toffee-rich sponge arising from a lake of swirling cream. To stifle a yearning that simply would not go away, I rummaged in the bottom of the backpack and found a handful of the peanuts I had politely bought in Saint-Christophe seven days earlier, and chomped them around with a little of the Coca-Cola. It was better than nothing, and at last I was able to get to sleep.

There was a full moon, and once again it was bitterly cold in the early morning.

Maps were a problem, because they were both expensive and heavy. The best I could carry were on a scale of 1:100,000. If you take into account that the distance between la Rochelle and Lake Geneva was about four hundred miles in a roughly straight line, and that distance was covered by six maps, there was a minimum of sixty miles fitted onto one map page of about twelve inches wide. A scale equivalent to five miles to the inch left almost no room for such minor details as footpaths, for which I needed 1:25,000 scale maps, and to cover the distance I was going to walk I would have needed over forty of them and a wheeled device to tow them in, which would have looked rather foolish. During the months I had trained I had wasted so many hours, and walked so many unnecessary miles, due to insufficient map detail, that if I wanted to be certain of not getting lost I had to stick to the major roads, which wasn't much fun, but reliable. On one memorably beastly day, finding what I thought was the marked footpath, I followed it doggedly as it disintegrated into a deeply ploughed field that I had to scramble across to reach the edge, and then circumnavigate, which took over an hour. Then there was a live electric fence to negotiate — with the backpack; another ploughed field; and a small track, which finally led into a farmyard where a freshly slaughtered pig was hanging from the front of a JCB, and two large and grumpy old dogs chased me. So I was very wary of venturing off the tarmac.

The footpaths should have been well marked with *balises*: painted dashes in various colours, on trees, fences and stones, indicating changes of direction or dead ends. However, the winter weather had taken its toll, fence posts had fallen, plants had climbed to obscure the signs, and it would be later in the year before the local walkers set about refurbishing the marks, because only a fool would be hiking round at the beginning of May.

To reach Charroux from the campsite, there was a choice of a long walk along the road, or a brief footpath. I decided to live dangerously, and opted for the footpath. After a false start leading to a dead end located in a stagnant pond, I pushed through thigh-high grass and nettles and was shortly rewarded by arriving at a little iron bridge, marked with a *balise*. It gave onto an overgrown path leading into Charroux, passing the Commonwealth War Graves cemetery which sits high on a hill overlooking the town, and where three Royal Air Force officers are buried. The Blenheim bomber they were ferrying to the Middle East had crashed a mile away, on 18 June 1940, killing the twenty-year-old pilot and his two crew.

The path continued through the twelfth-century portals into the town centre, past the majestic polygonal tower which is all that remains of the Saint-Sauveur abbey, reputedly founded by Charlemagne. There are several cockleshell symbols along the way — Charroux was an important staging-post for pilgrims travelling to Compostela. Unfortunately it now forms part of the route for juggernauts plying their way across central France, thundering endlessly along the main road, shaking the pavements and rendering conversation impossible. There is talk of a bypass, but in the meantime the monsters rumble on.

There is said to be immense treasure buried beneath the town, below the crypt and in the network of tunnels which honeycomb the surrounding area. In the Middle Ages the abbey was an important place of pilgrimage for kings, princes and emperors, who came to worship there, bringing gold, silver and priceless jewels, only a fraction of which have ever been found. There are many underground passageways in the area, some leading into the cellars of local houses, and during the Second World War the Resistance made good use of them. Another current legend is that many years ago, in a long-forgotten loft, a mummified body was discovered. From its unusual height, being well over six foot, it was believed to be that of Richard the Lionheart, who was killed about fifty miles away, at Châlus, whilst engaged in a minor and unnecessary skirmish with one of his vassals. However, it is well documented that in accordance with Richard's last wishes his heart was buried in Rouen where, as Duke of Normandy, it belonged; his body at the Royal Abbey of Fontevraud with his father and mother; and his entrails at Châlus, his gory legacy to the people of the Limousin in recognition of their treachery to him. So what there was left to mummify couldn't have been very much, let alone six foot, and as to what became of it, nobody seems to know. You might wonder whether these legends are simply an attempt to make Charroux seem more interesting than it appears; because to be honest, even though it is a quiet and pleasant place inhabited by generally quiet and pleasant people, it doesn't have an awful lot going for it apart from a couple of good bakeries, an excellent restaurant and a small antiques shop run by a helpful and friendly English couple.

The sun was shining; my feet, festooned in wrappings, hurt only slightly, and finally I was enjoying my mission. I marched happily eastwards towards Availles-Limouzine, twelve miles away. After a couple of hours I turned into a quiet grassy lane in the Bois de Charroux (which for just a few hundred yards falls into the northernmost tip of the Charente département), and lay on the poncho soaking up the sun. In the cornflower blue sky overhead, two airliners crossed, their vapour trails carving a perfect white X in the sky, which thirty seconds later had faded to nothing. It was as if some celestial being were saying: 'Look — this is you. Here for just a brief moment, then gone for ever.'

Tilted forward under the weight of a backpack, I had ample opportunity to study the surface of the road and the dozens of insects which so recklessly occupied it. Why did they want to be there on the tarmac, when just a few feet away they could be in the comparative safety of limitless acres of fields and forests? Hairy caterpillars, ants, spiders, beetles, bees and centipedes all took their chances, or had done so unsuccessfully. I couldn't bear leaving them at risk, and was kept quite busy persuading them into the grass, thick with giant thistles, clover, cow parsley, and wild orchids. Each time I bent forward the backpack threatened to tip me on my face. One stunning caterpillar was well over four inches long, a shiny, ruby-red giant with an extravagant frilled yellow petticoat, which rippled sexily as it humped along, conspicuously overdressed for an afternoon stroll in the countryside. She was a stubborn character who used her flamboyant under-wear to anchor herself to the tarmac with limpet tenacity, but I managed to catch her unawares with a piece of card and knocked her off balance before scooping her up and depositing her safely in the undergrowth, wondering what sort of moth or butterfly she would become.

All along this road, pink, blue, yellow and white splatters of wild flowers broke up the green of the roadside, as if someone had walked past carelessly flicking a paintbrush. Cowslips, bluebells, great white daisies and yellow buttercups pushed their way through the long grass; the fields of lurid oilseed rape were fading, the hawthorn was in bloom, and tempted out by the heat of the sun lizards chased each other through piles of stones.

So far the terrain had been virtually flat,

but now the landscape began to undulate, mostly upward. The pastures were lush and rich, and the oak trees in bright green, perfect new leaf. Behind the thick hedgerows, sheep sheltering from the scorching afternoon heat scattered in quite unnecessary panic as I passed.

★   ★   ★

Right on the banks of the river Vienne, which is spanned by a handsome stone bridge bedecked, in summer, with pots of scarlet geraniums, the campsite at Availles-Limouzine was very peaceful. There was no-one else there, although in the adjacent car park a large group of travellers had set up home, and hosts of wild children scrambled around and played with tethered dogs. A couple walked by leading a donkey cart containing three young children, the little donkey bobbing his woolly head patiently up and down. In the river an alligator floated motionless, pretending to be a log, but it didn't fool me for one minute. I knew an alligator when I saw one. I was raised in the colonies.

Well, OK, so it was a log.

A fine new crop of blisters had sprouted like mushrooms during the journey. By the time I had swathed them in more thick layers of cotton wool and plasters, my feet looked like something a yeti would flaunt, but at least they didn't hurt. I studied the red rash that now enfolded both ankles and had reached my left thigh, as I lay cool and relaxed in the tent beneath a huge dark pine tree, with nothing much on. On the other side of the tall mesh fence voices shouted to each other as two girls cycled down the lane, and suddenly there was the rasping sound of tyres skidding on gravel, a clatter of metal, and then silence.

'Are you there?' squeaked a tearful voice. There was no answer. The speaker started to sob quietly.

I began hunting for my discarded clothes, then heard her friend's voice: 'What happened? Oh, my God, are you hurt?'

'I don't think so.' Then the first girl let out an earthshattering scream. '*Merde!* Look at the brakes! Look at the brakes! They will kill me when I get home. *Merde! Merde!*'

'Calm down, it's OK. I'll explain to them that it was an accident.'

The first girl started to shriek in earnest. 'They'll kill me! I know it. Look at the brakes! Look at them!'

'Let me see if I can fix them. Ah no, look this is broken off.'

'AAAAAH!' bellowed the potential murder victim. 'You'll see, they will kill me. All of them. *Merde! Merde!* The brakes!'

'No, no. I will be your witness. They will believe me.'

Clutching my pile of clothes, I listened in dismay as the hapless one worked herself into a frenzy. Either she was the product of lunatics who overreacted to small incidents, or else, having gained centre stage and an audience, she was not going to let her moment pass too soon. She screamed and wailed alarmingly, while her desperate friend tried to comfort her, but she didn't want to be comforted, she wanted her brakes repaired. I certainly couldn't mend the damaged bicycle and I doubted I could console the girl either, so remained unseen in the tent as the voices continued, one shrill and hopeless, the other low and calm, until eventually they both moved off, wheeling their bicycles.

Later, in the pleasant cool of the early evening, I crossed the bridge and strolled round the sleepy little town. An old lady, sitting on her doorstep outside a timbered house in a narrow alley leading to the river, smiled and beckoned me over, asking what I was doing and where I was staying. I told her about my journey, and she nodded wisely.

'Then you must be English. You're very brave. Aren't you afraid, all alone?'

Well, it was comforting when there were other people around, but I couldn't say I was ever frightened. I'd walked hundreds of miles on isolated footpaths in the previous months, stopping to pass the time of day with total strangers, who had never been anything but friendly and courteous. No, I wasn't afraid of being alone.

What a pretty little town Availles-Limouzine is, I said.

She nodded. 'Ah yes, it is pretty, but it is dying. There is no employment here, except the industrial bakery that supplies the prison in Poitiers. All the young people have moved away. All the lovely houses here are now holiday homes. For two months of the year the town comes alive, and then when the holidays end, it dies again. I am fed up with it. There's nothing to do except watch television.'

I invited her to come with me, and she cackled loudly.

'If I was a young girl again, like you . . . ' Her voice tailed off. At the time I was fifty-two.

We stood together and watched the river for a few minutes, and when I looked back from the campsite she was standing on the riverbank, waving.

The ground at the site was a well-mown lawn, free of any inconvenient lumps and bumps, so it wasn't too uncomfortable, and the river flowed past silently. I settled down confident, for the first time, that I would make it to Lake Geneva. And it would not be a matter of stamina, or determination, or fitness, or encouragement. Now that I believed I could do it, I knew I would. It was that simple. There was no longer any doubt at all. It would take longer than I had planned, it would be harder than I had anticipated, but I was going to get there. Just by putting one foot in front of another, one step at a time, day by day.

I drifted off to sleep to a chorus of bellowing frogs.

6

Being Insistent

The shortest distance between Availles-
Limouzine and the next stopping point at
Bellac was twenty-two miles, which I knew I
couldn't make in one day. I hadn't been able
to locate anywhere to stay overnight between
the two points before leaving home, so I
wandered into the Tourist Office, where the
girl was charming and as helpful as she could
be, but no use at all in finding anywhere for
me to stop en route. She pointed out
campsites, hotels, rooms and gîtes all of
which were either closed, in the wrong
direction or even further than Bellac, so the
only thing to do was to set off and see what
came up along the way. The Mandrake
footpath was well marked on the map and
offered an attractive alternative to walking on
the road, so I followed it to Abzac, crossing

from the Poitou-Charentes into the Limousin region, and into the département of the Haute Vienne. I'd been travelling for eleven days and covered about 120 miles, through one region and four départements.

There was a sign indicating a château close by, and I thought it might be worth a detour. The path rose 525 feet over a distance of half a mile, and I arrived gasping for air and sweat-streaked to find that the château was privately owned and not open to the public.

Once I had recovered my breath I headed on along the footpath, down into the welcome cool of the Forêt de Monette. Still winded from the climb to the château, I sat on the forest floor to rest and rewrap my feet, watching amongst the crisp dead leaves a tiny ant grappling with a huge load — a twig or piece of dead wood, six times its own size. It went one way then another, painstakingly manoeuvring its load over massive obstacles and back again, looking utterly disorientated. I knew just how it must feel. In the stillness, faint creaks and groans came from the ground, as if seeds were bursting and roots mining their way audibly through the earth. A tiny transparent green cricket, half an inch long, jumped onto my leg and sat grooming its perfect, diminutive body, and it was quite impossible to imagine that a whole self-sustaining life form could be condensed into so tiny a space.

The path was well marked for some distance, until unexpectedly a gravelled road appeared which was not on the map, and from which a network of tracks led off in all directions. There were no *balises* anywhere. I followed the road for twenty minutes, as the forest became denser, darker, and very humid, and I had no idea where I was going. The long grass hid rocks and bricks which had been dumped into ruts and could easily lead to broken or twisted ankles, and still the woods grew denser. The trees became thin and wispy, and brambles and nettles snaked across the path, which had deteriorated into a set of ruts brimming with black sludge. Millions of unpleasant little winged creatures whined and whinged around my face. The choice was between walking in the sludge, slithering about on the edges of the ruts, or beating a path through the thicket on either side. I tried the last, and after a while reached a fetid lagoon which had engulfed the ruts and extended for fifteen feet on each side. The only way was through it, hacking at the undergrowth and paddling through the black mess. The slime oozed to the very top of my boots, and I slipped on a submerged root, splashing filth all over my clothes. Only the hiking stick saved me from falling face down. I was sure I could hear groaning coming from the woods, and I began to feel panicky. Covered in sweat, slime, thorns and twigs, I ploughed onwards, and after about twenty minutes reached a junction and a well-defined path. Wherever it led, I was going to follow it, because I had to get out of this ghastly place. It led to a tarmac road on which I found a *borne*, the sturdy concrete pillar which indicates the road number, and from there I was able to pinpoint my position.

I wasn't too far off route, but I was frantically thirsty, and very stinky. Turning onto the busy national road, I was just in time to see a woman disappearing into the back of a dilapidated house, so I trudged to the back door and knocked. There was no reply. I knocked again, and again, and again. Louder. At length a shrill voice screeched: 'What do you want?'

'Some water, please.'

'Go away!'

'Please, I need some water.' I banged the door again.

There was a long silence, then a scowling face appeared at the corner of the house. 'Come and stand here, by the front door.'

I obeyed, while she scuttled into the house,

locking the door behind her. It was so long before anything else happened that if there had been any other houses in sight. I would have abandoned my quest. I thumped on the door again.

The lock rattled and the door opened about six inches. Out came a large plastic bottle connected to a grubby hand.

'Thank you very much,' I rasped.

'Take it, and go away. Go on, get away from here!' The grubby hand flapped threateningly, the door slammed once more, and the lock turned. She didn't seem to want me around. I hoped she hadn't done anything unspeakable to the water. What a very disagreeable person she was to meet on a sunny afternoon, I thought. She was probably thinking much the same.

Despite having spent several hours roaming around, I hadn't made much progress eastwards, and it was midafternoon. The next town, Mézières, was still nine miles distant, and I wouldn't make it. About three miles to the south was Brillac, the nearest village of any size, so I set sail to find out what it had to offer in the way of overnight accommodation, rubbing off as much of the now dry mud from my person as I could.

The village shop could suggest nowhere, but recommended the local *mairie*, where I met two ladies who shook their heads sorrowfully when I asked if there was somewhere I could camp for the night. No, there was absolutely nowhere at all. Did they know of anybody who could rent me a room, or let me stay in their garden, or a barn? No-one could do that. We sat around in silence for a few minutes, then one suggested perhaps a chalet in the holiday village, although it was not yet opened for the season.

The other lady was despatched to find the *gardienne*, who had last been seen helping widow Moreau with her garden. Fifteen minutes later she returned with the *gardienne*, who clutched a cabbage in each hand.

'You would like to stay in a chalet tonight?'

'Yes, I would be very grateful.'

It was no problem, although I would have to use one of the older chalets; the new ones weren't quite finished. That was fine.

'It will be two hundred and fifty francs.'

I groaned and shook my head. My total daily budget was a hundred francs, which had to feed me, pay camp fees and cover telephone calls home for a daily check-in and report on the animals, and allow for spare torch and tape recorder batteries, films and emergencies. Two hundred and fifty francs was out of the question.

They expressed their desolation. There was

nothing else they could do. I shrugged and grinned gormlessly. It was just after 5.00 p.m. and they started closing down the office for the night. I unlaced my boots and settled deeper into the chair.

'I truly can't go any further,' I said. 'I am sorry.' It looked as if we had reached an impasse.

The three of them withdrew to an adjacent room and talked quietly amongst themselves — perhaps they were drawing straws to see who would have to accommodate me. They returned, looking perplexed.

'Look,' I said. 'I only need a tiny patch of grass, nothing more. Maybe behind the church?'

'Oh, then you have a tent?' one of them exclaimed, a note of astonishment in her voice.

'Yes, of course.' As it was strapped conspicuously to the outside of my pack, which was occupying most of the floor space in the *mairie*, I thought they would have noticed it.

'Ah. You should have said! You can camp at the holiday village, if you don't mind being alone there?'

No, I didn't. To our unanimous relief, the cabbage lady drove me the half-mile to the site, which was deserted, and had an immaculate new sanitary block, complete with hot showers and a pay phone. The fee for a night's stay and as much hot water as I could use was just twenty francs.

As usual, Jennifer was enjoying herself. Gloria had taken her to Charroux, where Gloria had a doctor's appointment and thought it would be nice for Jennifer to see the tower of Saint-Sauveur. The weather was perfect, hot sunshine and a few wispy clouds, and at the small café in the shadow of Charlemagne's splendid tower they ordered a ham and cheese sandwich and a Pepsi.

To know that Gloria had found someone to keep her company and have fun with was excellent news, because I'd felt bad about going off and leaving her while her hapless spouse was locked up in the pokey. Bill's arrest had come just a few weeks before my departure date, and with Jennifer's ticket booked and all the arrangements in place it was rather late in the day to call the whole thing off.

The fine weather was holding, and the sky was a deep clear blue; by now even my tiny mind had worked out that a clear sky forecast a cold night, so I swaddled myself thickly in all my clothing and wriggled into the sleeping bag.

I was quite pleased with myself, because I

had managed to get the grubby-handed woman to give me water, and Brillac to find me somewhere to sleep. It shows what you can do when you have to.

Each day since leaving la Rochelle, I had heard a cuckoo calling. It called today, towards dusk.

Later, when the darkness fell, the nightingales started singing.

7

Yes, It's Very Close. No, It's Miles Away

A herd of silvery-cream Charolais cattle lay clustered together in the meadow beside the campsite, heads raised to the misty early morning sun. In the centre of the group a single tiny calf, darker than the adults, nestled between its mother and a regal and relaxed bull. Twenty-two lustrous eyes watched with mild interest as I folded the tent and loaded the backpack.

I was on the road by 7.15 a.m., following a footpath through the still sleeping village, en route to Bellac, fifteen miles away. Apart from a solitary black redstart perched on a fence post, tail switching up and down, calling his loud 'tchak, tchak', the lanes were deserted, and pleasantly cool, and the footpath here was clearly marked.

In the dappled shade of the path, a stout

103

black and yellow fire salamander stood foursquare and motionless, so well camouflaged that I very nearly stepped on it. I watched it for ten minutes to see if it would do anything. It didn't, even when I walked around it and touched its tail gently with my stick. It was still for so long that I began to wonder if it was real. I prodded it again very softly, and elicited an almost imperceptible movement of its stumpy tail, ever so slight, as if it was too weary to bother. It would have recently emerged from hibernation, and was charging its batteries from the sun. Wherever there were trees, caterpillars dangled from them by delicate threads, waiting expectantly to metamorphose into butterflies and moths. Often they hitched lifts on my clothing or backpack, or by dangling from the brim of my hat.

After a promising start, the *balises* did a vanishing act at a crossroads, and I was lost again. Across a steep valley a large farmhouse spread over the crest of a hill, and I headed for it. Children's toys were scattered all over the place, and in the fields horses, ponies, and goats were making the most of the spring grass. A smiling young woman called out from where she was hanging up the washing.

'Are you thirsty?'

'Yes!'

'Come in,' she called. 'We're so lucky here. We have our own spring, and it never dries up. Come and enjoy some of our wonderful water.'

I followed her through the garden to a large swimming pool, where she reached for a glass from a table, and bent down to the pool. She turned and laughed.

'Look — it comes straight from the ground, and fills the pool.'

The water emerged from a small slope and flowed down a pipe to a joint just above the level of the water. She filled the glass and handed it to me, and refilled it twice.

From where we stood, hills and meadows and oak forests covered every aspect; and a river curled through the valley.

'How lucky you are to live here. It's beautiful.'

'Oh yes, this is our paradise,' she answered.

She and her husband had four school-age children; they had opted out of the rat-race by moving from Bordeaux two years previously, and were planning to develop a small holiday complex catering exclusively for disabled people.

Trying not to sound too lost, I enquired where we were.

Bussière-Boffy. She showed me on the map. I was well off course, nearly four miles south of where I should have been, but it had been a very pleasant diversion. Refreshed, and promising that if I ever passed that way again I would be certain to visit her, I set off to find some lunch.

There was a field, with about twenty large humpy-shaped animals in it. I blinked and peered, because they looked startlingly like American buffalo, and after all, this was central France. But American buffalo is what they were, with four or five calves, grazing peacefully amongst bushes of bright yellow gorse. They were too far from the fence to photograph clearly, and did not reciprocate my interest. After a few minutes of tongue-clicking and arm-waving which they ignored completely, I gave up, and abandoned any attempt to attract them closer. Along with ostrich, alligator and kangaroo, buffalo meat is currently in vogue in France.

At midday I walked off the right-hand edge of the second map, and an hour later arrived hungrily in the little town of Mézières-sur-Issoire. From the open window of a small bar/restaurant in the village centre came the clatter of plates and cutlery, animated conversation, and garlic-laden food smells. I had walked for almost six hours and not eaten since the previous evening, so I pushed open the narrow door and stepped into the noisy room, which fell silent and still. There were a dozen workmen eating at a trestle table, and they sat, forks halfway to their open mouths, gazing incredulously at the weird apparition in jungle hat, rolled-up shorts and giant boots, topped with a bulging backpack and armed with the great stick. Nothing moved.

I inhaled deeply.

'*Bonjour,*' I said brightly.

'*Bonjour, madame,*' they answered, and resumed their meal.

English people are not accustomed to walking into rooms full of strangers and speaking to them. We don't do that sort of thing. The French, on the other hand, do, and, like so many French ideas, it's a winner, because once you have broken the ice you are instantly accepted as part of the crowd and can fade into anonymity. Walking in and saying nothing is regarded as ill-mannered, and only a foreigner or very ignorant person would do so, and could expect to be the target of frequent stares.

Not surprisingly, the lunch menu was all meat. It almost invariably is, in the small workmen's cafés. The chef was very obliging, however, and produced a platter of freshly prepared crudités, sliced tomatoes, diced beetroot, grated celeriac and carrots, served with a jug of vinaigrette and followed by a small mountain of potatoes crisply sautéed with garlic and parsley, and a large cheeseboard that was left on the table to be attacked at leisure. With two Coca-Colas, the bill came to fifty-five francs.

Décor was not the strong point of the establishment, which looked as if it had last been updated in the 1950s and then by someone suffering from a frightful mental illness or bilious attack. Grey pebbledash haphazardly coated the panels on all four doors and the front of the bar, and most of the woodwork was smeared with a cheap-chocolate-ice-cream-coloured paint. Various fragments of ghastly and diverse wallpapers unpeeled from the walls, revealing further murky layers beneath, and every vertical surface was smothered with ancient nicotine-stained and fly-blown posters, calendars, mirrors and plaques, all promoting beverages, many of which had probably long ago ceased production, and all hanging cock-eyed. Even the ancient pinball machine stood lopsided, sloping from side to side and diagonally, with its hind legs propped upon uneven heaps of old newspapers. However, the cordial atmosphere more than made up for the lack of elegance.

Refreshed and knowing that a room full of

strangers would never again intimidate me, I set off for Bellac. To avoid the endless stream of heavy vehicles on the main road I followed a longer, minor road, and was soon lost as usual. The lady in whose garden I arrived after dragging the backpack through a barbed wire fence was very helpful and sympathetic. She acted as if it was perfectly normal for eccentric foreigners to materialize on her doorstep, and steered me back on course.

A flock of guinea fowl scratched around in a cluster of trees, shrieking and screeching their blood-curdling racket. With their spotted grey chiffon skirts and bright red crowns, bald heads and scrawny necks, and cheeks thickly smeared with turquoise make-up, they looked like a collection of ancient dowagers. Among them a single golden pheasant swaggered, his magnificent plumage glinting in the sun, a Beau Brummell amongst a bevy of harridans.

On the outskirts of Bellac I met a lady working in her garden, which sloped up at an angle of about 60 degrees from the road. Large stones served as footholds, and the steep bank was a dense cloudy mass of pink and blue, dominated by a wisteria in a shade of palest pink. It was beautiful, and I stopped to admire it. The gardener negotiated the bank skilfully.

'The garden is nothing this year,' she said sadly. 'Too much rain in spring, and now too much sun.' Gardeners are the same the world over.

She invited me in for a cold drink, but I had been walking for ten hours and wanted to get to the campsite and get my boots off, so I declined politely.

'Promise you will come back then, one day.' She smiled.

Was the campsite close by, I asked?

'Yes.' She pointed. 'Just after the cross-roads, about two hundred metres.'

With a repeated undertaking to return one day, I headed for the crossroads, expecting them to be just around the corner. They were not. The road wound down, down, down, and above the valley into which I had now descended the town sat perched on top of a steep hill.

On the floor of the valley, I met another lady and her cat. Was it very far to the crossroads, I asked?

'*Oh, là là!*' she puffed. 'It's a long way. You must climb up there' — she indicated the hill — 'then walk right through the town. You will come to the crossroads where the four big national roads meet, and then carry on from there. The campsite is signposted.'

Climb, climb; it was very hot, and every

twenty paces I had to stop and catch my breath, but finally I reached the town square, where three people sat on a bench.

'Where are you looking for?' called out one of them, a lady with tight rust-coloured curls like coiled snakes which slithered in a rather sinister way as she talked.

'The campsite. Can you direct me, please?'

'Ah yes, it is very simple. Continue up the road until the bakery, then turn left. No, it would be quicker to carry straight on. When you get to the post office, cross over and then turn right. No, no, wait a minute. Don't go by the post office. After the bakery, carry straight on. Turn right at the *épicerie*, then cross over and turn left.'

I shifted my weight.

'On the other hand, you could go via the tabac. That would be quite quick. Not the first tabac, the one after. Where they sell the Loto tickets. Go past that, then when you reach the crossroads, take the left hand, which will bring you out by the post office, and then . . . '

It was frightfully hot, and I felt like toppling over. I wondered how long she would keep this up.

Her female companion murmured something. She nodded.

'But if you want,' she continued, 'you could

111

go down to the bottom of the hill and turn right, then follow the road up to the *mairie* . . . '

'Thank you very much, I think I will take your advice and go via the *épicerie*,' I said, and made my escape. I headed for the bakery, and behind me her voice continued: 'Now don't forget to turn right before the bakery, otherwise you will end up at the post office. But if you do get to the post office, the best thing would be to carry straight on . . . '

I started walking faster, almost jogging.

' . . . left, tabac, or post office, straight on, no, possibly right . . . '

Something was panting over my right shoulder, and I turned to find one of her companions, a dark, short little man, running to catch up.

'I will take you to the campsite,' he announced. 'I know where it is. We foreigners must help each other.'

He was from Portugal, and had lived in Bellac since fleeing his country as a refugee from the dictatorship of thirty years ago. Every dozen or so steps, he stopped to talk at length to anyone who would listen. His French was excruciating, but he was obviously popular in the town. After fifteen minutes we still hadn't reached the cross-roads: he seemed to know everyone, but he obviously didn't know where the campsite was. We arrived at the post office and I was starting to feel extremely bad-tempered. And then there it was — a sign pointing to 'Camping Municipal — 200 metres'. Thanking my new friend, I said I would find my way from there, but he was not going to be shaken off and kept trotting along beside me. People called out to him, and he hesitated between them and me. He stuck with me.

Once at the campsite I turned and shook his hand, thanking him for his help. He followed me in.

'Thank you very much, and goodbye,' I said cheerily.

'I had better make sure you find somewhere to put your tent.'

That wasn't at all necessary as the huge site was empty but for six caravans. He hovered around as I offloaded the backpack and started putting the tent together. He tried to help.

'Look,' I said, 'you have been very kind. Now I can manage perfectly, so you don't need to stay any longer.' I pumped his hand again.

Still he stood there as if he was going to take root.

'Really, it would be better for you to go now. Thank you so much for your help, but if my boyfriend finds you here with me he may be very angry. He is violent and unpredictable and I've no idea how he might react. There could be trouble with the police. Please go quickly; he could arrive at any minute.'

He hesitated.

'Quickly, please!' I implored him, wringing my hands despairingly and rolling my eyes in what I hoped looked like terror. As he turned to leave, I called out: 'If you see six big men with long hair and leather clothing and lots of chains, on big motorcycles, English number plates, that will be my boyfriend and his friends. Please will you direct them here?'

The washing facilities were poor: there was a single toilet to serve the whole campsite, and where there should have been washbasins there were just pipes poking up from the floor. It was dirty. A Frenchman wearing tartan carpet slippers and carrying a large plastic bowl shook his head and muttered angrily.

'Disgraceful. It's absolutely disgraceful.'

It certainly wasn't very impressive, but at least the water in the sordid showers was hot. The French municipal campsites are usually clean and well equipped. Doubtless Bellac would have improved by the time the holiday season got under way.

I had regretted abandoning Nick and would gladly have carried his weight given a second chance. The evenings could be long, and although I had picked up a couple of French scandal magazines they were frustratingly difficult, and often impossible, to understand without the help of a dictionary. The way they were written, I couldn't work out if somebody had done something they shouldn't, or hadn't done something they should. An English couple stopping on their way to the Dordogne asked if I would like an English book, and kindly invited me to help myself from a library of paperbacks they carried in their caravan.

Although I had eaten well at lunchtime, I couldn't resist the call of the town's restaurants, and found a small bistro. After studying the menu and changing my mind several times, I decided on a crêpe with a salad. The waiter gave me a funny look. I had meant to order a crêpe with smoked salmon filling, and a green salad. But tired and eyesore, I had asked for a green salad with smoked salmon, and a green salad without. I was surprised when it arrived, but realized what I had done and ate it anyway. Not to be deprived of the crêpe, I ordered a lemon one for dessert. It was a truly vile thing, gooey, sugarless, sour and very sharp. Even after washing it down with a glass of cider, its pasty texture and bitter flavour stuck to my throat. When the *note*[1] arrived, the crêpe was not included. I wrestled with my conscience and decided that (a) the crêpe was so nasty it didn't deserve to be paid for, (b) it was the restaurant's responsibility to get the bill right, and (c) I needed the extra francs far more than they did. I left without pointing out the omission, and have felt slightly guilty ever since.

★ ★ ★

Back at the ranch, Jennifer was having fun and games. When she and Gloria returned from their visit to Charroux, Gloria found her water had been disconnected because Bill had forgotten to pay the water bill that was due in January.

She'd asked a French-speaking friend to call the water company, and they sent someone to the house right away to collect a cheque and turn the water back on for her.

The next call she received was from the French national police, to say that one of her truck drivers had been pulled over at the Spanish/French border and fined for driving

---
[1] bill

116

over allowed time and using two tachograph discs in one day. To top it off they had found drugs on the guy, so he was in jail and the truck, with someone's furniture in it, had been impounded.

'Oh my,' sighed Jennifer, 'poor Gloria.'

'Don't worry, she may be small, but she's a very tough cookie. She'll be fine.'

'I sure hope so,' Jennifer said.

I took my regular evening cocktail of four distalgesics. At the end of every day everything hurt, but it didn't really bother me. As long as it didn't keep me awake, it didn't matter.

Following three days of walking, the next day was a rest day. It dawned hot and bright, and I enjoyed the luxury of lounging in the tent and watching a family of magpies through the mesh curtain. There were two enormous babies who bumped around on the grass about eight feet away. Their parents worked hard to feed them, and on seeing them approach the two giants would rock back onto their avian elbows and flutter their wings helplessly, shrieking piteously. It must have been a heart-rending sight for the adults, who flew off time and again to hunt for food for their helpless little ones. Once they had gone, the infants happily flopped around picking insects and assorted morsels from the ground. At the first sign of the parents' return, it was back to helpless and hungry mode. I named them Laurel and Hardy.

Bellac is a town of five and a half thousand inhabitants, built on the side of a high hill just inside the border of the Limousin region. Dating back to the tenth century, it had prospered during the Middle Ages on the back of the tanneries established there. It still has a tannery today, which processes beef hides into leather for saddlery and orthopaedic use.

It was the birthplace of Jean Giraudoux, the French diplomat and writer, many of whose works were modern adaptations of Greek mythology. In the courtyard of the *mairie* is a fountain erected in his honour, and every year the 'Giraudoux en Limousin' festival of arts is held in Bellac between June and July.

If you wanted to in Bellac, you could climb down 136 steep stone medieval steps to explore the valley of Vincou below, with its stone humpback bridge. I didn't want to climb down and up anything, so I opted for a couple of hours' reading in the sun, before aiming for the Bar du Commerce for lunch. I was getting awfully greedy and at the very limit of my budget.

Lunch came to sixty-five francs for a plate of crudités, a cutlet of sea bream flawlessly cooked and served with pasta and a saffron sauce, and an excellent cheeseboard and ice cream, accompanied by a half carafe of wine and cup of coffee (decaffeinated if you asked). The owner of the Bar du Commerce was a big burly man like a grizzly bear, with an easy-going manner. His wife was wearily pregnant and footsore, treading down the backs of her espadrilles and frequently kneading the small of her back with a fist. She still maintained a bright smile and had a friendly word for all her customers. Each time she passed the bar on her way to the kitchen, her ursine spouse patted her rump affectionately. Apart from her forward bump, she was slim and chic. They were both nearer to forty than thirty, and already had a teenage daughter.

Trade was lively; there was a single vacant table next to where I sat. A trio ambled over to it and settled themselves silently. He was a defeated-looking little man, with slumped shoulders and a threadbare moustache. His wife was huge and broad-shouldered, with man-trap jaws set in a down-turned glare. Her moustache far outdid the little man's. It bristled ferociously all over her top lip and straggled spikily down towards her chin. Its

119

wiry black hairs glistened with good health. With them was a teenage girl, twice as fat as she should be, and of a curiously boneless appearance, as if fashioned from pink almond paste. She had beautiful thick fair hair, and the smile of a saint. I supposed she was their daughter. The harridan ordered for them all: hamburger and fried potatoes. They didn't speak one word to each other as they ate. The only sound was the scraping of cutlery and munching, chewing and swallowing noises. They didn't look at each other either, keeping their eyes on their food. I watched, fascinated.

The resident dog, a grimy little apricot poodle, came over and stood with its paws on the table and the almond-paste girl clapped her hands together and grinned at me. She had perfect teeth. She reached out to stroke the dog and indicated that she wanted me to stroke it too. I did so, and she patted my hand, her big pink face alight with pleasure. The parents munched and swallowed.

In the corner a large television screen was showing the weather forecast. A thin blonde woman appeared, wearing huge sunglasses, with her hair piled in a massive beehive, and dressed in a yellow bikini top and black toreador pants. She was holding a toy seal in her arms, and standing on a raft in the sea somewhere. There was a bewildered-looking donkey on the raft, too. The beehive person said lots of things that I couldn't understand, but gave very little information regarding the forthcoming weather, except that the temperature had reached 27°C today. Then she dived off the raft and disappeared.

At the next table, they were slurping large bowls of ice cream. Suddenly the marzipan girl stood up, pushing her bowl away. Patting me affectionately as she passed, just as she had patted the little poodle, she marched towards the door. The parents abandoned their ice cream wordlessly, and leaving a handful of notes and coins on the table marched silently out after her.

I followed shortly behind them, and wobbled rather unsteadily back to the campsite, the lunchtime wine taking effect. I slept until after 6.00 p.m. and awoke to a beautiful evening, as the sun, the brilliant red of an Edam cheese, folded itself down gently over the horizon. Since abandoning the inflatable pillow at home, sleeping had been even more uncomfortable than previously, but now I found that by stuffing the sleeping bag's nylon sack with an assortment of rolled-up clothing I could make a perfect pillow, customized to exactly the right density. Despite the afternoon's long siesta, I had no difficulty falling asleep.

8

In a Pool of Nice Cold Water

Yesterday when I went to the newsagent to buy postcards, looking relatively normal, the shop assistant had been charming and friendly. This morning, when I arrived in full hiking regalia and armed with the huge pole, she was highly suspicious when I handed her a hundred-franc note to pay for my weekly Loto ticket.

She took the note, and holding it by each edge jerked it violently sideways several times. When it failed to yield, she held it to the light, turned it back to front and upside down, and stroked each side with her fingertips. Setting her lips in a tight hard line and slitting her eyes at me, she demanded: 'Where did you get this?' Obviously she considered it unthinkable that anybody looking as I did would have come legitimately into possession of such extraordinary wealth.

'From the bank on the corner — Crédit Agricole.'

'When was that?'

'This morning, just five minutes ago. Why, what's the matter?'

'I don't like the look of it,' she replied. 'It doesn't look right, and it doesn't feel right.'

I held out my hand and examined it. It looked just like any other hundred-franc note to me.

A queue of interested spectators was developing in the shop.

'What is it exactly that you don't like about it?' I asked.

'It's just not right. Have you another one?'

Was she mad? Did she think I was made of money? I did actually have another note, but if there was anything wrong with this one I wanted it sorted right now, while I was still near the bank.

I shook my head and we stared at each other meanly for a few moments.

'OK. I am going to trust you. But just this once,' she announced magnanimously, handing me my change.

'You are too kind,' I muttered, feeling like prodding her in the belly with the stick, and swung out of the shop, nearly knocking over a stand of greetings cards with the backpack.

I needed some shopping, and here the backpack became a serious obstacle. As it contained everything I owned at the time, I dared not leave it out of sight, but trying to manoeuvre through the narrow alleyways of the supermarket was just about impossible, as every time I turned towards a shelf I either bashed another customer or threatened the contents of the shelf behind me. None of the staff were prepared to look after it, so I loaded it into a trolley and pushed it around with me, under the watchful eye of the cashiers.

One thing it was vital to carry was toilet paper, because you never knew where you would or wouldn't find it. Sometimes the grubbiest campsites or restaurants would offer a generous supply; conversely some of the classiest and most expensive establishments offered none at all. Some of life's little luxuries I could manage without, but not that. However, the smallest quantity sold on the supermarket shelves in Bellac was eight rolls, in a great mountain which would have filled the backpack, had there been any room left in it. So I brought a box of tissues which I eviscerated, plus a very large bag of cherries for my lunch. The cashier looked quite startled that I had struggled so hard to navigate round the store with the backpack, to her obvious entertainment, for such an insignificant purchase.

The most foolproof route to Châteauponsac was the D1. It was far too hot a day to get lost. Sweaty farmers oozed in their tractor cabs cutting hay, and herds of cattle and sheep drowsed beneath great oak trees, too hot to bother grazing. Beside the road wild orchids flourished, and there were several dead adders on the tarmac, together with a few very beautiful lizards, their lifeless skins glistening in fantastic iridescent blues and oranges. Every little corpse represented a small tragedy to me. Each dead bee or moth or beetle had once been a perfect, intricate and unique being which was gone for ever, and I wondered why their designer had gone to the trouble of creating so many beautiful creatures without including the gift of road sense. It seemed such a waste.

Because the Limousin is associated with the great golden cattle that bear its name, it had always been in my mind a vast plateau. Cattle roam prairies; sheep ramble about in hills. Everyone's heard of the Limousin Plateau. I hadn't expected to encounter any hills at all until I reached the Jura; in my mind, again, a nice flat road meandered almost all the way between la Rochelle and Geneva, avoiding any inclines. But the

Limousin is not a plateau at all. No. What I saw of it, which was quite a lot, was an enormous collection of hills stitched together as far as the eye could see in every direction.

There is also a breed of Limousin sheep, and a Limousin pig, and at Bourneix, in the south of the département, two tons of gold are mined annually. Gold was being mined in the Limousin in the fifth century BC, and Julius Caesar, when he arrived, named the area 'gold-bearing Gaul'.

Rich thick forests of oak and fir offered a cool refuge from the midday sun as the terrain started to become seriously hilly. At Rancon, a pretty village trickling down a small hill to the river Gartempe, I stopped for an unbelievably expensive Coca-Cola, and to admire the flower-filled streets. For a very small village it had several restaurants, each offering enticing gourmet menus at prices well above average and well out of my range, so I sat on a stone bench in the shade of a large oak tree, watching the sheep grazing the floor of the valley below, and delved into the bag of rather hot cherries. A few yards away stood a *lanterne des morts*, a round, hollow stone column about twelve feet tall. These structures, which can be round, square or octagonal, stand on a few steps and are pierced with holes at the top, and occasionally surmounted with a cross. A small opening at the base allows access to a platform on which a lighted candle can be placed, and which can then be hoisted to the top of the column by a pulley. Sometimes, at head height there is a flat stone, like an altar. Archaeologists date them to the twelfth century, but many people believe them to be much older. I've no idea how old they are, but this one certainly looked pretty ancient.

Their purpose is open to speculation. They were often placed in the middle of a cemetery, presumably to watch over the dead; they could equally have been erected by a pagan cult, possibly a sun-worshipping religion, and could also have served as a beacon in the dark for travellers and pilgrims. You can choose which explanation you prefer.

For half a mile the road out of Rancon surged upwards into clouds of vivid yellow broom, pointing into which was an engaging sign indicating a footpath: a stiff-limbed couple marching purposefully, rigid legs and arms parallel with each other as they progressed in giant strides. The male was armed with a stick and wearing a backpack. He led the way. His well-endowed and modestly-skirted partner shadowed him at a respectful distance. Neither appeared to have any feet.

Over the hills to the south, skyscraper clouds were stacking up into the blue haze. Sweating like a racehorse, I fixed my thoughts on the Châteauponsac campsite that had just about every facility anyone could want, including a swimming pool. In a few hours' time, I would be soaking in an ocean of cool water. Even the clover, ranging in colour from palest pink to dark mauve and one solitary clump of vermilion, drooped in the heat. It was a great deal hotter than I had expected at this time of year. I usually wilted at anything over 70°F, and it was far above that. In the bar at Rancon the thermometer had indicated 86°F, but as long as I kept moving and kept my jungle hat on it was no problem. I was getting to the bottom of the bag of cherries, spitting the stones out onto the roadside in an unladylike fashion at regular intervals, imagining in years to come an avenue of cherry trees.

The campsite at Châteauponsac was beautifully situated, standing at the foot of the once fortified medieval town and overlooking the river Gartempe. I was the only person there. The *gardienne* was young, very enthusiastic about her job and proud of the site. She pointed out all the facilities available. Just as the brochure promised, there was a bar, restaurant, swimming pool and games room. They would all be open in another month's time, and the René-Baubérot museum in the town, showing Limousin life in the Middle Ages, which I had planned on visiting, would be open at the beginning of June.

I rang Jennifer to see what sort of a day she'd had.

She said she was feeling that it had been one of those days when it just didn't pay to get out of bed. At around midnight the previous night the electricity had gone off during a storm. The dogs were frightened of the lightning and thunder and it was very windy, so she'd let them all into the house to ride out the storm together. Around one thirty when it was over she put all the animals back in their respective nests.

She headed up to bed, still with no electricity, and had just about fallen asleep when there was a horrendous crash and the sound of breaking glass. She had no idea what it was. Could it be the dogs trying to get back in, or had someone driven their car through the sliding glass door? She searched around in the dark for the torch, made her way down the stairs and started looking around. There were shards of broken wine-glass all over the kitchen floor, knocked over by the cat. It took her about thirty minutes to get the splinters up off the floor with only the torchlight to see by. When finally she was certain she had all the glass cleared up ('All I needed now would be for someone to get cut'), she headed back to bed. The electricity came on at about two thirty and woke her up as the lights and radio came on.

Gloria had phoned at seven to tell her she was leaving to go to the border to get her truck, and asked Jennifer to feed her dogs.

Slightly weary, Jennifer had got up and decided to do the laundry as the sky had cleared and it was a beautiful sunny day. She'd cleaned and dusted and washed the sheets, moved the horses to where they could have some nice grass to eat and gone out to pull more weeds from the flowerbeds. She got into her swimming costume and lay out in the sun for about an hour surrounded by the dogs. There was a pleasant breeze blowing and it was just right for being outdoors.

She heard nothing more during the day from Gloria — maybe they'd arrested her too, she thought.

When she went to get her nice white sheets and duvet covers off the clothes line, the birds had crapped on them. That didn't surprise her. The real surprise, she said, was that it was Friday the fifteenth and not Friday the thirteenth.

Later she had a call from Carole in Sauzé-Vaussais: Gloria had called her and asked her to let Jennifer know she was being detained at the border. Apparently now the Customs were insisting that the truck be unloaded so they could search it.

Afterwards Gloria did phone and said she wouldn't be home until the next day. The Customs had brought in ten men to search the truck, plus a sniffer dog that was flown in by helicopter. Jennifer told her not to worry about her dogs, she would feed them until Gloria got back, but she was concerned because they'd let the driver go, so if they did find drugs on the truck would Gloria have to go to jail?

'Well,' I said, 'we'll just have to wait and see. If she does, you'll have a whole lot more dogs to look after, won't you?'

Life certainly wasn't dull for my new friend.

The stifling heat had killed my appetite, so I settled for a tin of raspberries, a pot of crème fraîche (that product which initially fools so many of us English into thinking it is fresh cream), a chunk of cheese and a bottle of cider. The air hung motionless and heavy.

It was like trying to breathe warm cotton wool and I could smell the approaching storm.

After a shower, I sprawled out on the emerald grass and started a tentative exploration of my feet. Blessed with a squeamish disposition, and having once keeled over at the sight of a child's wobbly tooth, I didn't want to look, but they were now buried beneath several layers of unsavoury dressings ranging from a few hours to several days old, and it had to be done. I needed to know gangrene wasn't setting in.

They looked like an advertisement for leprosy. Flaps of skin dangled vaguely, uncertain what to do with themselves. Having used up all the available space under my toes, a more enterprising brigade of blisters had squeezed in between them. I still had a small piece of the miraculous Second Skin left, and I applied it to the worst-affected parts, enfolding the rest in wads of cotton wool and securing the lot with yards of plaster.

While I had been occupied with my feet, two ants had fallen into the bottom of my cider, and lay lifeless on the bottom of the cup. I scooped them out and laid them on my towel in the sun.

The evening air was incredibly hot and

heavy, and I sat on the grass in the long shadow of a skinny tree, reading and munching cheese. Every so often I checked on the ants, and after ten minutes the first one was starting to move its legs. The second one followed a while later, and within half an hour they were both exploring the edges of the towel, faltering, looking as if they were nursing hangovers, but definitely alive.

Pleased with this small miracle, and having finished the book from Bellac and a litre and a half of strong cider, I settled down for an early night and went out like a light.

★ ★ ★

There seemed to be an earthquake happening. The ground was shaking, the tent flapping and billowing wildly, and there was water everywhere. Massive explosions smashed the night, and the sky was impossibly bright. The storm had arrived and it was more like being in a small boat on an ocean than in a tent. Water flowed in a brisk stream through the seams. The earth trembled, the air was shattered by enormous cracks of thunder, sheet lightning bounced all around making the ground judder, and I wondered what to do. Could the lightning reach me through the nylon? Would the sleeping bag zip attract it? Could it set the tent on fire? Should I do something? Like get out of the tent and run to the washing block fifty yards away? Then I could sit there, soaking, if not struck dead by lightning on the way, until the storm abated. It was too much trouble, and for once I was not freezing, so I stayed where I was. Just as I had hopefully imagined a few hours earlier, I lay soaking in a pool of cold water.

Having reached the decision to stay put, I went straight back to sleep.

It was thirteen days since I had left la Rochelle, and I had walked 135 miles, without taking into account all the long cuts, and walks to and from local shops. Allowing for the three rest days, it averaged thirteen and a half miles per day, which although not as much as I had originally hoped to achieve wasn't bad.

By morning the sun reigned again. Almost collapsed under the weight of the water, the tent looked very sorry for itself. I was sorry too. Common sense had advised me to buy the lightest tent I could find, weighing a little over four pounds, but had stopped short of checking out its suitability for the job it was expected to do. It was composed of a single nylon skin with a polyamide floor, supported by one glass fibre folding pole which went through an exterior channel and formed an arc, and anchored by six pegs. This gave it the profile of a headless, legless and tailless chameleon. Access was suggested via two minuscule triangular flaps which half unzipped at either end, both lined with an inner flap of fine net. There were two very tiny net triangles in each side, presumably to provide ventilation and combat condensation, which they didn't, covered by nylon caps on the outside. The two walls of the tent sloped up to the central pole at an angle of about 45 degrees from the ground, and unless I slept right in the middle of the tent the condensation which poured down the inside would run onto the sleeping bag, or my face, or whatever other part touched the nylon. It was described as a two-man tent; it might possibly have suited two anorexic people lying on top of each other, or a pair of pygmies end to end, but it was hard to see how two standard-sized persons could spend a night in it. The manufacturers, a well-known name in the field of outdoor activities, claimed it was a three-season tent, suitable for spring, summer and autumn. It gave no protection whatsoever from cold, and not much from the ingress of water, and provided an interior atmosphere which would be ideally suited to growing mushrooms. I really didn't like it at all.

Leaving the sodden (sic) tent and towel (left outside for the ants, and forgotten) to dry over a hedge, I hiked up to the town to the bank. Châteauponsac was a medieval town of narrow windy lanes and old houses, in a state of some disrepair, but nevertheless rather charming. There was a spacious central square with virtually nothing in it. Most of the shops were either butchers, bakers or hairdressers, spread very far apart from each other. It was Friday and market day — the market consisted of three stalls, one selling plants and vegetables, one meat and the third fish. The town centre seemed to occupy a large area filled with very little.

A group of four people were waiting for the bank's doors to open. I joined them. We waited. A cleaning lady was pushing a mop around inside. We waited. It was nearly ten minutes past opening time, and still we waited. The queue started growing restless. Someone rapped on the glass door and waved to the cleaning lady, who continued mopping. Expostulations began, at first good-humoured, then becoming increasingly irritable. I wandered off to explore the 'Chemin des Anglais', the 'English path' which tumbled unevenly through a small narrow alley with a splendid view down to the Gartempe valley. The bank queue had grown when I returned five minutes later, but the doors were still closed. An old man with a poodle, a woman with a wicker shopping basket and another in a startlingly bright dress were now all talking happily, apparently resigned to a long wait. The sun was shining; there was no rush. Why worry?

Still, I had fourteen miles to walk, and wanted to get going. I learnt from the basket lady that there was a cash dispenser at the supermarket three-quarters of a mile outside the town, in the direction from which I had come yesterday and in the opposite direction to which I was going today. I trotted off, then back, and folded up the still-saturated tent. The camping fees were fifty-five francs, and I dug my heels in.

'It's very expensive.'

'Ah yes, but look at all the facilities here. It is a very good campsite.'

'Yes, I know. But the facilities aren't open yet.'

'But they will be next month,' she replied, a little illogically.

I told her, quite truthfully, that the most I had paid for camping during the last fortnight was twenty francs for a night, so we settled on that.

'I was worried about you last night, in the storm. Were you very frightened?'

'No, I wasn't frightened, just wet.'

'I wanted to come and get you, but my husband said he was sure you would be all right.'

How nice — a man who had so much faith in the weaker sex.

Usually, she said, storms were attracted to Lake Saint-Pardoux to the south, and missed Châteauponsac, but occasionally they would rage up the valley, causing chaos. Last night's storm had only been a small one. I was impressed.

There were no open campsites within thirty miles to the east, so I had to track north up to la Souterraine in the département of the Creuse, a favourite area of writers and artists. It is a land of hills and plateaux, where 40 per cent of the land provides grazing for cattle and sheep and the large numbers of Anglo-Arab horses raised in the area, and 20 per cent produces grain for animal feeds. Forests and woods cover more than a quarter of the terrain. For fishermen, there are 908 lakes and six hundred miles of fishing rivers. In the west of the département the landscape is characterized by pastures bordered with hedges, and in the east by dry-stone walls. It is truly an unspoilt, rural paradise. The air here has an intense clarity: it is like looking through freshly cleaned windows.

Morterolles-sur-Semme arrived just before midday. It baked in the heat, and there was not a sign of movement. No cars, no people. Just a field of magnificent Anglo-Arab horses on the outskirts. I headed for a cold drink at a canopied restaurant/bar in the deserted main street. Empty tables slouched disinterestedly on the pavement. The whole place had the air of the village of the damned.

Pushing open the restaurant's door, I was struck lightly on the head by a tin ashtray, which had been balanced astride it to act as an early warning signal for the staff. It tinkled to a halt beneath a table, and a big fat man waddled out from behind a curtain, served me with a shandy, and then sat morosely at the bar talking to a horsy-looking young woman with large buttocks in tight trousers. They both appeared very bored, which was hardly surprising if the place was always as lively as this. Disregarding his insistent advice that I stick to the busy main roads I cut obliquely towards la Souterraine by a network of small lanes, passing a series of prosperous villages, with houses in good repair and well-kept gardens. At Fromental, I lay on a lawn of daisies in the shadow of the old church. The village clock struck the hour, twice, as it does in many rural parts of France for the benefit of people working out in the

139

fields. If they fail to hear the first note and are unable to tell the hour, if they wait for a moment it strikes again.

On the following Sunday night I planned to stay in a *gîte d'étape* at Noth, between la Souterraine and Guéret. These guest houses normally offer overnight accommodation for about sixty francs, which buys a clean and comfortable bed, pillow and blankets, sometimes in a dormitory, sometimes in a private room, clean sanitary facilities and plenty of hot water. Some offer cooked meals, or you can make your own. They are a blessing for people travelling long distances and needing a place to sleep, and many also offer stabling for those travelling by horseback.

Advance booking with the local *mairie* was essential for the Noth *gîte d'étape*, said the brochure. As tomorrow was Saturday, and the *mairie* would be closed, I phoned from Fromental to book for Sunday night.

The man who took my booking told me that this was a three-star *gîte d'étape* and cost 395 francs per night. I laughed. I thought he was joking. I spelt out my name. How would I be paying, he enquired. I realized he was serious, and explained that I was just a humble backpacker with very thin pockets and certainly couldn't afford 395 francs. Wishing me luck, he said he didn't know of anywhere within twelve miles where I could stay, cancelled my booking and put the phone down.

Thinking about the place called Noth, I wondered why so many French words have a 'th' in them when it is always pronounced 't'. There is no word in the French language with a 'th' sound in it, so the 'h' is quite redundant. Most French people find it an impossible sound to enunciate. Ask a Frenchman to say 'thistle' and see what happens.

On the other side of Fromental was a congregation of huge rocks. From a narrow cleft in the centre of one a handsome oak tree thrived, a monument to the determination of a tiny acorn. The lane twisted its way through Chégurat, a peaceful farming hamlet drenched in sunshine, and an old lady came slowly towards me, wearing a sun hat, cotton frock and huge rubber boots, and carrying a very long wooden pitchfork. She peered at me suspiciously. Behind her three people worked in a hayfield, one driving a tractor which cut the hay while the other two raked and forked it into neat rows of piles. Springing through the stubble, a ruthless tortoiseshell cat exploited the small terrified animals which fled from the advancing tractor.

'*Bonjour, madame,*' I called.

She smiled and came over. 'You're English,' she said.

'How can you tell?'

She laughed. 'It's your accent.'

It was a dispiriting fact that after four years of living in France, I still couldn't say *'bonjour'* without betraying my nationality. I practised saying the word in every conceivable way. I mimicked the postman, the cashier at the bank, the librarian, my neighbours. Still it defeated me.

'My children.' The old lady waved a hand at the workers in the field. 'It's good weather for haymaking.'

The two who were not in the tractor were using old wooden rakes to scrape the hay together, and I wondered how much longer we would be able to enjoy such sights before mechanization destroyed them for ever. The old lady lamented the advent of the tractor that had replaced the horses that used to do the heavy work. Of course the tractor is much quicker, but . . . She sniffed.

She had lived there for over sixty years, and still ran a working farm. Spanning the départemental border between the Haute Vienne and the Creuse meant she was obliged to pay taxes in both départements. She clucked disapprovingly, and asked whether I would like a drink. Reluctantly I

142

turned down her invitation. What stories she would have been able to tell of rural life in this remote area! But I couldn't linger, because there were still at least seven miles to go and it was already late afternoon. I followed her helpful directions across a field and got lost again. Which crossroads did she mean, I asked myself? The one formed by the converging paths at the end of the field, or the one formed by the two main roads fifty yards away? I tried the first, and ended up in a field with a very beautiful Arab mare and her new foal, which flicked its bushy tail furiously as it tormented an ancient and very overweight companion. The latter stood tolerantly, letting the foal nip and tug at her head collar, while its mother took advantage of the situation to yank up mouthfuls of grass. They eyed me warily as I crossed the field to link up with the road.

The countryside was peaceful, pulling steadily uphill, and hard going, especially with the added weight of the wet tent and towel. It was extremely hot. The first sign indicating la Souterraine appeared on the south side of the N145 motorway. Just before then, a bulky four-wheel-drive vehicle towing a caravan towards me pulled up abruptly in the road, nearly causing the following car to hit it.

'Camping?' bellowed a gingery-faced man.

'Excuse me?' I called.

He beckoned me over impatiently, and I narrowly missed being mown down by passing traffic.

'Is there a campsite in la Souterraine?' he bawled.

'Yes,' I replied, 'I know there is one, but I don't know precisely where.'

'What do you mean? How do you know there is one, then?'

'Well, I have a brochure.'

'But are you sure it's there?' he yelled. His wife sat grim-faced, glaring at me as if I were failing in my civic duty.

I assured him there was a campsite but couldn't say exactly where it was.

'Maybe,' I suggested, 'I could ride with you and we could look together.' After all, I had walked to the town, and a lift as far as the campsite wouldn't be outside the rules.

'Ah no, there is no room,' he sighed, indicating the spacious, empty interior of the vehicle and the caravan. The ugly wife shook her head.

I left them trying to turn the rig around on a sharp bend, on a hill, and kept walking until I reached the town centre, about one and a half miles further on. A man who had been watching me for a while came up and said: 'I see you are walking the roads.' Now what could have given the game away? The boots? The stick? The backpack? Or was it dust- and sweat-stained me? He offered to drive me to the campsite, and I wearily accepted. It was awfully hot. I said I would have to buy a few things at the supermarket first. He nodded and promised to wait in the car park. I stocked up on two large bottles each of cider and wine, cheese and salads, some fruit and bread. When I staggered out with two heavy bags full of shopping, he had gone.

A skinny girl sauntered across the road.

'Excuse me,' I said in French. 'Do you know where the campsite is, please?'

'I am English,' she said haughtily.

I bit back the urge to say 'Never mind.' I was very tired.

Finally someone knew where the site was, still over a mile further on. It took me almost an hour to reach, and I had to keep changing the heavy shopping bags from side to side, hoping they wouldn't burst because then I really would have a problem. The cardinal rule seemed to be that the more tired you were, the further away the campsite was. But when I limped in, it was perfect, beside a large lake, with plots bordered by hedges, and surrounded by beech, pine, and oak trees. There were plenty of other campers there, and even the bar/restaurant was open. The heated washing block was immaculate, with limitless steaming water. It was obviously going to cost a bomb. But I would worry about that after a night's sleep. A wrigglesome black Labrador puppy helped me put up the tent, jumping on it and tugging at the guys, until, bored with this game, it squirmed off up the hill.

By 7.00 p.m. I was already in the sleeping bag, but sleep wouldn't come. I lay in the dark for a long while, aching in parts of my body I didn't previously know existed. Over the last fortnight I'd taken so many pain-killers that I was worried about getting addicted, but without them I wasn't going to get to sleep. There was no water in the tent, and too tired to struggle out and walk fifty yards to find some I took some small pieces of cheese and poked the tablets into them. They slid down well enough and eventually I fell into a deep sleep.

In the night, with no warning, the tent collapsed onto the sleeping me, accompanied by a ghastly grunt and something sharp sticking into my face. A heavy moving object pinned the nylon to my head. Everything was still for a moment, and then the moving object began rapid, heavy breathing in my ear and the sharp things found new places into which to stick. Emboldened by the knowledge that there were other campers within no more than ten yards, I groped for the torch and managed to push myself upright, tumbling the heavy breather to the ground. The tent re-erected itself, and I shone the torch through the mesh curtain, into a grinning black face with wet pink gums and bright pointed teeth. The black puppy had come back. She was ready to play.

After stroking her for a few minutes, I explained that she couldn't come in. I would be leaving on Sunday, and couldn't take her with me, with several hundred miles still to walk, and six more dogs at home. It was no use building up a relationship. She threw herself down across the doorway, and went to sleep. I woke several times during the night, and she was still there. She had managed to climb part way up one of the tent 'walls' and lay upon it, further narrowing the tiny sleeping space inside.

When I opened the flap in the morning she pounced in, a shiny black writhing and uncontrollable mass, beating the condensation off the tent and all over the sleeping bag with her delirious tail, washed my head and face thoroughly, then vanished.

Saturday was a perfect day for laundry,

with a light breeze tempering the hot sunshine. The washing block included enchanting laundry basins. To distinguish them from washing-up basins, which sported a picture of a plate, knife and fork cavorting in a sudsy bowl, the laundry basins bore pictures of an equally merry shirt and sock bouncing around in a tub of bubbles. It just made me want to let all my travel-stained clothes join in the fun.

The spotless porcelain basins were deep and spacious, and the front edge had a ridged sloping platform on which to rub and pound the clothing. A gratifying quantity of sludge exuded from the slope as I hammered away, and I kept rinsing until the water was absolutely clear. Leaving the spotless, soggy garments festooned on the hedge, I set off into town.

Trading was lively at the market place, with stalls of glossy vegetables, colourful flowers and plants, jars of honey, cheeses, fresh fish, garlic, onions and olives. The shoppers looked prosperous and happy. From the market place there is a fine view of the thirteenth-century Porte de Saint-Jean, sixty-five feet high and flanked at each corner by fifteenth-century towers, the main gate in the former city ramparts that extend nearly 2,000 feet around the town. Until the nineteenth century, it served as a prison. The church, with its thick walls, tall, narrow windows and prominent buttresses, a mixture of Gothic and Romanesque architecture, looks as much like a fortress as a place of worship. Started during the twelfth century on the site of an eleventh-century church, it took nearly one hundred years to build. Many medieval houses line the narrow streets, solid old buildings with granite walls and slate roofs, and there are plenty of shops, cafés and restaurants, although I was unable to locate either of the two regional specialities I had wanted to taste — potato pie and clafouti[1].

Situated right in the middle of France, la Souterraine once stood at the crossroads of the Roman Imperial Highway, and passed backwards and forwards between the English and French during the twelfth and fourteenth centuries. The town takes its name, meaning underground, from the crypt beneath the church, and a number of underground watercourses. It is a town rich in history and architecture, with thriving commercial, industrial and agricultural activities, set in an unspoilt landscape. Until the previous evening it had been nothing more to me than a name on a map and I was surprised that

----

[1] batter pudding with fruit, usually cherries

such an attractive and interesting town was not better publicized.

At the tourist office a very helpful lady confirmed that the *gîte d'étape* at Noth had indeed become a luxury hotel. Between la Souterraine and Guéret the only accommodation she could find was at le Grand Bourg, where there were *chambres d'hôtes*[1]. This type of accommodation is more sophisticated than a *gîte d'étape*, and consequently more expensive, but on this leg of the journey there wasn't any alternative.

Back at the campsite the exuberant black canine hurled herself at me. Happily she had been reunited with her owner, the barman, who had spent half the night searching for her while she had been lying contentedly curled up on guard outside my tent.

As I lay reading in the sun, a dragonfly flew onto my book, its slender, gunmetal-grey, inch-long body and filigree wings gleaming in the sunlight. From the page where it had landed, it cocked its face sideways and regarded me from disproportionately large silver ballbearing eyes, a miniature work of art. Overhead, two crows mobbed a lazy buzzard which flapped away into the distance; over the bole of an oak tree two six-inch-long

---

[1] guest rooms

lizards scrambled, one predominantly green and the other more pink, stopping periodically and waving their forearms in a frantic and distracted fashion, as if telling each other tales of appalling disasters. I thought what a very enjoyable time I was having.

Anticipating at least a hundred francs in fees for the two nights at the site, I was very pleasantly surprised to receive a bill for just thirty francs. I headed for some liquid refreshment with the hypothetical seventy francs I had just saved.

Being Saturday night the bar and restaurant were packed, the bar completely taken over by a squad of men in their mid-twenties with weird haircuts, smoking hard, tattooed and earringed, laughing and talking quietly amongst themselves. Despite their appearance they were all charming and polite. One, devoid of any muscle or flesh, just a skeleton draped in skin, wore a silver earring, a tattoo on his left shoulder, a blue vest, and jeans so shredded that they were more not there than there, exposing one scrawny knee and a pair of startlingly red tartan boxer shorts.

After an exotic cocktail I walked back in the moonlight, and tried to find a way of reducing the condensation problem by draping the poncho over the tent and securing it with clothes pegs to the pole and guy ropes, leaving an air space between it and the fabric of the tent. It didn't do any good at all — by morning the inside of the tent was just as saturated as ever.

The belligerent ginger man and his wife never did arrive.

9

Castration Techniques and a Tale of Murder, and Jennifer's Having a Bad Time

My blisters were healing well after a day's rest, but the sharp edge of the insole where I had cut it away was beginning to slice into the underside of my toes like a razor blade, so I cut up a section of my thin mattress to make two new double-storey insoles.

Just in case I should find somewhere to camp before reaching the *chambres d'hôtes*, I left Châteauponsac with some emergency rations including six bananas, a one-pound tin of apricots, a two-pound tin of mixed vegetables, a tube of mayonnaise, two fruit compotes, a medium-sized cheese and a half-litre bottle of water leaning precariously from a side pocket. The backpack was impossibly heavy and stretched to bursting. For about five miles, walking on the

experimental mattress insoles was like floating on a cushion of air: then they deflated and
compacted into a mass slightly thinner than
tissue, from which they never recovered.

South-west towards le Grand Bourg the
road wound through long, shady cool lanes,
and in a field was a herd of huge grey
boulders which looked, from a distance, like
hippos. By blinking rapidly and shaking my
head from side to side, I could make them
move about.

In this part of the Creuse region, the
granite subsoil and consequent shallow earth
means cultivation yields meagre results.
During the nineteenth century, much of the
great building work in Paris was undertaken
by Creusois masons. Unable to earn a
living in an overpopulated and agriculturally
impoverished area, each year, until the arrival
of the train, they walked the two hundred
miles to Paris at the beginning of March, and
returned at the end of November. The
simple lines of Limousin-Roman architecture
resulted from the hardness of the granite with
which the masons worked. Although now
used less for paving stones than previously,
the granite is still used for municipal
buildings, and for sculpting.

The sun reflected from the polished copper
coats of a large herd of Limousin cattle,

which as I passed studied me with that air of sadness and hope that is peculiar to all cattle, unlike the mixture of arrogance and fear displayed by sheep. There was something else in their eyes this morning. Curiosity. They advanced to the flimsy wire fence, which clung listlessly to wispy posts that a sturdy mouse could have pushed down and was all that separated them from me. I smiled and called out 'Hello' in English to give them something to think about, and moved smartly on.

The journey continued uneventfully, up and down, mostly up, and through the delightful village of Salagnac, a mixture of modern and older properties, some undergoing restoration. Behind neat hedges the gardens were tapestries of blue irises, purple lilac, scarlet peonies, golden wallflowers and roses of every hue on an emerald background. Two bare-chested men were building a drystone garden wall around an interesting house with a narrow, ivy-coated circular turret on one corner with a steeply pointed slate-tiled roof topped by a weathervane. Rapunzel would have lowered her hair from a turret just like that.

A two-inch-long black beetle trundled into the road about six feet ahead. It swung its antennaed head towards me, jerked to a cartoon-style halt, and rocked backwards, its posterior touching the ground, front legs rigid before it, then swivelled through a 180-degree turn back into the grass, where it crouched immobile as I passed. When I looked back from ten feet away, it had resumed its course. Occasionally I wondered whether it was the same giant beetle which seemed to pop up so often in my path.

The address for the *chambres d'hôtes* was simply 'le Grand Bourg', but they were nowhere near the small town with the big name, but four miles further on, a hot, hard climb to a very large farmhouse standing in grounds of about thirty acres. In a paddock beyond the swimming pool a thoroughbred chestnut mare was showing off her day-old filly, the result of her romance with a Portuguese Lippizaner stallion. A converted outbuilding served as a boutique selling the farm's own produce, primarily foie gras, confit de canard and other assorted poultry products. Wrapped around two sides of the house, the dining room was a smart, pretty glazed terrace at ground level, full of well-dressed people in various stages of post-prandial relaxation.

Despite my laundering efforts the previous day, I was conscious of my rumpled, bedraggled appearance, and distinctly uncomfortable at walking in and spoiling these people's elegant Sunday afternoon. As I was searching for a tradesmen's entrance where I could slink in unobtrusively, one of the diners, a stout bearded gentleman, rose from his table and came over and held open the door, ushering me in with a small bow. The elegant assembly all smiled and greeted me cheerfully, moving cane chairs aside so that I could manoeuvre the bulging backpack to the rear of the restaurant. A waitress disappeared to look for Madame, and while I waited the customers started dispersing, each coming over and shaking my hand warmly as they filed past.

Madame la Patronne didn't bat an eyelid at my appearance and unannounced arrival, but led the way up the narrow, dark oak staircase, shiny with age and polish, to a cool room in the eaves, with an en suite bathroom and shower. The swimming pool was at my disposal and looked bluely inviting, but the water temperature was such that I wondered how it had managed to stay in liquid form and not coalesced into a single frozen block, so I sat beside it watching the mare and her foal, and a large gelding which pranced frantically backwards and forwards on the other side of the electric fence.

One other couple was staying overnight,

the stout gentleman and his wife, Charles and Dominique, who came from Angers. We shared a table for the evening meal of tomato salad, omelettes with fried potatoes — mine without bacon and carefully isolated from the others on the platter — and a delicate pear mousse with caramel. Madame la Patronne joined us. Conversation skittered around until it settled on the castration of cockerels, a highly skilled art, apparently, in which Madame had been trained. She described the process in distressing detail, and Charles blanched a little. Then, regaining his equilibrium, he matched her story with one from Argentina, where a man he had met said the shepherds castrated lambs with their teeth. I smiled politely, and felt smugly vegetarian.

Dominique changed the subject. Their daughter was cycling alone through China, Tibet and Nepal. It made my voyage seem very prosaic and cosy.

We discussed different nationalities. Madame said she found the Germans extremely difficult to please and very arrogant, while the English were courteous and appreciative; but their offspring! She raised her eyes and hands in horror. Intolerable! Uncontrolled, ill-mannered. Why, she asked, did nice people permit their children to be so socially unacceptable? I wished I knew the answer. The local hostelries made a point of warning each other about undesirable guests: you might get away with not paying, helping yourself to something, causing damage or making unkept reservations, but only once. Nobody could afford even small losses if they wanted to remain in business. The tourist industry was suffering because of the strong French franc, which had discouraged foreign visitors, and the recent introduction of a tax on holidaymakers which was discouraging everybody.

Charles was a gentleman with strong opinions and agreed about English children. He added a further criticism. The English, charming as they were, had one serious fault — their practice of driving on the wrong side of the road. He felt that they must come into line with the rest of the European community and start driving on the right, because how could one expect people to drive into a tunnel on one side of the carriageway, and emerge having to drive on the opposite side without causing accidents? He does have a good point, but imagine the logistics involved in changing a country's driving habits in one move. And almost certainly there would be some English die-hards who would maintain their right to drive on the side of the road they always had — can you visualize the pandemonium *that* would lead to?

Sitting in company and comfort with these friendly and lively people made a welcome change from solitary evenings in the little tent and it was almost midnight before we adjourned to bed. Madame apologized in advance if the nightingales kept me awake, because they lived just outside my window. They sang all night, as I threshed about in the comfortable, warm bed. It seemed I was unable to sleep in comfort any more: I needed a cold, damp, lumpy environment.

Over a breakfast of freshly squeezed orange juice, piles of hot buttered toast and the most delicious homemade marmalade I had ever tasted, we discussed the forthcoming World Cup football, a massive international event to which France was playing host and which had been the sole topic of conversation and media attention for several months. Charles felt it his patriotic duty to watch the games, although he abhorred the violence associated with football. In his opinion, the only team who understood the meaning of 'le fair play' was Brazil. Dominique and I both declared that we loathed the game and that nothing would tempt us to watch a single match. (When we spoke some weeks later, however, we had both watched the final and cheered

France to her victory.)

After we had exchanged e-mail addresses and photographed each other, and armed with a plan showing a short cut to the D4 towards Guéret, I set off on another glorious sunny morning. The little map led me through coniferous woods that were cool and dark, and I emerged at the other side onto a startingly golden hillside of gorse that was dazzling after the darkness of the trees. Giant white marguerites and delicate blue forget-me-nots danced in the grass, and on an ancient electricity control box was a notice banning bill sticking in accordance with the law of 29 July 1881.

Just outside la Brionne the body of a female chaffinch lay on its back in the road. It was uncrushed, and as I picked it up to move it from the road it made an almost imperceptible movement, and the tiny eye was still bright. I cradled it against me for a few moments until I felt a faint flutter of life, and carried it well away from the road. As the strength began to flow back into its body I placed it in the long grass where it could recover in the warmth of the sun. When I left, it was standing upright and tentatively moving its wings.

A contingent of about a dozen madly galloping wire-haired dachshunds were racing uncontrollably round a garden, with a fox terrier and a miniature poodle in hot pursuit, all yelping and barking. They hurled themselves at the fence as I passed, making enough noise to waken the dead. Behind them a harassed lady was trying to round them up into a pen, but they didn't want to go and she was no match for them. She explained that they were her husband's hunting dogs: seeing this stumpy-legged and noisy rabble in hot pursuit must have been quite something and I could still hear their frenzied racket and her breathless curses from a long way down the road.

It would be unjust to give an opinion of Guéret, départemental capital of the Creuse, because I only passed through the unpleasant centre in search of the campsite. The town square was spacious and surrounded by imposing buildings, but the overall impression was of austerity and little charm, and nothing tempted me to explore further. A large man, dressed in a suit and open-necked shirt, wearing a gigantic orange velvet sombrero with orange velvet bobbles dangling from it, was singing loudly as he weaved unsteadily across the square and tried to climb into his car. The car was not very much larger than the hat; consequently a considerable struggle ensued. It didn't look as if the hat was coming out of this at all well, and by the time the still-singing man had succeeded in getting into his vehicle the hat was more rectangular than round, and pulled right down over his face.

The campsite was about a mile and a half out of town, up a mini-mountain, but it was cool and shady, and there were other residents. I lay on the grass beneath the fluttering leaves of beech and silver birch trees, watching an aerial combat between a crow and a magpie. The crow was half-hearted and bored, and flapped lazily away leaving the battlefield to the magpie.

Once rested I walked down to the nearest supermarket a mile away, then climbed the mountain once more back to the campsite, where a small travelling circus had appeared in the car park. An assortment of pygmy goats, tiny ponies and a llama were tethered on the grass, and around the vans and trucks scores of small dogs and children chased each other. I had always wanted to befriend a llama, and here at last was an opportunity. I spent a long time and a lot of bread rolls trying to establish a relationship with the disdainful creature. It would eagerly snatch as many rolls as I offered, but after eating its fill it folded its ears flat on its elegant head and sneered through its cloven lips with that arrogant expression which llamas have perfected, and refused to let me stroke it. I persevered, until finally it came towards me, ears pricked forward and the great limpid eyes, fringed by luxuriant lashes, gazed innocently and deeply into mine. I put my hand gently over its muzzle just in time, and thus managed to deflect the jet-propelled spit/sneeze which it projected at me. Fortunately its mouth had been empty, so my hand was not soiled by this demonstration of good will.

When I phoned home I was unable to raise Jennifer, so I called Gloria. She assured me all was well, and so, blissfully unaware of the events that had been unfolding behind me, I settled down for a peaceful night. The area has a volcanic history and is known for its frequent mild earthquakes, which generally pass unnoticed. If there were any that night, they passed unnoticed by me.

★   ★   ★

Following an unruffled sleep I woke at 6.00 a.m., and was soon en route for Gouzon, three map-folds away. I was going to have to get there in one day, even if it meant arriving at midnight, because there was absolutely nowhere else to stop en route.

After an hour of walking in circles, I had managed to reach the outskirts of Guéret, which didn't seem to be a very well signposted town. The D4, on which I thought I was, seemed unnaturally busy for a départemental road. The edges were very narrow and bordered by robust metal crash barriers which left a space of about twelve inches between them and the tarmac. The continuous flood of fast traffic meant I was unable to cross to walk facing the oncoming vehicles, and found myself being buffeted at close range from behind by a stream of pantechnicons. It was a most unpleasant experience, and absolutely terrifying. I began stepping sideways like a crab, facing the road so that the backpack overhung the metal barriers and allowed me a few valuable extra inches of walking space. A dark green Renault Espace drew up alongside, and a perplexed-looking driver asked if I was going far. No, I replied nonsensically, I am just arriving. The driver frowned, shook his head and drove off with a long look through his rear view mirror.

Nearly two and a half miles of very disagreeable walking passed before I discovered I was actually on the N145, and that very shortly it would cease to be a dual carriageway and become instead a quadruple one. Of this major road, there was no hint on my map. There was no question of turning back, so I carried on until a turning off to the right led into quieter waters and linked up with the elusive D4. Passing the Guéret-Saint-Laurent aerodrome the road rose and fell energetically, dipping down to Pont à l'Eveque and over the river Creuse. Silhouetted above me, against the brilliant blue of the sky, a herd of cattle grazed on the brow of a hill; they raced downhill to examine me with bovine wonderment, standing in an orderly row by the hedge as I passed, and moving on in unison to reach the corner before me.

In the village of Pionnat I found a phone box and called Jennifer, as I hadn't spoken to her the previous evening.

'Hi,' I said. 'I was worried when I couldn't get you last night. Is everything OK?'

'Just wait till you hear this,' she said ominously. 'I got up at six thirty yesterday morning. First time for everything. The farrier was coming at nine thirty, so I figured I could do some gardening while it was nice and cool. Then I would feed the animals and wait for the farrier.

'First of all, the weed eater — her name for the strimmer — would start but wouldn't stay started. So I got the lawnmower out instead. After about an hour I took a break, and when

I went to restart the mower the pull cord broke. So there I was wide awake and no tools to work with. I was just on my way into the house to get the dogs' food when they all started barking at the gate. A lady got out of an estate car. She had short blond hair, a red blouse, white pants and little kd lang boots. As a matter of fact she looked a little like her too. She introduced herself and said she had come to shoe the horse and would drive around to the gate by the road. I put a rope on Cindy and took her to the gate so she could get her shoes redone.

'I watched the farrier setting her stuff up. In the back of her wagon she had a butane heater to heat the metal shoes. I asked how many woman farriers are there in France and she said six.

'Cindy was pretty good while her feet were being cleaned, cut, nipped and filed. When the farrier had finished shaping the shoes and had burned them into the hoof (I have never seen this done before — they actually take the red hot shoe and put it on the hoof. It makes a whole lot of putrid-smelling smoke), we moved to the shade and the shoes were nailed on. At long last Cindy could be set free. I removed her rope and she took off running. It was about twenty past ten when the farrier left.

'I hadn't fed the dogs yet so I went into the house to get the food I had fixed earlier. When I went to feed them two dogs were missing. Vulcan and Wizzy were nowhere to be found. I was panic-striken. I looked everywhere. I walked and walked and then decided I had better get the car and start looking. I looked for about an hour. I decided more extreme measures would have to be taken.

'Since I can't speak French, I made up some little flyers and got a picture of the dogs out of the photo album. I gave a flyer to the postman, three men on tractors, the lady driving the bread truck and all the neighbours. Then I drove to all the little villages, down all the little roads, and stopped at every house and showed the picture of the dogs and gave them the flyer so that if they saw them they could call. By this time it was one thirty and still nothing. I started getting a big lump in my stomach. How would I ever be able to face you if I had carelessly let your boys escape into the French wilderness? How would I live with myself if I didn't find them? By four thirty the dogs had been missing for six hours. I knew there wasn't much more I could do except wait for some word, from somewhere, that they had been seen. But I couldn't just sit and wait.

'I went and told Gloria the dogs were missing and I didn't know what I was going to tell Susie when she called. I had already got out the maps and found exactly where you were because I was ready to go get you and bring you home. I thought maybe if they heard you calling them instead of me they would come back.

'Gloria tried to calm me down and said you had already called from stop number fourteen, about a hundred and ten miles from here. I said, well I don't know what else to do, so I am going to get her. Gloria said the boys have run off like this before a couple of times, so why didn't I wait awhile and see if they came back? I thought about it and decided I would wait until seven and if they weren't back I would have to tell you. I prayed and watched and waited. I was going nuts.

'I decided to work on the lawnmower; at least if I was concentrating on something the time would pass. I fixed the lawnmower and mowed half the village and along the street. Waiting, watching, hoping, praying that by some miracle they would show up. I couldn't find anything else to mow so I put the mower up and went to get a drink of water out of the hose. As I was drinking I looked up and there was Vulcan peering at me through the fence, sitting very still and looking at me with this innocent look as if to say: 'What did you leave me out here for?' He was alone, his brother nowhere in sight. I thought, what if he was somewhere hurt and Vulcan came home to tell me.

'Gloria came back to ask if they had showed up. I said: 'One is here, but not the other.'

' 'Well,' she said, 'at least now you only have half the problem. The other one will show up soon, you'll see.'

'In the meantime little Max had something wrong with his foot. I don't know if he had been bitten by something, or had a thorn in his paw. When I tried to check it he yelped real loud. Lord, I thought, isn't this day ever going to end? Now it was coming up to six thirty and guess who was waiting to get in the gate by the driveway? Wizzy had come home. I have never been so relieved by the sight of an animal. I could breathe again.

'Gloria said, 'Now you can relax a little bit. I'll just go put the kettle on.'

'I said, 'I need something stronger than tea.'

'I was exhausted, my legs were hurting. I had a nice cold beer, then another and yet another. Gloria was reading to me out of the AA books she has. At midnight I retired for the night. Rest assured I will not get up at six thirty any more.'

'I'm so sorry you had such a bad time. Are you feeling OK now?'

'Oh, sure. We're all fine, and don't worry, I won't let them escape again.'

'Well, just look after yourself, and remember that things can go wrong no matter how careful you are. These things happen. I know you're doing your best, so don't let anything get you down.'

* * *

Outside the village school children were squealing in the universal language of playgrounds. I removed a vivid two-inch-long scarlet and black butterfly from where it quivered dangerously in the road to a safe ledge on an old stone wall, where it could continue its sunbathing. After the delicious extravagance of the *chambre d'hôte*, frugality was the order for the next few days, which was a pity as there was a tempting restaurant in the village centre, with a mouth-watering menu. Propped against the bar, and slurping at a cloudy yellow glass of pastis, a thin and very red-faced man was earnestly recounting a complicated story about something that had happened to his bicycle to the barmaid, who

171

listened with patient good humour while she polished and stacked glasses. The narrator could only seem to get so far in the story before he forgot what happened next, and had to start again. It was 11.00 a.m.

Back on the road again, a few miles further on, a very tanned, wiry man with shoulder-length grey hair and beard and penetrating grey eyes stood watching me from a farm gateway, wielding a lethal-looking implement with which he was mending a fence. As I approached he stepped into the narrow road and I braced myself for trouble. He had all the makings of a maniac, I was sure.

What to do? I'd never outrun him — I was having enough difficulty in walking. Turn and calmly go back the way I'd come? No, I didn't want to return to Guéret. I wanted to get to Geneva. Stand and fight? The great hiking stick seemed frail in comparison with the fencing tool, and the knife was trapped in the pocket of my shorts.

'Hello,' he said. 'You look heavily laden. Do you have very far to go?' He tossed the fencing tool into the grass and held out his hand.

I told him I was walking to Geneva from la Rochelle. He nodded.

'Ah yes. You're English, are you?' They always knew.

He bred Appaloosas. For a living? I asked. Did he sell them? No, he loved them. He bred them for pleasure. The previous week he had lost a mare and foal, during the night, and his eyes filled as he recounted the sad tale. Across a small valley a spotted stallion raced up and down, snorting, head high and tail streaming; beside the hedge three mares grazed, and a newborn foal lay sleeping among the buttercups. After admiring the horses and snatching a brief rest I moved on, and the man continued twisting wires onto fence posts. When I looked back from the corner, he waved a brown stringy hand.

At Jarnages I stopped on a refreshing patch of newmown grass beside a lake and tennis courts, eating bread and cheese and prodding some more cotton wool into my socks to cushion the latest crop of blisters, admiring the rhododendrons, azaleas, roses, and geraniums exploding into colour all around.

The road temporarily levelled out, which was a relief. I wasn't ready for the Massif Central. In fact, I hadn't realized that it had managed to work its way this far north. Geography had never been my forte; I had never had an interest in maps until I embarked on my pilgrimage, and other than that there was a mountain range just before Lake Geneva I had absolutely no idea whatsoever regarding the terrain I would be crossing. I could recognize a river and forests, and that was about it. Up until now, the steepest climb I had ever attempted was the beastly enforced slog up Box Hill on Saturday afternoons while I was at boarding school. In my mind, when I started out on this journey, I had a vague concept of a long, slightly winding level road linking la Rochelle to Geneva, and it had not crossed my mind that there would be any struggling uphill until the Jura.

At Goze, still a long way from Gouzon, I was thirsty and dehydrated, and spotted a lady weeding in her garden. Undeterred by my previous experience, I called out and asked for a glass of water.

'Go around to the front of the house,' she shouted.

She disappeared through a back door, and I tentatively hovered around until the front door opened and she called. 'Come on in! Take your pack off and come and sit down.'

Sitting at a long scrubbed kitchen table, I demolished a jug of iced water, which she refilled. She came originally from Normandy, but said she was very happy in Goze. Most of the other residents were from different parts, she said, and everyone was very friendly, but she warned me about another village a little way south.

'They are terrible people. Someone murdered the local nobleman, and the culprit was never found. Nobody trusts anybody else. They hate outsiders.'

'When did this happen?'

'Oh, about two hundred years ago. But they still talk of it. They are very suspicious of strangers. It would not be a good idea for you to go there.'

I promised not to, and continued on my way.

Just before Gouzon, a man and a woman came out from a house, smiling, and said they had seen me on the road in Chénérailles only an hour before. They were surprised I had got so far so quickly. So was I, as Chénérailles was at least six miles south, and I had never been there in my life. I said so. They had seen someone with the same backpack, the same boots and carrying a map, but slightly taller. So there was another of us about somewhere. It was a comforting thought. They asked where I had come from, and where I was heading. I told them.

'Ah, then you must be Dutch.' Madame at le Grand Bourg had said my accent was Dutch. I wondered whether or not that was an improvement.

By walking slowly, stopping frequently and setting out with a very positive attitude, I had covered three folds of the map today, and a distance of twenty-six miles. I felt as if I'd been hit by a steamroller, and the undersides of my feet were raw from pounding the tarmac all day. But I was pretty pleased with myself. I had walked for over twelve hours.

The neat and spacious campsite was beside the river Voueize. There were two dozen caravans there, but I still had not met one other tent-dweller. The *gardiens*, a diminutive couple, gave me an enthusiastic welcome and escorted me to the shade of a huge fir tree, where I collapsed for half an hour before walking to the local supermarket to buy my evening meal. With only eighteen francs in my pocket it would have to be a modest menu, and I ended up with a two-pound tin of peaches, two litres of Coca-Cola, and a small pot of crème fraîche. The temperature on the digital display outside the pharmacy read 86°F at 7.30 p.m.

The large tin of peaches cost the same as one which was only a third of its size, but made up for its small stature by having a ring-pull. I felt that the extra fruit was worth more than the ring-pull, even though I had no can opener. Next to the tent was a smart English-registered caravan with a giant awning, two bicycles and a Range Rover attached. I wondered whether they might have an English book or newspaper I could borrow, as well as a tin opener. I called out. Twice. The awning opened fractionally and a man's face peered out. 'Yes?'

'I'm sorry to disturb you, but could you possibly lend me a tin opener?'

I could see Mrs Range Rover through the crack in the awning, sitting within and working on a tapestry. She asked Mr Range Rover what was happening.

'She wants a tin opening,' he reported.

'Oh.'

The tin vanished, and reappeared two minutes later, opened, and was passed through the gap in the awning. I took it and thanked them. I didn't think there was much chance of borrowing a book.

*   *   *

As I was limping back from the sanitary block after a freezing shower, a voice called out in French: 'Do you have a bad back?' It came from a Dutch caravan.

'No, it's my feet,' I said.

'Will you have a drink with us?'

'Ah, no, that's so kind . . . ' Why was I saying no? 'Yes, I'd love to.'

We continued in fractured French for a few moments. Ab and Berdien came from Zaandam, having recently retired after twenty-eight years developing and running three businesses, and were on their way back home after spending seven weeks touring Spain. They were both fit and very tanned, and spoke excellent English. They wanted to know why my feet were sore. I explained.

Berdien said something in Dutch to Ab, and disappeared into the caravan, emerging a few moments later with an electric foot spa. Ab was despatched to find an extension lead, and five minutes later I was installed in an armchair, plumped up with cushions, with a large whisky in one hand and both feet immersed in warm, fragrant water. After half an hour in the spa, Berdien took my feet in her lap, patted them tenderly with a fluffy towel and then massaged them into a state of bliss. This was my first experience of Dutch kindness.

A short distance from where we sat, a top-of-the-range silver Mercedes estate car was parked. Next to it was a folding table, and two chairs occupied by an elderly German couple. As daylight began to fade, Frau Mercedes departed for the washing block armed with a vanity case. She returned ten minutes later, in a quilted dressing gown, devoid of make-up and climbed daintily into the back of the car. Herr Mercedes shut her in and produced a metallic, padded silver cover which he draped over the car, before disappearing to the washing block and returning some minutes later in his dressing gown. He disappeared into the front of the car, pulling the cover into place as he went.

'Why would anyone who can afford such a car sleep like that?' asked Ab. It really did seem rather bizarre.

It was very pleasant sitting and listening to Ab and Berdien talk about their life in Holland, and later, brimming with Scotch and painkillers, I slept very well until the early hours, when there was a thick silver frost on the ground and it was too cold to do anything but shiver.

M. et Mme les Gardiens reigned over their kingdom with a regal dignity that would have put the crowned heads of Europe to shame. Neither more than five feet tall, Madame more amply padded than her tiny spouse, they strolled slowly around their empire, side by side, stopping to exchange a few majestic words with each resident before proceeding, with a noble inclination of their heads, on to their next subject.

When they arrived at the tent, I felt I should curtsey or bow. Had I been too cold in the night? Yes, I said. They shook their heads sadly. The little king likened the area to the

Sahara: sandy soil, very hot days, very cold nights. I asked him where the camels were.

'Oh,' he replied, deadpan, 'they'll be here later.' With a small appreciative smile and tilting of her head, Madame clapped her hands gently, and, wishing me a safe continuation, they sailed off.

When I phoned home, Jennifer said she had heard from Arizona that her father's condition had worsened, and he had been diagnosed with cancer. She was very upset, but insistent that she wanted to stay until I had finished my trek.

Ab and Berdien went off on their bicycles to explore, and I left at midday after an enjoyable hour wandering around the lively and pretty little town of Gouzon. I set off for Evaux-les-Bains following what the Dutch called the 'yellow road', referring to the map colour of the départemental roads. The road was flat, shadeless, and busy, bordered by hedges and fields and dotted with a few sheep and cattle. The pampering of the previous night had inspired my feet and they performed well, eating up the miles, but it was a fairly boring journey. I did pass a glass-blowing workshop, which was closed for lunch.

Crossing départemental or regional boundaries was always a milestone, as was reaching a new fold in the map or arriving at a new campsite. Very shortly after Gouzon the third map ran out. This was a major milestone, a satisfying moment when another map could be folded up and consigned to the backpack. I had covered about two hundred miles so far.

Over my shoulder came the sound of voices and the tinkling of bicycle bells. Ab and Berdien arrived, armed with a bowl of chilled, sugared strawberries which we ate in the shade of a large oak tree before they set course for Chambon-sur-Voueize. Half an hour later they pedalled back into view. Berdien's bicycle had developed a brake problem, and the descent into Voueize was too steep to risk. Once again we sheltered in the shade, chewing gum, before they headed back to the campsite where Ab would mend the bicycle. I watched until they had disappeared from sight, with a final wave and tinkle of their bicycle bells.

★   ★   ★

So that I could keep a record of what I saw while I was walking, I carried a small cassette recorder, and in the evenings used it for writing up a journal of the day's events. The recorder had a dual purpose. Whenever I found myself in a particularly isolated place and saw a car approaching, I would hold the recorder between my mouth and ear, and talk and nod, as if I was on a mobile phone. Although I never felt threatened in any way, it gave me a feeling of security.

The downhill road into town was very steep and winding, and hot, and gave an excellent view onto Chambon's turrets and towers sprawled over the hillside at the junction of the rivers Tardes and Voueize. The town is dominated by the enormous abbey of Saint Valérie, containing the saint's relics, and is one of the largest Romanesque churches in the Limousin. Like the age and purpose of the *lanternes des morts*, the cause of Valérie's martyrdom comes in several versions. One is that she was abducted by Caligula, but the official version is that as a young noblewoman she was promised in marriage to the Roman governor of Limoges. However, as she had already made up her mind to become a nun, she refused to marry the man. He expressed his disappointment by cutting off her head, so she had probably made a very wise decision, as he would certainly have made a very petulant husband. As we really don't know quite what did happen to her, you can make up your own story if you like.

The interior of the abbey was dark and

intimidating and creepy and I didn't stay in it long enough to enjoy the works of art for which it is renowned. Instead I went to admire the ancient picturesque bridge, with its three unequal arches, that spans the river. The stone sides are worn down where the local tanners used to scrape their hides — cow hides, not their own, of course.

A little way from Chambon, in the gorges of the Voueize, stand the ruins of one of the castles that belonged to the French 'Bluebeard'. This was the extraordinary and notorious Gilles de Raïs, a noble knight, devout Christian, connoisseur of the arts, brother-in-arms and companion of Joan of Arc, fabulously powerful and wealthy *maréchal*[1] of France. Not content with all that, he indulged in alchemy, Satanism and murdering children. He confessed to having been responsible for the gruesome murder of 140 young boys during satanic rituals and experiments in alchemy, but it is believed that 400 is a more likely number. He was simultaneously hanged and burned in Rouen in 1440, in the place where Joan of Arc had been burnt by the French nine years previously. This was another spot I decided not to explore.

---

[1] marshal — very senior military officer

Between Chambon and Evaux-les-Bains a 325-foot-high viaduct spans the river Tardes, a daring metal bridge built to facilitate the encroachment of the railway network across the region. Designed by the great French engineer Gustave Eiffel, the bridge was blown down by a storm during construction, and the celebrated engineer had to recalculate the wind resistance. Seven years later, older and wiser, he designed and supervised the construction of the Eiffel tower, which has so far successfully defied any attempts to blow it over.

En route I passed the once wealthy gold-mining town of le Châtelet. Colliery engineers discovered a deposit of gold-bearing quartz there in 1896 and by 1914 the place had mushroomed into a prosperous town with schools, a town hall, offices and even an early version of a supermarket, while six hundred miners destroyed their lungs working in appalling conditions using toxic materials. The mine closed down in 1956, although the seam had not been fully exploited. Now the twenty-six miles of tunnels are flooded and irrecoverable, and all that remains of the buildings is a windswept ruin, covered with a shifting layer of coppery dust. It wasn't until I passed here that I realized I had taken a long cut to

Evaux-les-Bains, by following the wrong road.

After twisting gently alongside the river course for a while, the road started zigzagging upwards into a seemingly infinite succession of hairpin bends. Under the merciless heat of the sun, it turned and climbed, climbed and turned. At every bend I was certain I must have reached the top, but still it went on. A new problem had developed with my left little toe, and putting it to the ground was like walking on burning coals. As the road continued twisting endlessly upwards, I started feeling really cross, and wondered why they had to build this damned place quite so high. I was totally exhausted by the time I reached the town at 6.00 p.m., and I absolutely hated the place.

10

Really, Truly, Absolutely Frozen

According to legend, long, long ago to the north-west of Evaux, at the massive, precariously balanced blocks of granite known as the Pierres Jaumâtre, the pagan population sought treatment of their ailments from the hot springs which rose there. But when Christianity arrived the people turned their backs on the springs. This rude ingratitude sent the fairy of the Pierres Jaumâtre into a frightful tantrum; she sprang onto the highest stone and, stamping violently on the rock, caused the springs to dry up instantly. Hurling a heavy hammer (with astonishing strength for a fairy), she cried: 'Where this hammer falls, the springs will flow.'

It landed at Evaux-les-Bains, where forty years before Christ the Romans came to ease their aching bones, after all those trying hours of marching and conquering. A great fire in AD 260 burned the town into disuse, and it wasn't until the nineteenth century that the therapeutic properties of the springs came into their own again and a treatment centre was created, now greatly enlarged and modernized, offering cures for rheumatic, neurological and gynaecological disorders. Situated between the valleys of the rivers Cher and Tardes, at an altitude of over 1,500 feet, the air is pure and the climate temperate. From 1 April to the end of October each year, patients come for treatment, which is available under the French national health service, and consists of bathing, hydromassage, and drinking the waters from the two radioactive springs in use today, whose temperatures range from 56 to 60°C.

The pleasant campsite was tucked away down a quiet lane, and about half full. As soon as the tent was up and I had washed, I went in search of food. I was famished, having eaten nothing but a tin of peaches with crème fraîche and some sugared strawberries in the last twenty-four hours. Evaux-les-Bains fell far short of my expectations of an elegant, spacious town, lively and well served with restaurants. I found it a dead and dull place. In a deserted square a van was selling pizzas, but I didn't think they would be pleased to accept a tiny cheque, and I had no cash. One restaurant had apparently closed down and the only alternative looked as if its clock had stopped in 1910. Having no choice, and by now feeling murderously angry with Evaux-les-Bains, I ventured into a dim lobby, where an old man transparent with age was slumped over a newspaper, and Madame la Patronne sat behind a high counter looking as grim as I felt. There was only a set menu and I asked cautiously whether there was a possibility of substituting the meat with something I could eat. You risk life and limb asking such a question in a French restaurant, and can unleash a torrent of scorn and contempt and a look which says they would like to spit in your face. However, Madame was most accommodating. Would a nice omelette be acceptable? She would tell the chef.

The restaurant was a nightmare. It was full of decrepit old people talking in whispers, and dipping into assorted containers of pills, which occupied so much room that there was little space on their tables for plates. Remembering my manners, I said 'Bonsoir' as I walked in, and they all momentarily stopped whispering and stared at me suspiciously. None spoke. They resumed their whispering. The walls were smothered in grubby cream paint and a violent flock wallpaper of that furry texture which makes you want to scrape it off. Dusty chandeliers dangled from the ceiling, but each table was decorated with a small vase of fresh flowers, and the cutlery and glasses gleamed on crisp white cloths.

Service was not swift. The sole waitress smiled patiently as her decaying clients debated whether to have red or white wine, still or gassy water, dessert or cheese, coffee or not. It seemed to take for ever before they finally made a decision. I wondered whether I could escape from this frightful place, but the narrow doorway was right in the centre of the room, which meant passing all the staring whisperers. Madame had been most kind, and I was awfully hungry, so I stayed grumpily put.

A salad of tomatoes, egg and tuna arrived in the fullness of time, without the tuna. By the time I had managed to re-attract the attention of the waitress, I had eaten the rest, but asked what had become of the tuna.

'Ah,' she explained, 'that was the lunch menu.'

'But,' I said, 'it was the same menu you showed me for dinner. It said 'tomato, egg and tuna salad'.'

She shrugged. 'OK.'

Off she went, and returned shortly with a heaped plate of tuna.

'I opened a whole tin for you,' she said.

The omelette, with green beans, was excellent, and so was the raspberry ice cream, and as I worked my way through it one by one the slow old people tottered out of the dining room. When the bill arrived, it included a reduction, in homage to the omelette. It was the first time I had ever been charged less than the quoted price. Madame came over and enquired whether I had enjoyed the meal, whether it was sufficient, was the omelette good? Despite her grim expression, she was quite charming and hoped I would enjoy staying in Evaux-les-Bains. Privately, I very much doubted it.

The transparent gentleman nodded and raised a frail old hand as I left. '*Bonsoir, madame,*' he croaked.

Revived by the meal I felt less irritable, and rather ashamed of my earlier bad temper. The path back to the campsite led through the lovely gardens of the abbey of Saint Peter and Saint Paul, which dates back to the eleventh century. A whole choir of blackbirds sang, and white acacia blossoms scented the air.

A three-inch-long black beetle with exaggerated antennae and sturdy legs was trying to block the road to traffic. I dragged it off, its limbs waving furiously at such indignity.

By the time the church bells tolled 9.00 p.m., I was entombed in the sleeping bag. As the blackbirds' song faded into the night, the cricket chorus took over, and shortly the nightingales joined in. Today was the first day since leaving la Rochelle, twenty days previously, that I had not heard a cuckoo.

Next morning the church bells started thundering at 7.50 a.m., which was rather a shame as the previous night had been one of very few that I had actually managed to get through comfortably, and I would probably have carried on sleeping for several more hours. Their tone was a deep echoing roar, which throbbed on the air, and all the birds were singing along, and there was no point in continuing to lie in the ghastly little tent, so I went for a shower. At Gouzon the royal couple had warned me that the camp fees at Evaux-les-Bains would be very expensive, because of the luxury heated washing block. In the event it was only thirty-nine francs for two nights and two showers. The washing block was indeed heated, very modern and clean, but there was no loo roll.

I changed my opinion of Evaux-les-Bains. If you are not in a filthy mood, it is a most charming little town, with winding, narrow streets, a mixture of elegant houses and small cottages, magnificent trees, intriguing alleyways, a splendid hilltop view of the surrounding countryside, and tubs of flowers at every window and balcony. The church is imposing, and its gardens a delight. Pasted to walls and doors were posters advertising a forthcoming disco, which conjured up an image of a room full of jiggling skeletons and clicking dentures gleaming under fluorescent strobe lights, as I hadn't seen anyone who looked under the age of seventy-five, apart from the waitress.

It was a rest day, and I walked half a mile to the supermarket on the town's outskirts to stock up my mobile larder. A group of elderly people stood in the sunny car park, talking animatedly. They looked very French, but the language didn't sound right — more like Spanish or Portuguese; musical, lilting. I edged closer. They were talking in the Creusois dialect, derived from the *langue d'oc* — the ancient language of the southern part of France, and the original language of the troubadours, as distinct from the northern *langue d'oïl*, the root of modern French, to which it bears almost no resemblance.

After doing my laundry, I wandered down

to the thermal baths, passing a small park where a herd of about sixty fallow deer grazed. I tried feeding them. One young buck, more adventurous than the others, took bread from me, whilst the others stood at a distance, watching suspiciously and flicking their tails. So elegant, so beautiful, until, like Eliza Doolittle at the races, they gave voice, a disgustingly vulgar mixture of a spit, a sneeze and a burp, which seemed to be their primary means of communication and was quite at odds with their refined appearance.

It was very hot, and the swimming pool looked luxuriously inviting, and was closed for Ascension Day. After a brief look at the buildings of the spa thermal centre, which the Vichy government used as a detention centre during the Second World War and which were slightly sombre, I climbed back up to the campsite, sticking my head round the door of the abbey, which like the one in Chambon was huge. I found these massive old buildings intimidating. Their damp, dark, hard and melancholy interiors and musty smells depressed and unsettled me, and despite the craftsmanship which had gone into their construction I didn't like them, and wasn't comfortable in them alone.

★ ★ ★

Every day when I set out for a new destination, I had no idea where, what or when my next meal would be, which was rather disconcerting. The remedy was to carry plenty of provisions, despite the unwelcome extra weight. I had bought two sliced loaves, a packet of grated Emmental cheese, and an onion, and made a monumental stack of cheese and onion sandwiches. I frequently craved something piquant, and would have sold my soul for a jar of Marmite, that quintessentially English delicacy that only the English palate seems able to appreciate. When I had given Jennifer a taste she pulled a face and asked incredulously: 'Do you mean you eat this for *pleasure*?' Oh yes, we certainly do.

The sandwiches would last for several days, and the older and more squashed they became the better they tasted.

With the sandwich mountain crammed into the backpack, I spread map No. 4 on the grass to plan the following day's route. A passing Frenchwoman asked what I was doing, and was extremely enthusiastic about my journey. I found that with all the French and Dutch people: they all wanted to know the why and the how and the where, and wished me well. The Frenchwoman and her husband were staying in their caravan for ten days while their elderly cousin, who was blind, took a cure at the baths.

Beside the tent a tiny coal tit cheeped from the shelter of a low laurel hedge which formed the boundary of my site. It had fallen from a nest in the birch above and its parents kept bringing it food. Watching the little family I couldn't understand how the creature seemed to be moving around in the hedge so rapidly. I investigated and found there were three babies, all as small as bumblebees, and heartbreakingly vulnerable. But they were well hidden and protected in the hedge and there were no cats around.

Behind the *gardienne*'s office, a psychopath was torturing a saxophone; every so often by sheer mischance a perfect note escaped, and it was beautiful. And all day, from dawn until last light, the blackbirds sang their dazzling songs. They were already in full voice when I woke at 7.00 a.m. the next morning and shook the dew from the tent. Evaux-les-Bains, sleeping still, floated in the mist.

In the gutter of the road leading from the campsite, a lump lurched around. It was a fledgling blackbird and it was in a very bad place. It was not easy to catch, or pick up, as it struggled wildly and its parents jumped up and down angrily. I pushed it through the hedge onto the peaceful lawn of a hospital, from where it tried furiously to clamber back into the gutter. Then I found another baby, and had a similar battle with that. They struggled so hard, and I was so afraid of hurting them, that it became a trial of wills until finally I managed to get them both to stay on the safe side of the hedge. Before setting off I had a good look to see if there were any more babies, and found the third, squeezed between a shrub and a wall. Unlike its siblings, this one didn't object to being picked up. It tilted back on its elbows and gaped widely and hopefully, and crossed to the other side of the hedge without a fight. The parents watched all the time from a nearby tree. It seemed that everywhere I went birds and insects were intent on suicide.

A wide avenue of copper beeches in full leaf flanked the road out of Evaux. The sun shone onto the grass, damp with morning mist, highlighting its many different varieties and colours. There were maybe twenty types along the roadside, in colours ranging from mauve to silver and many shades of green, blues, oranges, grey and pink. It came in thick, thin, tall, short, broad and narrow-leafed, with seedheads and without, and it was the first time in my life I had consciously thought about grass being anything other than green and spiky stuff you had to mow.

For much of the time when I walked, my

mind was something of a vacuum, which every so often would hoover up from some crevice an idea or a fact; today it dredged up some advice I had read in a French hiking book, which recommended '*le knickers*[1]' as the most suitable garment for walking in. What a vision this produced — the countryside dotted with all ages and sizes and both sexes, carefree in boxer shorts, bikini pants, thongs, large pink bloomers, Y-fronts. Personally, I found that when shorts were not appropriate, jeans were ideal because they provided warmth at night, protection from nettles and thorns, and didn't show the dirt. They doubled as evening wear, too.

The road spiralled down and down through peaceful, still woods thick with the deeply gnarled trunks of tall acacias, and into a valley where the hamlet of Valette was still asleep at 9.30 a.m. Suddenly I picked up the strong, unmistakable smell of cigar smoke. It hung on the air, and was rather disturbing. I looked around, up the hillsides, and into the depths of the woods, but there was neither sound nor sight of the perpetrator. I supposed the smoke had been left trapped in the valley from a passing car, but it must have lingered there for a long while, as since I'd left

---

[1] like plus-fours

Evaux-les-Bains I hadn't seen any traffic.

Beside the road the river Cher flowed fast, the water crystal clear as it rushed over polished rocks embedded in the brown sandy riverbed. Ahead, a patch of forest had been cleared on the hillside, and the gorse had invaded the space, leaving a great splash of yellow. On the river banks, shallow shingle ledges gave access to the water for the cattle in the adjoining pastures.

'Beware of the dog,' warned a sign on a garden gate. Below someone had added an additional warning: 'And the lady owner.'

At this point the river Cher divides the regions of the Limousin and the Auvergne, the land of extinct volcanoes, and forms the boundary between the départements of the Creuse and the Allier. The division was painted at the mid-way point on the bridge across the river. A double milestone passed. About a hundred yards the other side of the bridge was a very small and humble café, only distinguishable as such by the ancient red metal chairs and wonky tables sitting haphazardly beside the road. A bent old lady emerged with an overflowing laundry basket, and I asked whether the café was open.

'What would you like?' she asked.

'A *grande crème*, please.' I sat down on a rickety chair, soaking up the sweet bright morning. Two dilapidated old dogs dragged themselves over and collapsed beside the table. The coffee was quite a while arriving. In the meantime a car drew up and the driver disappeared into the kitchen, carrying two baguettes. Shortly afterwards another car arrived. The driver carried a packet of milk. A large cup on a tray materialized five minutes later, with a jug of scalding coffee, another of foaming milk, and apologies. The old lady had had to phone for milk; there was none in the house. Very few French drink their coffee with milk; they say it is indigestible. She placed a saucer of sugar lumps on the table, which by rolling their eyes and producing strings of shiny saliva the dogs gave me to understand were their prerogative. There was a continual stream of visitors in and out of the kitchen and a lot of laughter coming from within. Everyone passing called out: '*Bonjour.*' When the bill arrived it was a tiny six francs, the best-value coffee I ever came across. The old lady wished me good luck and was standing waving when I looked back.

The river tracked the road for some distance, through sparsely populated countryside. In one village I passed, out of twelve houses only one was occupied. Rotting shutters and flaking paint adorned the rest, which were losing a battle against dense undergrowth. There was an air of total desolation apart from the one inhabited house, which stood defiantly smart in a beautiful garden and flanked by great tubs of scarlet geraniums. Beside the river a young woman knelt planting pansies and begonias in a neat bed.

When the road seemed long, as it often did, I divided it into one-and-a-half-mile lengths and related it to the distance between my house and the nearest village. Thus six miles was only a walk into the village and back, twice, and didn't seem very far.

The road wound its way steeply up towards Marcillaten-Combraille, flanked on the left by dense copses of skinny trees and on the right by great rocks sprouting ferns, mosses and lichens in gold, lime green, cream and beige, the rock face glistening in the sun as if threaded with diamonds. They were cutting hay on the outskirts of the town, and the air was thick with its sweet smell.

In the town centre there was a modern restaurant/bar advertising 'snaks'. My destination that night was a farm campsite, and as far as I knew there would be no food there. Although armed with the cheese and onion sandwich mountain, a 'snak' didn't sound like a bad idea.

The proprietor was a burly young woman

with arms like hams and an expression that could freeze fire. I asked politely if there were any snaks that didn't contain meat. She indicated a poster offering hot dogs, hamburgers, croque monsieur, quiche lorraine and pizza.

'None of those have meat in them,' she announced.

I was nonplussed. 'What about the hamburger?' I asked. 'Surely that is meat?'

'Well, yes, but the rest don't have any meat in them.'

'What about the hot dog?'

That too she conceded.

But the croque monsieur only contained *jambon*[1] which she assured me vehemently was not meat, and the quiche lorraine contained *lardons*[2], which also were categorically not meat.

'Do you have anything to eat which doesn't have meat, *jambon* or *lardons* in it?' I struggled.

The pizza, she said stonily, was free of all. She gave me her oath. I didn't believe her, but ordered it anyway, and as expected found a dozen finely chopped pieces of bacon, cunningly obscured by a thick layer

---

[1] ham

[2] small pieces of bacon

of sweet tomato paste and some bubbles of cheese. I excavated them and their surroundings, and piled them ostentatiously on the plate.

There was a strange atmosphere in the bar; people came and went in a silent and subdued way, not wanting to upset this miserable giantess, I supposed. A dark unhappy-looking man ate his meal sadly, punctuating each mouthful with a fascinating clicking, smacking sound which he made inside his cheeks. I was glad to leave, and continuing through the town found several far more inviting restaurants offering proper meals at the same price as the horrid snaks. Never mind — next time.

The farm campsite was several miles north-east. As I turned a sharp bend, a gardening lady called out and asked where I was going. She came to the gate, brandishing a pair of secateurs and a handful of prunings.

'Take the short cut, just down here,' she indicated a pathway of trodden grass, 'go to the end, and it will bring you out on the lane. It saves a long walk on the main road. Don't walk on the road here, it is very dangerous. And be careful, the *pompiers*[1] are exercising in the fields at the bottom, and the

---

[1] firemen

gendarmes[1] are around.' She rolled her eyes expressively.

She didn't specify what sort of peril this might involve, but I said I would bear it in mind, thanked her and followed her short cut which cut off, just as she had said, a winding and busy road leading north to Montluçon. It led to a pretty lane cocooned by buttercup fields dotted with cattle, and scattered oak trees and hawthorn hedges, and I neither heard nor saw the *pompiers* or the *gendarmes*. A slight breeze stirred the afternoon heat. In a chilly, dark valley lurked a strange building, probably an old mill, with heavy machinery, enormous cranes and pile drivers surrounding it; a couple sat serenely eating their lunch from a small table set with a blue and white gingham cloth, amongst the surreal scenery. Beside them a big brown dog snored.

A quarter of a mile further on, something was gasping. The sleeping dog, a very fat boxer bitch, had caught up, and was following me. I ignored her for a while, but soon she was shuffling on fatly ahead of me, stopping every twenty yards to check that I was still there before snuffling onwards. I took her collar and turned her back to the valley, shooing her on her way. She stood for a few

---

[1] local police

seconds, a perplexed expression creasing her fat face, then lolloped past me again. I raised my stick and pointed towards her home. She looked from the stick to me and continued onwards. I turned and started to run back in the direction we had come. She followed happily. I turned back on route, she followed. I shouted at her and waved the stick. She threw herself in a heap and lay on her back, wriggling and rolling her eyes. I was now over a mile from where she belonged, and wasn't going to walk back to the valley and certainly not climb back to this point again. I wondered what to do. Perhaps tie her to a tree with the piece of rope I carried? She had a disc with her telephone number on her collar. Surely someone would come along eventually and take her home? While I was contemplating this strategy, she wobbled happily along ahead of me towards a small lane beside a field of cattle, with car tracks leading down it. She turned in and began investigating, while I stood motionless in the hedge for five minutes. She didn't reappear. Tiptoeing as quickly and quietly as it is possible to tiptoe in hiking boots, I carried on. Gasp, snuffle, she was back again. I turned and headed down the lane, slightly apprehensively, wondering where it would lead, but needing to rid myself of this persistent canine before we went any further.

The lane led past a pygmy goat and a large white nanny which invited me to butt heads with it. Reassuringly there were children's toys scattered around the garden, so I called out. A face appeared at an upstairs window.

'Hello,' it called. 'I see Florette is with you.'

A young woman opened the front door, laughing. Beside her was another boxer.

'I know her owners well. I will ring them to come and get her. She and my dog are great friends. In the meantime she can stay here.'

Florette took off at a rate of knots and chased a cat into a barn. For a fatty she was fairly fleet of foot. Thanking her new custodian I resumed course, stopping to rub the white goat's forehead with my fist, which it seemed to enjoy. It wound its chain round my legs and nearly pulled me over.

The area was forlorn. Everywhere cottages were falling into ruin, and great houses boarded up, their rusty wrought-iron gates hanging from crumbling stone pillars. It was a heart-rending sight, each empty building the end of a family story, and I thought of the thousands of people who dream of living in countryside such as this, with views reaching forever, clean air, no traffic. There is much talk of France's dying rural areas; here was the depressing evidence.

The farm campsite was a new enterprise for a friendly Dutch couple. The camping area left much to be desired, being nothing more than a large sloping field with spectacular views, where a tractor had roughly cut the straw leaving hummocks of stubble: a hard uneven surface, suitable for caravans but not for tents. The kitchen, washing and communal dining area were housed in an old barn, which had totally preserved its unspoilt rustic exterior but offered excellent cleanliness and comfort within. It was particularly tastefully done, and expensive at forty-five francs per night.

Ronnet village was served by a tiny but well-stocked supermarket, and a pretty little church which was crammed with flowers. Its walls were stencilled with fleur de lys, and bedecked with colourful plaster Stations of the Cross, and it had a warm, cheerful atmosphere. Its doors were wide open and the afternoon sun streamed in, giving a glow to the interior. Unlike the imposing abbeys, it was comfortable to wander around and didn't smell of gloom.

The other four residents at the campsite were Dutch, all in caravans, and they all wore wooden clogs. I watched them striding around in them and couldn't imagine that they were comfortable. With nothing to read and nothing to do, I asked the owners whether they had any books, and was led to a well-stocked library offering hundreds of volumes, all, not surprisingly, in Dutch. Except one, which one of their children had studied at school. It was *Lord of the Flies*. With just one evening in which to finish it, I started reading at top speed, by torchlight in the lumpy lopsided tent, munching cheese and onion sandwiches and drinking cider. I thought it a particularly gruesome story, and marvelled at the skill of the writer and the nightmare atmosphere he created. Having finished the book, I dressed in all my clothes, including the poncho, and folded myself into the sleeping bag. It was desperately cold, colder than I had ever been before in my life.

I shivered through the night as the temperature crashed. I tried sticking my head inside the sleeping bag and warming myself with my breath, but it wasn't very successful. I was frozen and shaking. The cold seeped up from the ground and through the thin nylon of the tent and through the thin sleeping bag and multiple layers of clothing, and it passed to the very centre of my bones. There was absolutely nothing I could do until morning came. Had I known that I would spend the following night in a cosy bed beside a crackling log fire, I would have been greatly comforted.

First light broke at 6.00 a.m. Inside, instead of the usual running rivulets of condensation, there was a crisp film of ice coating the walls of the tent, and as I sat up freezing flakes dropped down the back of my neck and into my hair. Outside, the tent sagged under the weight of a lacy silver veil which crazed its blue surface. It was literally frozen. The only reasonably level place where I had been able to pitch it was on the eastern side of the field, with no trees or hedges to protect it. Shivering in the early morning sunlight, I breakfasted on iced cheese and onion sandwiches, and then used the small towel to mop the tent dry. Even my boots and insoles were frozen solid, and it took an hour of arm swinging, jumping up and down and generally frantic movement before my blood started flowing again and I could stop shaking.

I was making a detour to the south-east, to see the famous Chouvigny gorges in the Sioule valley. It was very peaceful on that Saturday morning, and by the lake just outside Ronnet fishermen were congregating around a long trestle table set with glasses and bottles of wine. It was just after 8.00 a.m. The small country lanes I followed served me well for a while, leading across the départe-mental boundary (another milestone) into the northernmost part of the Puy de Dôme, until I arrived in a farmyard at the hub of a network of small tracks. There wasn't much there apart from a sludgy pond, a giant manure heap and a combine harvester, and I stood around rather stupidly for a few minutes trying to find any distinguishing feature which would give a clue as to which direction to follow. Two odd characters materialized; they could have been father and son, or brothers; their faces were very alike. They didn't say anything, but just stood staring blankly at the Kiwi Trikers logo on the front of my T-shirt. They had the appearance of a pair of murderous simpletons.

'I'm on my way to my friends' house. They are expecting me,' I said rather unconvinc-ingly. They didn't look convinced, but continued gazing quadroscopically at my chest.

'Can you tell me the best way to get to Meaux, please,' I said, picking the name of a village not far distant. 'My friends are waiting, and I am already late.'

Eventually they pointed me silently down a path. With a cheery wave I galloped off over hill and dale, mostly hill, towards Saint-Eloy-les-Mines. To the west of the town the road climbed to 2,400 feet, followed by a shin-racking 800-foot descent. Once known as Saint-Hilaire-de-Montaigut, the town became Saint-Eloy-les-Mines with the discovery of a silver-bearing seam in 1695. The town's coal industry developed during the nineteenth century, employing at its peak 3,000 miners producing 700,000 tons of coal a year. The pit ponies spent one week at a time underground in the mines. Blindfolded, with their legs folded into their bellies and tied, they were slowly lowered tail-first down the shafts by means of sturdy slings attached to chains.

The mines saw their share of disasters, including one in 1950 when a methane explosion nearly 1,000 feet below ground left thirteen dead. In 1977 the mine closed and in its place is a large plastic factory, or should it be plastics factory? Anyway, a factory producing plastic, not one made out of it. There didn't seem to be much else in the town; it was just a long road with a variety of shops, several of which were closed down. I found a *boulangerie* and bought a couple of croissants, as a change from cheese sandwiches of which I had eaten three for breakfast and two en route.

Leaving Saint-Eloy wasn't easy. It had seemed to me for quite some time that the roads I was walking were often at variance with those shown on my maps, and when I examined the maps, which I had bought only three months previously, I found they had actually been drawn in 1994, and were hopelessly out of date. With the building of new roads they bore no similarity to the current layout, and I just couldn't work out how to get out of town. I stopped and asked a mechanic at a garage, who called over another man. They discussed between them the best route to Servant, and were joined after several minutes by a third man, who poured scorn on all their suggestions and recommended a completely different route, which he said was no more than three and a half miles; one of the others said that it was more like five, the third said that it was at least six. They started getting heated.

'Listen, I walk every weekend! I have walked to Servant at least twenty times. I am telling you it's five miles.'

'But no! It is only three and a half. I'm telling you. I've walked there many times myself.'

'Pah!' spat the five-miler.

Before they came to blows, I dragged the backpack onto my shoulders and said solemnly: 'So are we all agreed, then, it is somewhere between three and a half and six miles from here?'

'Yes,' they chorused in happy harmony, 'that is exactly what it is!'

It was, as a matter of fact, precisely six miles.

The climb out of Saint-Eloy towards Servant was fearsome. There was almost but not quite a breeze on the shadeless road. Occasionally a tiny puff of cool air wafted past, but mostly it was still and scorching. The weather was certainly very extreme in these parts, with sub-zero nights opening out into days when the temperature reached over 90°F.

The miles were the longest I had found so far; it didn't seem to make any difference how long I trudged, I was never any nearer my destination. Recently there had been very little wildlife to see — even the beetles and butterflies had been conspicous by their absence — but today there was a small adder beside the road. It appeared uninjured, but lifeless. The little body wasn't more than ten inches long, and it seemed strange that with all the larger snakes to be found in France — for instance the western whip snake and the grass snakes, which can both grow to over six feet — this delicate little reptile is the only one which can do serious harm.

The road climbed and dipped through meadows shaded by oaks and traced with streams and small lakes; glossy creamy Charolais cattle with young white calves grazed amongst the wild flowers, or occasionally stood cooling themselves in the lakes. An average-sized group seemed to comprise one bull and about twelve cows with young, and they looked happy, healthy and contented.

Sometimes I would reach a peak and look back at ranges of hills disappearing far into the distant west, and I would say to myself, 'I can never have walked all that way!' But I had. Somehow I could never quite believe it.

Very fortunately, as it happened, I missed the first turning off the road towards Servant, and by the time I realized my mistake it wasn't worth turning back. I took the next turning instead, and arrived in a pretty hamlet called les Berthons, where I sat beneath a horse chestnut tree cooling down before making for the campsite a mile further on. A small black poodle came and sniffed me, followed by a woman with an enormous smile, which completely occupied her face.

'You're English, aren't you? Are you going to the campsite?' she enquired.

I said I was, once I had cooled down.

'Wouldn't you rather stay at my house?' she asked.

I didn't quite know what to say. Maybe she had a *chambre d'hôte*. I thanked her, but explained that my budget didn't allow me anything other than camping.

'But no,' she exclaimed, 'I don't want any money. Just your company. And to speak a little English. Why don't you come and have a cold drink? My friend Yvette is coming to stay. It will be a nice adventure for us to have an English guest.'

Slightly uncertain, I followed her to a small cottage engulfed in Virginia creeper.

'This is Holympe,' she said, indicating the poodle. 'Olympe with an H.'

I remarked that it was an unusual name. My new friend, Laurence, explained: the year the dog was born, all dogs had to have names starting with H. However, one of Laurence's grandchildren had set her heart on naming the dog Olympe. So she became Holympe.

Holympe jumped onto my lap, curled up and went to sleep, while Laurence made a pot of tea.

'We always drink tea, it's much better for you than coffee. Yvette has to be very careful with her digestion. She can't drink coffee at all!' She punctuated every sentence with an explosion of laughter.

Yvette arrived, petite, neat and rather timid

and bearing three exquisite *chaussons aux pommes*[1].

'I must have known you were coming.' She smiled.

They were both widows in their seventies from Clermont-Ferrand, and had known each other for more than twenty years, since their husbands worked together as engineers at the Michelin tyre factory. Laurence's husband had suffered a heart attack sixteen years ago, and believed that if he could only have a small house in the country, with a garden, he would recover his health. They had bought the cottage as a weekend home in April that year, and he died the following December, and although Laurence found the village life too quiet, and hated gardening, she still came most weekends with Yvette. Her greatest passion was playing bridge, and she went out to '*bridger*' at least three times a week. This weekend she had been due to play in a tournament, but, fortunately for me, she had opted instead for a quiet weekend in the country.

By the time we had demolished the *chaussons aux pommes* and two huge pots of tea, I felt it was time I set off for the campsite, but Laurence's face fell.

---

[1] apple turnovers

'You don't like my house?' she asked sadly.

'No, it's lovely, you are very kind, but I can't impose on you.'

'Please stay. Please. Stay and talk with us tonight.' She added rather shyly: 'We don't have a lot to eat, but we would like to share it with you.'

It would have been ungracious to refuse. We went on a guided tour of the pretty little garden, and Laurence pointed out the wall of hate at the back of the house.

'It's the new neighbours. They are quite mad. They built this horrible wall.' She indicated a lopsided and higgledy-piggledy breezeblock construction nearly six feet high, running for sixty metres between the two properties.

Why did they build the wall, I asked?

'I don't know. They are just mad. I planted creepers all up the side, and they chopped them down. What's more, the wall is one metre inside my boundary. The police have been and said I can make them take it down, but I shan't bother. I shall just barbecue sardines every summer evening I am here. The wind will take the smell right into their house.' She roared with laughter and clapped her hands.

She had just bought an expensive new strimmer (one of Jennifer's weed-eaters), and

216

she threw up her hands in despair. The instructions for assembling it were impossible; she had wasted her money and would never use it.

I put the nylon reel in for her, and pushed the button. The machine screeched into life. Laurence was ecstatic.

'But you are a mechanical genius!' she shouted. I hadn't known that before.

The neighbours came to visit, friendly and charming people. It seemed they were all fanatical gardeners, and they stood around pointing at various plants, commenting on how well or otherwise they had done this year, offering advice and promising cuttings and seeds.

The downstairs of Laurence's house comprised a room which served as sitting/dining room and hallway, a compact kitchen leading off, and a tiny room where one could perform what Laurence described as 'our little necessities'. From the main room an open staircase led to a spacious landing which doubled as a spare, if rather exposed, second bedroom, and Laurence's room was off that. It was rather like a large doll's house and quite delightful.

I had anticipated that supper was likely to be a problem. In the face of Laurence's extreme kindness, I felt I couldn't mention that I was a vegetarian without possibly causing her embarrassment, so I kept quiet. A large bowl of vegetable soup with some cheese crackers was followed by a plate bearing two slices of ham. Yvette, who had a small enamel box containing an assortment of pills in different colours, which she dipped into throughout the evening, proclaimed that she was so full, she just couldn't eat anything else. Laurence pushed the plate towards me. It would seem dreadfully uncivil to refuse, and so for the first time in eighteen years I ate a piece of meat. And no, I did not enjoy doing so.

We drank port and red wine, and ended the meal with *fromage blanc*[1]. This was a revelation to me as I had always found it to be rather uninspiring, but Laurence explained that it is eaten with sugar and cream, or a fruit purée. She had no cream, but liberally sprinkled with sugar it was delicious. Yvette abstained. She had to be very careful with her liver.

'Adventure,' said Laurence. What was life worth if there was no adventure? And it was just on the doorstep. The most important thing was to jump straight into an adventure at the first opportunity — never hesitate. She

---

[1] soft white cheese, similar in texture to yoghurt

talked of many of her own, including extensive travels abroad which always seemed to include some nail-biting situation, and the six Cambodian refugees, mother, father and four children, she had found in a bakery when she lived in Paris. She had taken them home and installed them in her two-bedroomed apartment, so that when her husband returned from work he found they were now a family of eight, with the Cambodian man wearing his clothes and shoes, which were several sizes too large, and the children sleeping in a cupboard. The novelty of the adventure began to wear thin as the Cambodians dug in and wouldn't leave voluntarily as they had nowhere else to go, and the authorities wouldn't find them alternative accommodation because they already had it. But, laughed Laurence, she had eventually managed to find them an apartment and they had all lived happily ever after and prospered. The children were now adults, and she still saw them from time to time.

Yvette had a problem. Whenever she went away, her neighbour who had a key to the apartment would keep an eye on it for her. But now the neighbour had become insane. One day when Yvette had taken her car for servicing, the neighbour had telephoned

Yvette's daughter and told her that Yvette had been rushed to hospital. The daughter had telephoned the hospital, who knew nothing about Yvette. Unable to find her mother, the daughter had alerted the police who had launched a full-scale 'find Yvette' operation. When Yvette returned home with the newly serviced car, there were police and paramedics preparing to break into her apartment, as the neighbour refused to produce the key. During the night she sometimes went in while Yvette slept, and removed all her mail, and rearranged her ornaments. She was over eighty, and not at all *belle*, but kept complaining that men followed her in the streets and pestered her and that Mitterand himself had tried to make her his mistress. Many times she had stayed at his country home. Yvette shook her head despairingly. Now she wanted her key back, but didn't know how to go about recovering it without offending her neighbour. I suggested she changed the lock.

She mulled over this idea while she extracted and broke in half a yellow pill from the enamel box. Another pot of tea arrived, but Yvette declined. It was bad for her kidneys to drink tea so late. Laurence managed to persuade her to take a weak tisane of verbena and mint. She hoped it wouldn't affect her sinuses.

With a gust of laughter, Laurence announced that we would all rise at 6.30 a.m. It was nice to get up early, there was so much one could do. I hoped she was joking. She stacked the fire with logs and unfolded the bed settee, much to Holympe's disgust, as the settee was where she slept. She sat at the end, looking at me rather reproachfully before curling herself into a perfect circle with her neat black nose tucked up under her tail.

What a treat! A warm bed. The flicker and crackle of the fire, and Laurence's gentle snores, kept me awake for about two minutes.

11

The Hilarious Prospect of Freezing to Death

Just as Laurence had threatened, we all rose at 6.30 a.m., with some considerable reluctance on my part. We breakfasted on delicious toast made in a cast-iron frying pan, with crispy black bits on it, crowned with generous blobs of butter, and several bowls of tea. After a bear hug from Laurence and two delicate kisses from Yvette, I set off en route to the Chouvigny gorges which I had diverted so far off track to visit.

Outside the *boulangerie* in the village of Servant a cluster of baguette-bearing people talked cheerfully in the morning sunshine. In the village square, four-foot-high steel shell cases stood at the corners of the monument to the dead of two world wars, Indochina and Algeria. The names of everyone who had fallen were carved into the monument, and some families had sacrificed as many as four of their number.

As usual, it wasn't long before I was quite lost. A road that was prominently marked on the map wasn't where it should have been. It simply didn't appear, but confident that I was heading in the right direction I ambled along happily in the sunshine, descending into a deep valley and forest and back once more into the Allier département. Streams and small waterfalls tumbled through trees and rocks, and it was very pretty. I liked it there. Breaking out from the woods and climbing upwards, I caught sight of a long dark red tail scooting up a tree. I stood very still for a few moments, and watched the return run of the tail, which was led by a handsome weasel. Several green woodpeckers flew past, and two herons flapped lazily overhead, all folded up neatly. Eventually I reached a small village on a summit. There were odd noises coming from a vegetable garden, and through the hedge I could see a man wearing an ancient jester's cap, kneeling in his garden and crooning lovingly to a handful of seeds as he planted them. From ahead came the sound of rapid and heavy gunfire.

After several minutes of trotting up and down, calling out and waving my arms, I managed to attract the attention of the jester, who interrupted his incantations and asked what I wanted. He wasn't much use at giving directions, but summoned his burly neighbour who shook hands vigorously and said, 'You can't miss it. You'll see the sign once you get to the main road.'

Although I was on the right road to Chouvigny village, I had taken the longest possible course and could not actually get to the gorges from here unless I retraced my steps almost back to Servant; that would mean another three hours' walking, and suddenly the gorges didn't seem that attractive. The gunshots continued, and I asked where they were coming from.

'Are you afraid?' enquired the burly man hopefully.

'No. But do you know which direction they are aiming in?'

'Don't worry, they won't shoot you. They'll see you,' he assured me. So I took his word for it, and didn't get shot.

The sun burnt down from a sky that was busily stacking up large curly clouds. Chouvigny looked deceptively close on the map, but took three hours of hard, shin-racking climbing. Every corner I turned led to a new place to be lost in. Everyone I asked for directions ended by saying: 'You'll see the sign.' Not once did I see a sign for

Chouvigny, on any road, anywhere. A large dog came charging out at me in a small hamlet, wagging its tail furiously, followed by a wrinkle-stockinged and aproned old lady who berated it wildly. How dare it be so rude to a visitor, she wanted to know. It was a disgrace. It sniffed my legs and continued wagging its tail, disregarding her shrill curses and easily dodging the stick with which she attempted to thump it.

'Just turn right at the end of the cinder path — you'll see it signposted,' she called.

I did, and I didn't.

At last Chouvigny village appeared. At the *mairie* a very small car boot sale was in progress, three trestle tables spread with a sad array of chipped mugs, obscure electrical and mechanical pieces, and battered children's toys. A band of musicians in medieval costumes were playing and singing medieval music, their fine voices backed by fiddle, drum and tambourine. The *mairie* was followed by a hairpin bend, then the church, then another bend gripping a hotel/restaurant which I planned to visit once I'd set up the tent, after which I would hike to the gorges, which I so much wanted to see. A little further on, round yet another bend, was a small, picturesque medieval castle, once the home of the Marquis de Lafayette, amongst

225

other things a soldier, politican, popular hero of the American War of Independence, and creator of the modern French flag — he added the white to the original red and blue. The states of Indiana and Louisiana both have towns named Lafayette in his honour.

After the castle, nothing except more bends. No shops, no houses. I kept expecting the village to appear around the next bend, but it didn't. Nor was there a sign to the campsite.

A group of people were strolling up the hill towards the castle. I asked a beautiful man holding a squealing baby if he knew where the campsite was, and the dreaded expression I had come to know so well appeared on his face. It starts with pursed lips, puffed cheeks, raised brow and widened eyes, followed by an expulsion of air from between the aforesaid lips, and it always means bad news.

The municipal campsite was at Péraclos, at least another two and a half miles away. But there was another on the way; he had heard it was very pleasant. I would see the signs just down the road, and this time I did. They indicated a luxury campsite, which I found behind the cemetery. It was overgrown, dark, dingy, dirty and dejected, and sinister enough to have made the Bates Motel seem homely. Not surprisingly it was totally deserted. I retraced my steps over the bridge and tramped on towards Péraclos.

The road twisted and turned, and the edges were very narrow. From behind came the distinctive sound of ancient and expensive engines, and I flattened myself against the rock face as a magnificent procession of stately vintage cars growled up the hill — Bentleys, Ferraris, Citroëns, Rolls-Royces, a Bugatti, a Karman Ghia. Half a mile further on a chain of about fifty vast gleaming motorbikes throbbed past in the opposite direction, and as they did so the leathered riders all raised their hands in peace signs and salutes, as if we shared a common bond. Nice friendly people.

Five hours after leaving Laurence's house, which according to the map was no more than eight miles away, I staggered into the campsite. Idyllically situated on the banks of the river Sioule, it was totally isolated and would have been utterly peaceful had it not been for a group of French campers with a trumpet which they took turns blowing into, causing their dog to fall into an understandable frenzy of wailing each time they did so. They had obviously lunched well and were enjoying themselves. I stuck the tent up and crawled into it while I decided what to do next.

The nearest food was two and a half miles behind me, and I didn't even know if the restaurant would be open on a Sunday evening. There was no shop. I had four dried apricots, a small tin of smoked sardines, and a dozen of the three-day-old cheese and onion sandwiches, with which I was becoming slightly bored. There was an ominous feeling in the air, and if it rained tonight I would have at least a six-mile walk to the next town the following morning with a wet tent, and possibly in the pouring rain. It made sense to push on to Ebreuil, so after sleeping for a couple of hours, I folded up and headed out. As I walked from the campsite, a voice called out: 'Do you not like it here?'

It was a Dutch couple with a caravan. I said that although the location was lovely, being low on food and concerned about the weather I had decided to go on to Ebreuil, and abandon any thought of visiting the gorges.

'But we can give you food,' they offered.

I thanked them but said that I wanted to move on, because if the weather was going to deteriorate for long I would rather be somewhere a little less isolated.

'I will drive you there,' suggested the man, and I declined, explaining that I didn't take lifts.

He frowned. 'But the road is dangerous. It's very narrow. There's a lot of traffic. You may get hurt. Please let me take you. Also it's much further than you may think. It will take you at least three hours to get there.'

I kept refusing, but the couple became so agitated that I finally surrendered and heaved the backpack into the car. He deposited me at the municipal campsite in Ebreuil, which was, as he had said, a great deal further than it looked on the map. It was right on the banks of the river Sioule and there were notices posted all round the site advising what to do in the case of brutal *inondations*[1]; it was comforting to know that someone had thought about this likelihood, which if the skies were anything to go by was becoming a distinct possibility.

Ebreuil was a small town of winding lanes, topsy-turvy roofs, wrought-iron balconies, courtyard gardens, and higgledy-piggledy houses. Beside the market place stood the tenth-century abbey, and next to that a retirement home. Even at 5.00 p.m. on Sunday the bakery was open, selling fragrant, freshly baked pizzas, which were, most unusually in France, totally vegetarian. Armed with one of those and a bar of

---

[1] severe flooding

chocolate I felt secure once more. Funny how little it takes. The town was lively; a cycle race had just passed through, and spectators were packing up their picnics beside the river. I stopped in a bar for a shandy, but was soon driven away by three small and extraordinarily noisy children playing on a pinball machine. Having no money to put in it, they rocked it madly from side to side, banging on the glass and pulling the plunger out as far as it would go before letting it smash home, shrieking and howling with excitement each time the machine shuddered.

A short distance up the road from the local taxidermist (who was situated within a stone's throw from the retirement home) was a brief tarmac lane leading directly, down a slope and without hindrance, straight into the river, an ideal opportunity for careless drivers to become instant submariners. Dark blue cornflowers, pink and pale mauve scabious and scarlet poppies were scattered along the roadside. When I returned to the campsite, two fishermen had pitched a tent, the first I had seen since starting out twenty-four days previously. It looked warm and dry and cosy and comfortable, all the things which mine was not. One of the fishermen stood thigh-deep in the river, encased in green rubber waders up to his waist, flicking a line up and down for two hours without any success. The sky was ominously overcast.

I phoned home. Jennifer was in good spirits, despite the news about her father. She reported that poor Gloria's problems were increasing. Having been rescued from the clutches of the French Customs and their sniffer dog, her truck had continued to England to deliver two customers' furniture. The first customer, upset at finding holes drilled in his garden ornaments and the bottoms of his chairs and settee torn open by the Customs in the course of their unproductive search, had withheld payment and expropriated the vehicle. The second customer's goods were now immobilized in the first customer's garden. Nevertheless, said Jennifer, Gloria was managing to retain her sanity and good humour.

Just down the road from the municipal campsite was a superior establishment run by an English couple, and I went to see if I could buy an English book from the large stock of paperbacks available for residents. They most generously offered me not only my choice of reading matter, for which they wouldn't accept payment, but also the use of a bath, which was particularly magnanimous as I wasn't even staying there. The prospect of soaking in a tub of hot, clean water was almost too much to resist, but unfortunately my little towel was still stuffed into a plastic bag, wet and filthy from drying the tent at Ronnet, so I couldn't take advantage of the offer, feeling that to expect the loan of a towel too would have been rather a cheek. I selected Thomas Hardy's *Jude the Obscure*, which looked as if it would last for a while, and a bottle of wine, which certainly wouldn't, and settled down for another chilly night to the sound of the river slurping politely beside the tent.

Although the night was cold, the rain didn't arrive and the next day looked promising. As I packed up the tent in the early morning, a platoon of ducks came gliding down the glassy surface of the river and established themselves on a flat projecting rock where they proceeded to perform their ablutions. Fish were jumping right out of the water as if they knew that the fishermen had already left, on down to the Vercors, which they (the men, that is, not the fish) had assured me was a fisherman's paradise.

On the way back into town to buy some fruit, I stopped to admire an elegant arched doorway in a wall adjacent to the retirement home. It had automatic doors. As I watched, a large black car drew up and the gate swung open. Inside, a discreet sign read 'Morgue'.

Pasted to a wall in the centre of town was a poster depicting a cartoon dog addressing an assembly of similar dogs, explaining that the commune couldn't afford the expense of a mobile mess-collecting machine, so would everyone kindly use the gutters and not the pavements. From what I saw of the streets this friendly and humorous notice was entirely effective, and compared favourably with those blunt anti-canine notices in England which say, 'Owners of dogs fouling the pavement face fines of £50.'

The streets of Ebreuil were lined with tubs of pansies, salvia, petunias, antirrhinums and tobacco plants, and the sun was fierce by 9.00 a.m. In the wide fields the hay stood in the giant-sized rolls which have almost completely replaced the homely little bales, huge and unmanageable cylinders requiring a tractor to handle them. In someone's garden a litter of twelve collie puppies played in a clean pen; ignoring the rubber puppy toys scattered all around, they were enjoying a tug-of-war with a plastic ice cream container.

The whole of this fairly flat countryside was planted to crops, and the maize and sunflowers were neck and neck at six inches high. As compensation for missing the Chouvigny gorges, I made a detour of about five miles to visit the picturesque medieval hilltop village of Charroux, built on a circular plan and described as one of the loveliest villages in France, and not to be confused with the other Charroux which I'd passed through fifteen days ago. However, it was Benedictine monks from fifteen-days-ago Charroux who had come here originally and named it also Charroux. Smitten by the plague twice in the fifteenth century, leaving the population decimated, Charroux was also a frequent battleground during the civil and religious wars that ravaged France. The street names evoke images of a turbulent and bloodthirsty era — the Street of Sufferers, the Street of Sighs. However, on this very pleasant sunny day, 25 May 1998, all was well in Charroux. Beautiful stonework, old wells, narrow cobbled alleyways and a very peaceful atmosphere made the deviation well worth while. There was a shop selling local products including an impressive range of mustards, and a mustard museum, which was closed.

At the Auberge de la Porte d'Occident, seventy francs bought a tomato salad that bit back, trout fried until the skin was brown and crispy and the flesh still moist and tender, a platter of cheese and a vast pyramid of glistening strawberries. When the cheese course arrived, the waiter asked whether I would prefer *fromage blanc* or *fromage sec* — offering a choice between the delicious soft cheese I had eaten at Laurence's house, or a selection from a platter of hard cheeses. It was the first time I had come across this option, but from here on eastwards, it was the case wherever I ate.

Could the taxidermist from Ebreuil, seven miles away, be responsible for the décor here? On the main wall hung a wild boar skin; a group of three squirrels squabbled over a single walnut on a corner shelf, and above the fireplace a tragic vixen gazed proudly at her tiny cub. There was a set of antlers hanging over the bar. Those spaces not occupied by dead animals were filled with mugs and copper saucepans. In a murky aquarium a solitary goldfish swam around rather pointlessly. It was very rustic and the food was excellent.

I spent an hour wandering around the pretty town, before turning back towards Jenzat, about four and a half miles to the south-east. Sore feet and aching shoulders had long since become the norm, but occasionally sharp stabbing pains struck unexpectedly in diverse joints. These were signals to slow down, if indeed it was possible to go any slower than my current snail's pace. Today, overloaded with food and *Jude the*

Obscure, I ached all over. For three days a storm had been building up, the weather was hot and humid, and it was with relief that I arrived at the campsite at Jenzat, which sat twenty yards from the banks of the river Sioule. It was absolutely seething with mosquitoes.

Jenzat had been renowned for the production of hurdy-gurdies during the eighteenth century — beautifully worked instruments in exotic woods, intricately carved, inlaid and painted. So talented were the hurdy-gurdy players of Jenzat — known as *luthiers* in French — that they were said to be in league with the devil. Although I have the musical talent of a grain of salt, I thought it would be interesting to visit the hurdy-gurdy museum for which Jenzat is world famous. However, it was closed until 15 June, three and a half weeks away. So was the little twelfth-century church known for its superb murals. No doubt the keys were in safekeeping nearby, increasingly a necessity of life even in rural France where churches are targets for vandalism and theft. I ardently hoped that before arriving in Geneva I would find something, somewhere, that was open when I was there. Apart from a few dozen houses and a restaurant, that was about the extent of Jenzat. Despite the excellent lunch, the restaurant appealed to me. It seemed that the more I ate, the hungrier I became. The prospect of fighting the mosquitoes over a picnic was not attractive, and it was virtually impossible to eat comfortably within the tent, because its design meant that to sit up I had to keep my head bowed, as if in some yogic or devotional pose. Eating lying down was difficult, uncomfortable and liable to cause choking, and propped up on my elbows painful.

The menu offered, by my frugal standards, expensive meals or very expensive meals. I went in to ask if they could do a meal that I could afford. Madame was a little lady who looked as if she had stepped out of a 1940s film. She wore a narrow black skirt down to mid-calf, high-heeled peep-toe black patent sandals, a cream silk blouse with short puffed sleeves, and black hair parted to one side and cascading in waves to just below her ears. Her husband was a short, dark plump man with unbearably sad eyes and a tragic expression. He was also a chef of some renown. They were most obliging and would be very happy to produce a three-course meal for sixty francs.

A tiny vase of pale mauve chive flowers decorated the starched white linen cloth on each of the beautifully set tables. I was as ever conscious of my appearance — the baggy mohair jumper covering a crumpled T-shirt, wrinkled jeans and the great hiking boots, which I had brushed and oiled so that they at least looked cared for. The only other diners were a friendly and unbelievably scruffy couple whose dress made me feel positively chic. He was very thin, in crumpled beige linen trousers, sandals and an even more crumpled mustard-coloured shirt. He had a sparse scruffy beard which he picked at nervously and constantly. Compared to his wife, he was a model of sartorial elegance. She wore a shapeless orange T-shirt tucked half in and half out of the elasticated waist of her green and blue blobbed shiny polyester skirt, which reached to just above her knees. Her bare, unshaven legs ended in scuffed and cumbersome shoes and her hair didn't look as if it had ever had any attention, even a basic brushing.

They both talked at me simultaneously, in a very strong accent, very fast, and with their mouths full. Apparently what they were saying was funny, because they laughed uproariously every time they spoke. She prefaced each tale with uncontrollable laughter even before the story began, and her words came tumbling out like ants from a disturbed nest, in so much of a hurry that their order was irrelevant.

They came from Besançon, and warned me of what I could expect when I reached the Jura.

'You think it's cold here!' she shrieked. 'Wait until you get there! Oh, just wait until you get there!' Her husband nodded and picked quickly at his beard. He was a van driver delivering food supplies to hospitals and schools throughout the Jura, and knew the region well.

'Chamois, squirrels, wild boar, deer. There's plenty of wildlife there. New restrictions limit how many animals the hunters may kill each year, and now we are starting to see the numbers growing. The hunters don't like it, but it's a good thing. Not all of us want to kill everything that moves.' I was glad to hear that.

The melancholy chef had conjured up a plate of crudités, a fluffy omelette with sauté potatoes sprinkled with garlic and parsley, and after a bowl of *fromage blanc* with a raspberry purée a large tray of fresh fruit appeared. I helped myself to a couple of velvety apricots. It was pretty good value for sixty francs.

Reluctantly I prepared to go back to the mosquito-ridden site. As I stood up, the scruffy lady exploded into a cloud of coughs,

239

tears and food crumbs. She heaved and sobbed, waving her arms and hands so wildly that the horrid orange T-shirt came completely untucked from her skirt, and signalled that I should wait. Between gales of laughter and splutters, she said she hoped I wouldn't wake up one morning in my tent in the Jura, frozen solid like a log and encased in ice! So extraordinarily hilarious was this prospect that we all dissolved into tears of laughter. I waved goodbye to them, leaving her wracked in a paroxysm of hysterical mirth and her husband burrowing in his beard. What a jolly lady she was.

The air was still and soggy, and the night sky a black sheet unbroken by even a single star. Hoping for a warm night's sleep, I put all my clothes on, and closed both flaps of the tent. In the night I woke in pitch darkness, panicking, because I couldn't find the torch which I had forgotten to unpack. I struggled to unzip the inner mesh flap and then the outer nylon one which I tied back so that I could see the sky. Later the storm broke, and the rain battered the tent in torrents. It came dashing in through the mesh, which I had to open again and reach around in the dark to close the nylon flap. Rain teemed down my arm and into the tent and I cursed its wretched design.

During the night the slugs somehow managed to get in, and in the morning their glistening silvery runways criss-crossed the tent's wet walls, the floor, and the backpack.

12

Twelve Miles is a Long Way to Walk for a Loaf of Bread

It took several hours to get the tent sufficiently dry to pack, and remove the dozens of slugs and snails that had set up home within and upon it. I was still moving northwards to get back onto the la Rochelle-Geneva line, and was heading for the next nearest campsite at Paray-sous-Briailles.

I followed quiet back roads past a farmyard which looked as if it hadn't changed in two hundred years: chickens scratched in the central courtyard and a duck stood guard over her twelve ducklings on the compost heap; pigeons gurgled in their loft, and cattle dozed hock-deep in straw in their barn.

Wild geraniums and poppies were in control of the roadsides, their vivid colours of pale mauve and scarlet somehow managing not to clash, and embryonic apples were developing on the trees. A cool and brisk wind blew, and I reached Bayet, the halfway point, at 2.00 p.m. with perfect timing, because as I went into the bar the heavens opened and the rain exploded as if from a burst dam. It was forty minutes before it showed signs of abating, and I felt that was long enough for me to nurse one Coke, so with the help of a big-eyed brown-skinned lady who looked as if she had stepped off a Gauguin canvas I climbed into the red poncho and ventured back out.

It was not quite rain, but too heavy for drizzle, and penetratingly unpleasant. Cattle grazed each side of the road, and I wished the poncho was not quite so red. An exceedingly fat horse alone in a field demanded that I socialize, trotting alongside the hedge, whinnying and whickering until I went and stroked it. We stood wetly for five minutes, talking about nothing much, and as I turned away he galloped off, kicking up his heels and large clumps of muddy grass.

The countryside was peaceful and unremarkable, apart from an astonishing number of overhead electricity cables and pylons. It seemed that just as all roads lead to Rome, every electric line converged on Saint-Pourçainsur-Sioule, just to the west of

Paray-sous-Briailles. Although as navigational aids overhead power lines are very useful, I hated walking beneath or beside them, especially when they emitted pinging noises indicating emissions of invisible needles of electricity.

An encouraging sign after I had passed so many derelict buildings in the area was a very large château undergoing complete renovation. New red tiles covered the pitched roof of the main house and the numerous outbuildings. Newly gravelled drives carved their way through elegant lawns, bounded by a high wall and great ornamental wrought-iron gates. Somebody was spending a lot of money.

On the outskirts of Paray-sous-Briailles a fabulous tulip tree (*Liriodendron tulipifera*), maybe sixty feet high, and the first I had ever seen, was heavy with its huge tulip-shaped green and orange blossoms. A few yards further on was a purple-blossomed acacia. They both looked wildly exotic, as if they should be growing in tropical forests, and not this very green and wet French village.

The campsite was just beyond the village, next to an immaculate football field. The site was neat and well laid out, and there was a young family living there in a mobile home. I had been walking for the previous five days and was looking forward to a rest day with Jude, so I went to see what the village had to offer in the food line; the bar was open, but the adjacent restaurant, widely advertised en route, was only open by prior arrangement and definitely not tonight or tomorrow. There was neither a grocery nor a bakery. I had sufficient food for tonight and tomorrow morning. The nearest shops were six miles away.

There were sporadic showers during the night, but I was only moderately cold.

The *gardien* arrived in the morning to clean the sanitary block. He had a simple technique, which I mentally stored for future use. Armed with a giant lavender-scented air freshener, he opened the doors of the showers and toilets and blasted them for about fifteen seconds each. Nothing else. They certainly smelled very much more pleasant than they looked. It was doubtful that anything short of demolition and reconstruction could make them usable.

I asked him whether I should go to Saint-Pourçain-sur-Sioule or Varennes-sur-Allier for my shopping: both were the same distance away. Saint-Pourçain-sur-Sioule, he said. It was a pleasant town with an impressive church. Was I religious, he enquired. Just in time I detected a glint of zeal in his eyes, and a little warning bell tinkled.

'Are you a Catholic?' I countered.

'They are all thieves and liars,' he announced, rather sweepingly, I felt. 'I am a believer. A very strong believer. But I am not a Catholic. Have you heard of Jehovah's Witnesses?' He reached into his car and emerged with a bunch of leaflets, which he tried to hand to me, unsuccessfully as I doggedly tucked my hands into my armpits.

He launched into a ten-minute diatribe against the Catholic Church, and extolled the virtues of living in accordance with the word of the Bible.

'Twenty years ago, everyone thought I was crazy. But now they are starting to listen.' The leaflets hung suspended between us.

'Well,' I replied, 'I think everyone has the right to their own beliefs and should be free to worship as they please without interference. Me, I'm a Buddhist.' This was not untrue. Not a fully fledged Buddhist, but trying.

He shrugged, and produced another pamphlet, entitled *Automedication — can it harm you?*

He suggested that I might find the bundle of tracts interesting.

'You do read French, do you?' he asked.

Fingers crossed behind my back, I said, not really, I found it very difficult. I really didn't want to be converted, and as I relied heavily on automedication to help me sleep and conquer my aches and pains, I didn't want to know what harm it was doing.

However, he wasn't to be easily dissuaded, and peeling off the automedication paper tucked it under my arm — in case I changed my mind and wanted something to read. As I was morbidly entranced by the hapless *Jude the Obscure* and his tormented life, it was unlikely that automedication was going to distract me, but I took the paper anyway, politely.

It was unfortunate to have chosen to rest in a place where the nearest food was six miles away. When I talked to friends after my return, they would say things like: 'Why didn't you stop somewhere sooner?' or 'Why didn't you catch a train, or a bus?' or 'Why didn't you buy some new insoles before you got there?' Many people found it impossible to imagine that there wasn't anywhere sooner. There were no trains or buses. My route led through one of the most sparsely populated areas of France, where there wasn't anything but open countryside for mile upon mile. I had badly needed new insoles for my boots since leaving Châteauponsac a fortnight ago, but none of the towns and villages I passed through had anything resembling a sports shop. The occasional pharmacies along the way might, if they were adventurous, stock the thin foam insoles you put in shoes that are a little too large, but nothing like the high-tech articles I needed to make walking bearable. The first town where I could hope to find them was Mâcon, still many miles and at least twelve days away.

However, it was a pleasant, hot sunny walk to Saint-Pourçain through flat wheat fields and a great expanse of poppies, beautiful scarlet carpets stretching to the horizon, and cherries in abundance, and the walnut trees just starting to show the first signs of fruit. The town was busy, with endless streams of traffic ploughing the west-east axis between Montluçon and Mâcon and the north-south Moulins to Clermont-Ferrand. A young blackbird sat on a chimney pot practising singing. It was calling clearly: 'Little bir-dy, little bir-dy.'

Saint-Pourçain dates back to the third century, and claims its vineyards to be amongst the oldest in France. The Phoenicians are said to have planted the first vines there and since the twelfth century the area has been renowned for its production of dry, smooth white, fruity rosé, and rich red wines. Saint-Pourçain wines were served at the tables of the kings of France and the popes in Avignon, and during coronations at Reims. Over the years the town has survived invasions, pests, attacks by the beastly English, religious wars, floods, and the ravages of phylloxera. Now it is a bustling, thriving place, with well-preserved medieval timbered houses and a thumping great church, the Église Sainte-Croix, which when I was there was undergoing restoration.

As a change from the usual dolphins, it was tortoises who spewed water from a pretty fountain in a small square, where a grimy little boy wearing a moth-eaten jumper was happily occupied playing with a stick and a heap of dirt. I lunched in a small restaurant overlooking the bridge over the river Sioule, and lamented the never-ending stream of juggernauts barging uncaringly through the streets of another French town marred by their intrusion.

Back at the campsite, newly supplied with food, I sat by the football pitch watching three crows solemnly pacing up and down, staring at the perfect turf, like a committee of frock-coated Victorian gentlemen with their hands behind their backs, searching diligently for renegade weeds. The weather didn't look very promising and spots of rain were plipping onto the tent. The *gardien* assured me that the weather the following day would be perfect — these were just a few passing clouds. Having walked twelve miles to buy a loaf of bread, half a dozen bananas, some mayonnaise, and a packet of crab-flavoured shreds of fish, I hadn't had much of a rest day. I took to the sleeping bag early, and settled down with the torch to share Jude's ongoing miseries. If Evauxles-Bains had been the realm of the blackbird, here it was the kingdom of the crows. They were everywhere, strutting around and poking about in nooks and crannies, and surveying their domain from the high treetops. They laughed loudly, and with exaggerated slowness: haa, haaa, haaaa.

On the river the ducks hooted, and it began to rain in earnest.

Despite the *gardien*'s assurance that the weather would improve, it continued raining hard through the night and without let-up well into the morning. It was 10.30 a.m. before I was finally able to get out of the tent, which I dragged with its contents into the shelter of the football stands where I spread everything out. The crow groundsmen were out weed-hunting, occasionally conferring and uniting in examination of a particularly intriguing specimen.

In Saint-Pourçain the previous day, the Tourist Office had given me details of a campsite just a short distance away on the road to Varennes-sur-Allier. The skies showed little signs of clearing, and the thought of walking fifteen miles to the next scheduled stop at Jaligny-sur-Besbre was not particularly appealing. The tent was completely soaked within and without, and if I waited for it to dry I was going to be here for at least another day. I decided to move on, and rolled up the clammy bundle, hoping I would have an opportunity to dry it out before I had to sleep in it again.

Once the backpack was loaded and ready to go, it started to rain heavily again. It was almost 2.00 p.m. I really did not want to spend another day trapped in a wet tent between the Jehovah's Witness and the restaurant that didn't open, so I fandangoed into the red poncho again and started sploshing northwards. The field of poppies which had frolicked so merrily yesterday was now a limp mass of wet red tissue.

The dark soil smelt rich and clean, deliciously seasoned with wild garlic. Rain hammered down doggedly and the poncho had lost its impermeability somewhere along

251

the way. When walking in the rain I always wore shorts, so that my jeans would be dry and wearable in the evenings. The shorts would dry more quickly than jeans, too. The wet plasticized nylon of the poncho smeared itself lovingly around my bare legs, and rain seeped up the sleeves. It wasn't a very nice sensation, but at least it wasn't cold, and it wasn't far to the next campsite. According to the brochure, there were plenty of facilities there, including a snack bar and a laundry room, so I was confident of finding a warm meal and being able to dry the tent properly.

The river Allier rather inconveniently separated Paray-sous-Briailles from Varennes-sur-Allier, and the only crossing point was via the busy motorway. The distance between the edge of the road and the crash barriers was about eighteen inches, and I was forced to keep scrambling out of the way of thundering trucks, which while failing by a whisker to crush me with their wheels all managed to drench me with heavy spray.

I arrived at the entrance to the campsite. 'Closed indefinitely,' said the notice on the gate. Great. Wet through to the skin, with the wet tent, and another twelve miles to go to Jaligny, what now? It would have to be the cheapest possible room in town. Maybe I could get a mortgage.

Turning onto the N7 towards the town centre, I saw a sign. 'Camping Le Château de Chazeuil ****.' It seemed as if a guardian angel sat on my shoulder. Whenever a predicament arose, a solution invariably followed not far behind.

The sign led up a steep hill to a wide tree-lined avenue leading from the driveway of the château onto neatly trimmed, smooth, bumpless lawns. A tall man emerged from a building and showed me the best place to put the tent to avoid flooding — an alarming prospect as the château was at an altitude of nearly 1,000 feet. There was a Dutch-registered caravan and a Dutch tent, an old-fashioned dark green canvas structure with about thirty stout guy ropes anchored with crude wooden pegs. I put up my tent, which sagged despairingly under the weight of its soaking fabric and the rain, which was still beating down relentlessly. The prospect of spending a night in it was totally depressing. The sleeping bag was wet through, and I draped it over a basin in the sanitary block, next to my dripping clothes, and wondered what to do next. Sitting scrunched up on the mattress in the centre of the tent to avoid contact with the wet sides, I immersed myself in Jude's ongoing problems. Didn't this man have any luck? It took my mind off my own situation for a while.

Tomorrow was going to be a miserable day unless the weather changed. I'd be wearing damp clothes, sleeping in a wet bag in a wet tent. But I'd worry about it when it came. The tent bowed deeper and deeper beneath the downpour. Over the squishy noise of the falling rain, from the spires of the château came the sound of blackbirds singing a most complex song, while a mob of crows tried to drown them out with faultless trim phone imitations.

A female voice called out. The *gardienne* had come to collect the camping fees. I hoped they wouldn't be too steep. She stooped down and peered into the gloomy blue interior.

'Why don't you go and sit in the reading room? It's warm and dry,' she suggested, and went off to find the key. It was a comfortable room annexed to the château, with chairs and a table, and heaps of magazines and books, and absolutely weatherproof.

'You could sleep in here, if you wish,' she said.

I couldn't believe my luck. The heavy clouds were purple, and so were my wet cold limbs. Behind the reading room was a large barn full of firewood over which I draped the tent. While the sleeping bag dried in the heated shower block I sat and read for a couple of hours, watched at the window by a redstart which pecked furiously at the glass, hovering like a humming bird. Something had made it frightfully angry. In blissful comfort I demolished a plateful of plastic crab and mayonnaise, writing up my journal, and watching dusk fall soggily around the overloaded clouds above as the birds handed over the nightshift to the crickets. The cushions from the chairs made a thick springy mattress on the floor, and the sleeping bag was only slightly damp. I fell asleep quickly, wakening once during the night as sheets of lightning bounced around the room, and thunder shook the window panes. But I soon dropped off again. I had covered over three hundred miles and four of the six maps by now, and had been travelling for four weeks.

13

And Where are You From? And Where are You From?

By morning the storm had passed, and the tent was crisply dry. The *gardienne* came to ask whether I had slept well, and to say there was no charge for the use of the reading room. She wished me *bon courage*, and I set off down a slippery footpath leading through the dripping woods and past a herd of cattle wreathed in mist in a nearby field.

The *gardien* at Paray-sous-Briailles had given me directions to Jaligny-sur-Besbre — clipping the edge of the Forêt des Mouzières and then cutting through the Bois de Jaligny.

'Don't be afraid,' he had leered encouragingly. 'There are no werewolves there now. At least, not many.' He chortled.

The ersatz crab of the previous evening had

not been a very fulfilling meal, and I was hungry by 9.00 a.m. when I reached a small village where the bar/café was already doing a brisk trade. They served the smallest *grand crème* imaginable, not much larger than a thimble, and so overpriced that I thought they were joking. The shelves of the adjacent mini-grocery were virtually empty, but I bought a large marble cake and ate half for breakfast, sitting in the bar and listening to the other customers arguing about politics, weather and hunting as they sipped their breakfast wine.

I was suprised by the number of French people I had spoken to who said they no longer ate a great deal of meat. There seemed to be a growing interest in the welfare of both farm and wild animals. Once motorists had killed deer and boar at every opportunity, but now people were starting to appreciate that animals did have a place on the planet and not simply on the plate. Hunting was becoming more strictly regulated, to allow necessary culling without wholesale slaughter. This upset the hard-liners, but found favour with many people.

The French love their land. Their pride in it is very evident and everywhere *potagers*[1]

---

[1] vegetable plots

were well tended. In one garden I passed, a bent and ancient lady in a baggy grey cardigan and thick wrinkled stockings was hoeing her vegetable beds, propped up on a walking frame. Even the most dilapidated house or shed had a pot of geraniums, or a clump of pansies, or a little black cauldron of petunias decorating it, and in every village the war memorials were invariably bordered with colourful and lovingly maintained plants.

Ferns and baby trees struggled through the moist rich floor of the Forêt des Mouzières, beneath a lacy canopy supported by straggly beech trees. The interior was bright green and inviting, dappled with sunlight, the air as pure and fresh as spring water. The dandelion leaves were three feet long, and stinging nettles five feet high. I dodged a small red and green spider abseiling purposefully down a thread from an overhanging branch, as if it were on a mission of considerable importance.

From the courtyard of a long low farm-house, a mobile bedside rug masquerading as a giant hairy dog, sporting a jaunty blue and white checked handkerchief tied around its shaggy neck, sprang up at the fence, barking wildly and wagging its tail madly, and in the adjacent field stood a perfect pair of matching bay hunters, standing motionless tail to tail, like outsize bookends.

A very nearly perfect garden was blighted by the presence of a plaster Snow White and her seven sinister companions, to my mind a great deal more threatening than a werewolf. They must have sneaked in under cover of darkness and remained undiscovered so far, because it was impossible that anyone capable of creating such a beautiful garden would have allowed these grotesque characters into it.

At midday I stopped at a small bar/restaurant for a Coke. Perched on a stool at the bar was an exquisite dachshund bitch, with seductive black-rimmed eyes. She came over to introduce herself, and invited me to stroke her belly. With her short bandy legs she could only reach the bar stool reserved for her via a chair, and it was incumbent upon whoever sat next to her at the bar to place the chair correctly to facilitate her access to and from the stool. A heavy-set man, walking with the rolling gait of a seafarer and covered in tattoos, came in and shook hands with everyone. He started to sit down, then, noticing me sitting at the back of the restaurant, he came over and with a beaming smile shook my hand too, saying, 'Why not?' Why not, indeed. I felt like one of the locals.

The woman behind the bar, who seemed to

be the proprietor, was talking animatedly with a younger man about a fight which had taken place on the previous Saturday evening and during which a customer had assaulted her. She called her husband from the kitchen to verify the facts, and indicated a bruise sustained to her neck during the scuffle. From the little I could gather it was the young man's father-in-law who had attacked her, but though I listened avidly it was frustratingly impossible to understand the whole story. When I left, we all shook hands and the tattooed gentleman helped me on with the backpack and waved me off down the road.

There was a short cut to Jaligny, but I opted for the longer route through the Bois de Jaligny, as the weather was perfect and I was really enjoying the walking today. At a tiny picnic area just within the woods a single deep scarlet antirrhinum pushed through the grass, and honeysuckle twined up a sapling. The woods were oak and pine, peaceful and cool, and led to the main road at the intriguingly named Roundabout of the Dancing Stone. The distance between Chazeuil and Jaligny-sur-Besbre was twelve easy miles over gently sloping ground, under warm sunshine, with a cool breeze, through the glorious woods. It was the most perfect day so far on the journey.

The carved-up insoles were seriously slicing into the undersides of my toes. It was alarmingly painful, but did nothing to detract from my enjoyment of the day.

Two flycatchers hunted in mid-air, scattering clouds of moths and assorted titbits rising from the fields. Jaligny seemed to be a village with a sense of humour, because large roadside signs leading towards the centre depicted cartoon characters relaxing under canvas, and fishing, and a turkey in a poke bonnet taking a photograph of the château. From a sawmill on the edge of the village the delicious scent of resin filled the air.

Tall elms formed an elegant arched avenue into the village, where three thoroughbreds stood sentry by a green iron bridge decked with pots of geraniums and troughs of begonias and marigolds, spanning the willow- and ash-fringed river Besbre. Jaligny-sur-Besbre is well known for its weekly poultry market, and famous as France's turkey capital. Each year in mid-December thousands of the region's renowned free-range white turkeys are sold there, and traditionally a gift of one of the birds is made to a celebrity —Winston Churchill and Queen Elizabeth II have both been recipients.

The village is a mixture of half-timbered

and stone cottages clustered on a slight incline, an eleventh-century church and a strapping fifteenth-century château gazing as its own reflection in the river, and looking as if it would effortlessly withstand a nuclear attack. I learnt that it was the only château along the river Besbre that had not fallen to the English during the Hundred Years War. In the village centre stood a handsome war memorial topped by an arrogant cockerel.

The campsite was deserted but for one empty caravan, and the washing facilities were old but clean, and supplied instant hot water. There was a western style loo which was rather short on knee-space. It could only be sat upon in a sidesaddle position unless you were sufficiently uninhibited to leave the door open.

With the tent erected in solitary splendour, and armed with a bottle of wine and some fruit from the supermarket, I picnicked on a bench beside the river, in the shade of a willow tree. A white goose and two Muscovy ducks appeared almost as soon as I sat down, and helped me with the cheese and onion sandwiches which had travelled over ninety miles during the last six days and tasted better than ever. Once the bread was finished, the goose paddled off to her nest beneath a nearby bridge, from where she shrieked angrily every time a vehicle crossed above her, still keeping a watchful eye on the picnic bag. The ducks lingered hopefully. It was a perfect sunny afternoon, the river flowed quietly, and the leaves of the willow sighed contentedly in the warm breeze.

★ ★ ★

After the picnic I walked along the river for a while and met an elderly woman standing on a bridge, dressed in an apricot-coloured gabardine raincoat, under the baking sun. I stopped to talk to her.

'Where do you come from?' she asked.

I told her. I said I was camping in Jaligny for one night.

'Is that in the caravan?' she enquired.

'No, in a little tent.'

'And where do you come from?' she asked again.

I told her.

'Have you seen our splendid village memorial?' she asked.

I said that I had admired and photographed it.

'And where do you come from?' she asked yet again.

I told her.

'Perhaps you would like to see our fine

memorial,' she suggested.

I said I would.

She had difficulty in walking, but refused the offer of my arm. She was also nearly blind. We progressed very slowly towards the memorial, while she continued asking me where I lived, and whether I was staying in the caravan at the campsite. I kept answering her questions.

We admired the memorial, and in between bursts of repeated questions, she told me how happy she was to live in Jaligny.

'It has everything,' she said. 'Everything anyone could need. There cannot be a better place to live than Jaligny. There is an excellent hairdresser, too. I had my hair done this morning,' she added, patting her old head proudly. She told me of the turkey market, and asked where I came from and whether I would like to see the memorial. Someone had once stolen the cockerel from the top, she said.

I mentioned the ducks and the goose on the river. The goose, she said, had just appeared one day and taken up residence. One of the villagers had bought a gander for her, but it had vanished one night and now the goose was sad. The residents of the village all fed the birds and would like to replace the gander if they could be sure that it wouldn't disappear like the previous ones. Geese were expensive. She reminded me that someone had stolen the cockerel from the top of the monument.

Her husband had just returned home from hospital, having had an operation on his foot.

'His mind has gone. He doesn't know what he's doing or saying now,' she confided cheerfully.

I tried to imagine life in their household.

She asked the time. 'Well, we had better get back now, hadn't we?' she said.

'Back to where?'

'Well, the apartment, of course,' she replied, as if I was rather simple. 'He will be wondering where we are. Come on.' She led the way very slowly, and I followed not knowing what else to do.

They lived on the second floor in a small modern block of apartments. When we reached her door, she unlocked it and shoved me heartily ahead of her into the hall.

'Go on,' she ordered, 'go and talk to him.'

Her husband, with the remaining half of his foot wrapped in a reddened bandage and propped on a small stool, sat avidly watching the television, and was patently startled to find an unannounced stranger standing beside him.

I introduced myself. He grunted, and changed the channel.

His wife came in and sat down, and we all sat silently for several minutes, while her husband continually clicked through the channels.

'The lady has come to see you. Talk to her,' said his wife. With undisguised reluctance he wrenched his eyes from the screen, and asked where I came from. I told him. Then his wife asked. He rolled his eyes. And so it continued for about half an hour. He alternately watched the television and talked to me for a few minutes. His wife continued to recycle the same questions.

'Good God, woman,' he roared suddenly, 'you've already asked her that fourteen times. You've no brain left!'

'Then lend me yours!' she riposted, laughing good-naturedly. I managed to glean the information that they had farmed nearby for many years before their retirement, and that they had a son and a daughter, both living in Clermont-Ferrand. Once they had travelled extensively, including a trip to Russia, but now they were too old to go anywhere. The apartment was tiny, a combined dining/sitting room, small kitchen, one bedroom. It was bright and spotless and totally devoid of any character. It all seemed rather sad.

I started to take my leave, and the old lady

asked where I came from. Her husband grunted and turned up the volume.

'You must come back and see us,' she called, as I let myself out.

★ ★ ★

Walking back to the campsite I passed an English couple standing by their car outside a small hotel and enjoying a bitter row. The female of the pair unloaded the luggage, her face pale and tight with anger, while her short, fat spouse stood stamping his little foot and spluttering, his face red with rage. As I passed I said: 'I do hope you'll enjoy your stay here.' They both stared open-mouthed.

As the sun folded down, I dined beneath a canopy of leaves on the very last cheese and onion sandwiches, followed by marbled chocolate cake soaked in white wine.

There must have been a kennel somewhere close by, because all night long dogs barked and howled. My back was aching and it was absolutely freezing. In between the barking of the dogs, owls hooted and screeched.

The sun came up like a laser beam through the trees to herald another hot day. While the morning ritual of sleeping bag and tent-drying enacted itself, I attacked the second generation blisters which had taken up residence on the gravès of the first crop. Provided they were well cocooned in cotton wool, if I ignored the discomfort of the first ten minutes of walking the pain receded for several hours.

Ahead were two possible overnight stops: an *aire naturelle*[1] at Saint-Léon, or a private farm campsite further on at Saligny-sur-Roudon. I headed towards Saint-Léon. It was an unremarkable journey, except for the fact that there were no wild flowers growing on the roadsides, apart from a stray dandelion or buttercup, although the hedgerows were beautiful, laced with honeysuckle and wild roses in pastel pink and deep crimson. But to compensate for the lack of flowers, I saw a single large deer sprinking straight-legged up a meadow and disappearing into a small copse.

Saint-Léon with its colourful flower boxes adorning walls and window sills was small and neat, and absolutely closed for lunch. The campsite was at the top of Puy Saint-Ambroise, nearly two miles the far side of the village and a climb of four hundred feet, leading to a viewpoint which gave splendid panoramas of the more than

---

[1] campsite offering very basic facilities and usually rather isolated

200,000 hectares which make up the wild Morvan regional park. It was an idyllic spot, hidden in pine woods, but totally remote and too isolated for comfort. There was nothing and nobody there. High above, wispy clouds splashed the sky, and fluffy white mountains were building on the horizon. The heat was oppressive and I was learning about meteorology. There was going to be yet another storm tonight, and when it arrived I didn't want to be alone in a forest on top of a small mountain. I decided to push on to Saligny. I picked up the GR3[1] to Saligny which made a welcome change from following the roads and led through unspoilt countryside, but perversely I missed the security which passing traffic afforded. The GR crossed a farm, and one field away from the path were four men huddled in a corner with two madly barking terriers. I had an uncomfortable feeling that whatever they were doing, it was something not very nice. I walked as quickly and quietly as I could until I was well clear of the area.

In the fields the newly shorn sheep looked strange and rather embarrassed by their nakedness. Patches of purple foxgloves were popping up beside the hedges. On the

---

[1] Grande Randonnée — long-distance hiking trail

outskirts of Saligny a kite wafted, gliding, drifting on the wind, letting the up-draughts play with it. A wedding party stood outside the church watching the new bride and groom emerging. There was a lot of laughter, and as they all turned to stare at me I suspected I was a contributory factor. I was used to being a cause of amazement and mirth. Motorists regularly stopped to watch me pass, people stared from windows, and groups usually laughed aloud. It didn't bother me, and I couldn't blame them. I knew I looked peculiar.

I hunted in vain for signs to the campsite. This was a bad omen and generally indicated that there was still a long way to go. In the village shop I splashed out on two apricots, and asked for directions. The shop assistant assured me that it was no more than two miles to the farm, and pointed northwards. The toe-snipping machine was working overtime and I was greatly looking forward to getting my boots off. After half a mile of plodding a loud hooting caught my attention, and the shop assistant called me over to her car.

'It's on my way,' she said. 'I'll give you a lift.'

Had I but known it, the GR3 would have taken me right there, cutting off several miles.

270

The Moulin de Cropte was like a perfect oil-painting of a traditional farm, complete with its own mill where they produced a variety of flours. Good old-fashioned fat hens strolled around the courtyard, geese and ducks paddled on the small river, and behind the hedges sheep and cattle munched and belched. The farm's owners, Monsieur and Madame Beaupain, were delighted to have a guest, and he drove me the six hundred yards up to the campsite. It stood on a plateau above the farmhouse, amidst magnificent pine woods, about as far off the beaten track as you could wish. The sanitary block was simple, almost primitive, but immaculately clean, and delivered really hot water instantly. A large communal rustic table and benches stood underneath a covered veranda.

I decided to cover the tent with the two metallic survival blankets I carried, to see whether they would help with the condensation problem, provide any more warmth and exclude the rain, which was on its way. The tent looked very bizarre coated in the glistening golden sheets and secured with multicoloured clothes pegs. Tucked away in the trees at the far end of the campsite was a Dutch touring caravan, so I went over to introduce myself, and found a cup of coffee and slice of cake waiting for me. Martin and

Ine were a handsome and friendly couple, who had been coming to this site for eight years. We sat and talked as the skies darkened. They felt that, like England, Holland was being swallowed up by roads, sprawling commercial complexes and housing developments, and it was becoming ever more difficult to find somewhere unspoilt there. Furthermore, plans were afoot to make Holland the great port of Europe, entailing massive railway expansion to transport immense volumes of freight across the country. They were very distressed by what was being done to their country.

In the Vercors, they told me, where they had been staying, they had seen German tourists in bars and restaurants sitting waiting for service and being ignored by the staff. In some places the staff had refused outright to serve Germans, so Martin and Ine had carried their Dutch passports with them when they went out, displaying them casually and thus having no difficulty in getting attention. They advised me to use the same tactics if I was eating out and I said I would bear it in mind.

As expected, the storm attacked during the night, rain smashing down noisily onto the metallic sheets. In the spaces they didn't cover the rain seeped through the nylon and trickled in through the seams. It continued raining well into the morning, and when I woke there was a pool of water in the tent, which the sleeping bag and backpack soaked up thirstily. There was no way I could continue, with everything saturated, the next site almost twenty miles away, and almost out of money and food. The skies were black and heavy and there was no sign of improvement. What do I do now, I asked?

There were half a dozen caravans parked on the site, in small groves, each with a spacious awning, so I went down to the farmhouse and asked whether I could rent one for a day. That was no problem at all, Madame Beaupain assured me. Ten minutes later I was installed, and she returned shortly with a vast bowl of white fluffy pudding and a bottle of wine. With grey crinkly hair scraped tightly back from a permanently smiling face, apple-rosy cheeks and shiny smooth skin, she could be nothing but a farmer's wife, and she radiated calm and pleasure in everything she did. She very kindly drove me to the village, where I stocked up on food supplies, including a large baguette. When we returned, Ine and Martin had coffee, cakes and a dish of strawberries and cream waiting, and had set up an electric fan heater to dry out my possessions.

The deluge continued into the afternoon while I lay curled up comfortably on the caravan's cushions following the further tribulations of poor Jude. All the characters were absolutely infuriating, but the painstaking writing made every word worth reading. Even in the caravan it was chilly during the night, but the comfort of the thick cushions was a welcome change from the tissue-thin mattress. I thought how lucky I had been so far — all the heavy storms of the past month had occurred during the night, and I had only had to walk in real rain a couple of times. It could have been much worse, and although the nights were very cold the daytime was almost always delightfully warm. I firmly believed that the cuckoo which had called every day but one so far was my guardian angel, my Lady Luck, and was riding point for me.

Morning broke cold and overcast, and Ine volunteered to drive me back into the village to continue my trek eastwards. On the way we stopped at the farmhouse where I settled the bill for the use of the caravan — sixty francs. It was Monday morning, 1 June, Pentecost, and the Beaupain children, grandchildren and grandchildren's friends filled every corner of the house, as they prepared for lunch en masse. Madame Beaupain glowed with pleasure and the heat of the stove.

In the village I went to make a phone call home. With yesterday's large baguette strapped across the backpack, I managed to get myself wedged inside the small cubicle, unable to move the inwardly opening doors because the baguette had jammed against them. I was quite stuck. Panicking, I rapped loudly on the glass at a passing cyclist, who came to my rescue. By pushing very hard from the outside, he was able to snap the bread in half, thus releasing the pressure on the doors. I felt rather foolish, but from the large grin which he tried unsuccessfully to hide I think it made the cyclist's day.

Gradually the sun emerged, brightening the great expanse of green fields and hedges. The terrain was slightly hilly and several times I passed fields where cattle and goats grazed together happily, an unusual sight. Delicious, intoxicating smells came from piles of black shiny mush being scraped out by tractors from the barns where the animals had wintered. In a ditch beside the road a multitude of large green frogs (the French edible variety) plopped and splashed into the water as I passed. The road led to the Canal latéral à la Loire that runs beside the great river where it changes direction from north to north-west. I picnicked beside the canal, and then walked half a mile further on to discover a small snack bar beside the road where I had a plate of frites and a shandy. It was always just as well to eat at every opportunity, as I never knew what lay ahead. That was my excuse, anyway. The sun was out in full force, and people sat fanning themselves in the shade.

Alongside the canal a grassy footpath led to where I was going, and I shared it with impossibly slender dragonflies, velvet midnight blue damsel flies, colourful butterflies, swallows hunting over the water, and a heron which wasn't doing anything apart from maintaining a stately pose. Inexplicably, the footpath vanished without warning into waist-high grass, brambles and stinging nettles, only fifty yards from the end. The choice was between walking back a mile and crossing to the other side to walk yet another mile back to where I was, or battling through. Wearing shorts it was an unequal contest and the undergrowth won, leaving my legs lacerated and stung, but I gave the spiteful greenery something to think about with my stick.

I stopped to ask directions of a mother with two small children fishing in the canal, their tiny victims flapping frantically in an inch of water in a blue bucket. I hoped their little captors would tip them back into the water before it was too late.

Fifteen minutes later I crossed the bridge over the Loire into southern Burgundy.

14

Mowgli Keeps His Cool

If you ever wondered what happened to Mowgli when he grew up, he is alive and well, and *gardien* of the campsite at Digoin. Still skinny and tanned, with an ear to ear smile, an enormous shock of thick, glossy black hair and matching shiny black eyes, he has cast aside his little loincloth in favour of a pair of denims and a black T-shirt, and when I first saw him was sitting tilted back in a chair behind the counter, being patient with a pair of extremely awkward foreign women who wanted him to arrange train tickets to Paris for them immediately. Throughout a lengthy verbal assault which included threats of having him dismissed from his position, tears, pleas and footstamping, he maintained a relaxed attitude and friendly smile, no doubt remembering his happy days in the jungle with Baloo, Kaa and Shere Khan. Repeatedly he explained to the two enraged women that he had no control over the timetables of the SNCF[1] and that his job did not in any case include making travel arrangements for people staying at the campsite. He suggested the women should see a travel agent the next day. Couldn't he understand, they roared at him, *tomorrow would be too late!* With a sad smile and small shrug he turned his attention to me, leaving them to stamp out to their car and drive off with much grating of gears.

Mowgli led me to a patch of springy grass bordering the river, where I enfolded the tent in the golden wrappers again. There were two other tenters, who wandered past casually and repeatedly, gazing covertly at the gaudy little shelter. On the opposite bank of the river, a heron stood immobile. It was there when I arrived and set up the tent, and had not changed its position after I had walked to town, shopped, eaten a crêpe, and showered. Tangled rafts of bright green weed and a small duck whizzed by at top speed, swept along by the fierce current.

The site was about 80 per cent full, and seeing a caravan registered in the département where I live I went over to say hello to

---

[1] French railway

the owners. They were an elderly couple who talked simultaneously. He had lost nearly all of his family at Oradour-sur-Glane, the Limousin town where almost the entire population of 642 men, women and children were massacred and every building destroyed by the Nazis on 10 June 1944, and which remains just as it was left on that day, a permanent memorial and reminder of the barbarity of war.

Digoin is a solid Burgundian town with a titanic church and town hall and fountains playing in the streets, and is remarkable for the number of waterways which meet there. The rivers Loire, Arroux, Bourbince, Vouzance and Arconce all run through or around the town; the Roanne canal runs south; the Pont canal, an aqueduct 800 feet in length and 12 feet wide, spans the Loire, linking the Canal latéral on the western side of the town with the Canal du Centre to the east. The latter connects the rivers Saône and Loire, forming a junction between the Mediterranean sea and the English channel. I walked around for a couple of hours, dodging raindrops until dusk, then retired to the tent which rustled noisily through the night, buffeted by a strong wind.

Next morning, the immobile heron had gone. Which was the nicest route to

Paray-le-Monial, I asked Mowgli? He assured me that the footpath beside the canal was *super-joli*.

Cabin cruisers and barges smothered with tubs of flowers quivered gently in the marina on the canal. In the humid early morning air, fishermen stood amongst the long grasses, scabious and yellow irises, and once again the weather was gathering its resources in preparation for a storm. How much more water could the skies possibly hold? The silkiness of the grasses stroked my legs, soothing the scratches and stings inflicted yesterday by the nettles and brambles. Cattle grazed peacefully on a narrow strip of land sandwiched between the canal and the river Bourbince, and my constant companion the cuckoo called a three-note sound: cuck-cuck-oo. Bright pots of geraniums and begonias adorned each of the locks on the canal, and it was a relaxing and easy walk on level ground for the nine miles or so to Paray-le-Monial.

Tethered close to the entrance of the campsite there stood a thin, friendly goat. There was a restaurant, grocery, swimming pool and bar all within the site. They were all closed. After pitching the tent and spraying it with waterproofer, I followed the scented path bordered with philadelphus and honeysuckle alongside the Bourbince into town. It was a beautiful one-mile walk. At the end of the footpath was a length of thirty five-foot metal stanchions linked by chains at a height of about three feet. A man on a bicycle waited at the far end, while his Alsatian dog stood attentively at the other. At his signal, the dog started running towards him, weaving through the stanchions and jumping the chain effortlessly. As it reached the owner, he turned and pedalled away, his dog running joyfully beside him.

Paray-le-Monial is a handsome Burgundian town, and one of France's most popular places of pilgrimage, second only to Lourdes, visited by as many as 400,000 pilgrims annually. It was here that in 1673, and over the next seventeen years until her death, Marguerite-Marie Alacoque, a young nun, saw visions of Christ revealing his bleeding heart in the Chapel of the Visitation, and the Roman Catholic liturgy of the Sacred Heart was born. Pope John Paul II had visited the town in 1986.

A young monk dressed in a shiny black habit with a pointed hood, rope belt and sandals was guiding a group of Germans to the chapel, where a service was being held amidst hundreds of lighted candles. I followed on behind, and stood just inside the door feeling rather conspicuous in the big boots and rolled-up shorts. I rolled them down a notch and stood for a few minutes, listening to the priest speaking in French, Latin and German. From there I walked on to the imposing eleventh-century Romanesque basilica, built on the same pattern as the great abbey at Cluny and giving an idea of how that huge church would once have looked before it was demolished. Encouraged by the presence of several dozen visitors, I followed them inside, and marvelled at the perfect state of preservation of this church. On the steps outside sat a beggar with a small red plastic bowl. Dozens of people filed down the steps, talking animatedly as they passed him, doubtless on their way to a fine lunch, and one of them graciously dropped something into his bowl. Bringing up the rear, I saw the results of this collective generosity — a single half-franc piece. It made me feel terribly angry and sad and I wanted to burst into tears.

I enjoyed wandering around the streets, admiring the solid buildings, flower-filled balconies and steeply pitched roofs. The town hall, once the home of a wealthy sixteenth-century merchant, is an eccentric example of Italian Renaissance architecture, and the main shopping area is lively and prosperous.

Hay fever, that annual summer blight, had added itself to my current crop of aches, pains and abrasions, so that I sneezed constantly and could hardly see out of my swollen eyes. I had to spend sixty francs on some tablets, with the stern warning that I could drink no alcohol whilst taking them, which I ignored. As I roamed around, for once enjoying the bustle around me, the storm that had been developing finally broke, quickly turning the road into a shallow, fast-flowing river. The only thing to do was to sit in a bar and enjoy the house speciality, a long glass of sparkling wine with peach liqueur. At an adjacent table a group of four English people looked as if they had been there for some time, if their ebullient behaviour was any indication. They were spiritedly and laughingly arguing over who should sprint through the rain to bring the *voiture ici* so that the others could avoid *la pluie*. Finally a man in a Panama hat and Bermuda shorts made a dash for it, waving wildly as he sped out into the wet street, to the loud applause of the other three.

After an hour the worst of the weather had passed, and I walked back through the puddles, reading the wooden notice boards which volunteered information about the rivers. The last great flood here had occurred in October 1965, when the pedestrian area of the town was more than four feet under water, and in the river Bourbince there were an impressive nineteen varieties of fish.

The rain remarshalled its energies, and started hammering down again just as I reached the campsite. Swathed in the survival blankets and the layer of waterproofing, the tent stayed fairly dry. I went to pay the camp fees to the *gardienne*, who lived in a barricaded mobile home just beside the luxurious sanitary block. I rang the bell hanging at the gate, and nothing happened. I rang it again. A frilly net curtain twitched, and a face peered out and disappeared. I rang the bell again. The net curtain jerked angrily to one side and the window opened. A young woman scowled.

'She's not here. Come back later.' The window slammed shut, and the curtain fell into place. I sploshed back to the tent and read for a while, then tried again.

Several minutes of bell-ringing in the pouring rain resulted in a door opening. The *gardienne* appeared in a shiny purple clinging ankle-length garment which looked like a tight nightie, with a cropped matching jacket. Large gold rings swung from her ears, and the whole was set off by high-heeled golden sandals. From the doorway she shouted: 'What do you want?'

'To pay the fees.'

The door closed, and I stood dripping. A few minutes later she emerged with a small receipt book and a large umbrella, which successfully kept her dry. She asked my name and address, and would I spell it out.

'May I come in?' I asked.

'Ah, no. My dogs will bite you. They don't like people.'

So I stood in the rain and spelled my name and address laboriously until I was soaked through, and paid thirty-four francs for the privilege. Madame teetered back to her net-curtained, dog-protected home leaving me spitefully pleased at the sight of her golden sandals and varnished toenails covered in mud. There was an electric hand-drier in the washing block, and I used it to dry my hair and as much of my body as by various contortions it could reach.

Thunder rolled like cannon balls on a wooden floor, rain continued throughout the night, and the tent sagged precariously.

Beyond the early morning haze the sun signalled its intention to emerge a little later, and despite the nocturnal deluge the tent had survived unscathed apart from a couple of small patches which soon dried. While I was packing up, I could hear a low voice from the adjacent tent.

'You are my hat. You are my shoes. You are my saucepan. You are my stove. You are my blanket.'

This I had to see, so I hovered around for a few minutes and then called out: *'Bonjour!'*

The tent flap opened and a pale thin face squinted out, disappearing immediately and re-emerging with a floppy little hat on, followed by a thin body clutching a Bible in one hand and wearing a pair of ill-fitting trousers with the flies gaping undone.

'Good morning. Are you a pilgrim?' asked the pale thin face, blinking at me.

'No,' I replied. 'I'm just on a walking holiday.'

The thin body crawled back into his tent and dragged out a sheet of plastic which he flattened on the wet ground before starting to line up his chattels on it. Again, he explained to each item what it was.

'You are my saucepan. You are my shoes.'

I wondered if he might be slightly odd.

'You can come with me, if you like. I am going to Lake — ' He mentioned a name I couldn't catch. 'Do you have your Bible with you?'

I confessed that I didn't and thanked him for his offer of companionship but explained that someone was waiting for me in Geneva and I didn't have time to go with him. He wished me a safe journey in the love of Jesus, which I reciprocated, and returned to his one-sided conversation.

'You are my knife,' he explained helpfully to a piece of cutlery.

After unintentionally completing two comprehensive circuits of the town, I eventually found the way out towards Charolles. The canalside walk was the longer route, but worth it. It meant travelling north for nearly two miles, then turning east and finally south-east, but it avoided the very busy national road linking Paray-le-Monial to Charolles. A group of thirty-eight adolescent ducklings bobbed in the canal's sunny waters, and a brown spotted duck headed her flotilla of fourteen babies in a perfect V formation. On the banks of a large park carpeted with vivid emerald grass, young rabbits scattered into their burrows as I approached. Standing still, I watched them emerge cautiously a minute later. They hopped down the bank into the park, white tails flashing. From a small pond the resident frogs croaked deafeningly.

Just before the village of Saint-Just, I begged a cup of water from a weather-beaten old lady, obliging but unsmiling, and

288

surrounded by a retinue of geriatric dogs. After I had thanked her for the water, she bowed her head and walked silently back into the house. On the whole I found the people in Burgundy more reserved and less friendly than those further west.

From a field behind came a loud shouting. A bull was charging a person on a motorbike. Wowee! This really could be fun! (Probably not for the biker, of course, but certainly for the bull and me.) There was no exit from the field apart from a closed gate, and the biker skidded up to it with the snorting bull hot on his wheels. He leapt from the machine and snatched up a tree branch, and turned to face the galloping animal. I was impressed. Waving the branch about his head and bellowing loudly, he counter-charged. The bull veered off and slowed to a trot, finally coming to a standstill about a hundred feet away, and the hero walked backwards to his bike, all the time brandishing the branch and yelling. He wheeled the machine through the gate, watched by the perplexed beast, and with a final shout of triumph emerged safely onto the road.

Once this splendid entertainment was over, I lay on a cool narrow lawn beside a low stone wall in the village of Saint-Just, beneath a horse chestnut tree. It was rather ominous to see that conkers were already appearing, though it was only the beginning of June. Each year it seemed that the universal clock was speeding up inexorably and we were hurtling through life at breakneck speed. The temperature was in the low 90s, and from the cool of the shade I watched lettuce, beans and tomatoes growing contentedly in the garden opposite, while a mob of goldfinches squabbled in the trees.

Setting off again, I heard a familiar noise coming from behind. It was the sound of a panting dog. Like fat brown Florette, a young German pointer had decided to come with me to Geneva. I couldn't persuade her to leave me alone, so we turned back and started hunting for her owner. The village appeared to be deserted; there were no people, no sounds, no cars, and no responses to knocks on doors. The dog followed happily and looked at me as if to say: 'You're wasting your time. Let's get going.' The last house stood in spacious landscaped gardens, surrounded by fences and hedges, with several gates all of which were impossible to open. I climbed over the lowest, followed by my new friend, and by tapping on a large patio door managed to attract the attention of a fraught-looking woman with two tearful little girls wailing around her feet. Although taken aback by the appearance of a vagrant, she smiled politely and asked if she could be of help. I asked if she knew who owned a young German pointer, and indicated the dog which was examining a bush.

'Ah!' she shrieked. 'She's back!' The little girls squealed and rushed into the garden, hurling themselves at the dog. 'She's been missing for two hours. The children were desperate. Thank you so much. We must give you a reward.'

I said truthfully that finding her home was more than enough reward, but that a drink of water wouldn't go amiss, after which I set off once again, following the road through the Forêt dominiale de Charolles. Walking from the searing heat into the cool of the forest was like sinking into a bath of cool champagne.

Arriving hotly in Charolles, I set up the tent alongside the river at the smart campsite, and strolled around the small, pretty town with its narrow lanes and old houses with steeply pitched roofs. Traversed by the rivers Arconce and Semence, Charolles is famous both for its beautiful earthenware, produced in traditional and contemporary styles, and for the breed of cattle and sheep known as Charolais. It has an interesting history.

At the convent of the Clarisses, Sainte Marguerite-Marie Alacoque, who saw the visions of the Sacred Heart in Paray-le-Monial, had made her first communion.

On a slight hill in the town centre stand the remnants of the Diamond Tower, so called because of the stones embossed in its walls to deflect cannon balls. Beside it, the fortified castle of Charles le Téméraire now houses the municipal offices, and has lost its medieval character, but its fifteenth-century tower remains, four storeys high, its seven-foot-thick walls wreathed in ivy. Charles le Téméraire (Charles the Bold, or the Foolhardy — it's a matter of opinion and translation), Count of Charolais and last Duke of Burgundy, was the son of Philippe le Bon, who captured and sold Joan of Arc to his English allies, under Henry V, so that she could be burnt alive. What was Good about that? Charles lived up to his name, waging war relentlessly against Louis XI of France in his attempts to further expand the mighty Burgundian empire. He died in battle at Nancy in 1477, and his naked body was discovered days later, in a frozen pond, and partially eaten by wolves. After Charles's death, Louis XI installed a governor in Charolles, which for five hundred years previously had been independent of the French crown, and answerable only to Burgundy. Over the next three hundred years, the town passed backwards and forwards between Austria, Germany, France and Spain by various treaties and acts of aggression.

During the Second World War, Charolles was just outside the German occupied zone, and became the cradle of an active and highly effective Resistance movement, in recognition of which, on 14 July 1945, the town was awarded the Croix de Guerre with Silver Star.

In the cool gardens surrounding the tower, three teenage girls sat on top of a wall in the courtyard, dangling their legs over the edge. I thought they were living rather dangerously, with the town at about sixty feet below the wall, but looking over the edge I saw that no more than ten feet down was a small flourishing vegetable and herb garden on a wide plateau, high above the neighbouring rooftops.

I phoned and booked the *gîte d'étape* at Suin for the following day, and then swathed the tent against whatever weather might arrive. A Parisian couple had a caravan on the adjacent plot, and an elegant and friendly lady came over to complain that her husband always wanted to rush everywhere. He liked everything to be done in a hurry, so that they could speed on to the next thing. She found holidays quite exhausting, she laughed. From the caravan came anxious shouts aimed at her. She asked why I had decorated the tent in such a garish manner, and said that if it rained in the night I was to go and sleep under their awning. She would leave a space for the mattress and sleeping bag. If she didn't see me again, she wished me very good luck. They would be leaving at precisely 7.00 a.m. the next day; her husband insisted on meticulous forward planning and punctuality. As I thanked her, her husband's shouts became louder and more insistent, and rolling her eyes she walked slowly back to the caravan.

★ ★ ★

The Parisians had left by the time I woke at 8.00 a.m. the following morning, after a dry and warm night. Maybe from now on the night-time weather would improve, I thought hopefully. The sun was already high and I did some washing and hung it from a tree to dry while I went into town to check my Loto ticket at a café with a sheep-shearer's van parked outside. I had won thirty-four francs, which paid for the following week's ticket and a cup of coffee.

By the time the washing had dried it was 1.00 p.m., and I set off for Suin. It was always a mistake to leave late in the day, especially when the weather was so hot, because in the heat I moved even more slowly than usual, while at the same time there was still the need to reach that night's base before darkness fell.

A red squirrel bounced across the road in front of me, into the path of an approaching car, and I held my breath. But the car slowed down to a halt, and we watched the little animal clutch its way up an oak tree to hop along a branch and disappear into the leaves. Everywhere the countryside was bursting with colour and plenty. Houses were so festooned with baskets, pots, troughs and cauldrons of vivid plants in one small village that it seemed as if the residents must be in competition with each other to see who could attach the greatest number of plants to their property. Cherry trees dangled their ripe fruit overhead, and had I been a foot taller I could have reached it. As it was, I couldn't. Beneath an oak tree, a cow stood with her small calf, hock-deep in a cool stream, sheltering from the sun's furnace.

Ahead, the Butte de Suin reared up to 2,000 feet. It looked daunting. It was an agonizing climb, and a pulled back muscle didn't help. Every fifteen minutes I had to stop and sit to recover my breath and energy, and as at Evaux-les-Bains it seemed that no matter how far and high I climbed the end was never any nearer. The only consolation was patches of intensely flavoured wild strawberries growing on the sunny side of the road, of which I ate as many as I could find, despite nearly falling headlong under the backpack's weight each time I bent to pick them.

For the second time since setting out, I was ready to quit. My knees shook at each step and felt as if they were about to bend backwards, and every bone and muscle ached. I felt as if I had been stretched on a rack. It was very disappointing that notwithstanding all the months of preparation, and after walking at least 360 miles over thirty-five days, much of it uphill, I was no fitter than when I started. Each day was as much of a struggle as the one before, each incline hard work, and at every destination I arrived footsore and sweat-stained, frightening the natives with my wild appearance. If today was hard going, the chances of negotiating the mountains of the Jura were zero. Collapsed on a narrow strip of grass, listening to my heart pounding at top speed, I decided that when the next vehicle came along I was getting into it, no matter who with, and no matter where it was going. I simply couldn't walk another step and I didn't care what happened, as long as I could reach somewhere, anywhere, without having to walk. After an hour when nothing happened and there was no sign that anything ever would happen in this place, I pointed uphill again, panting, gasping, sweating and occasionally lying down until my heartbeat stopped drumming in my ears.

At 6.00 p.m. I at last triumphantly reached Suin village, and stopped to ask for directions to the *gîte d'étape* from a little gang of children who gawped openmouthed at the crazed apparition.

A delightful little boy with tousled hair and spiky limbs earnestly directed me, chewing his lip with concentration and gesturing with a skinny arm. 'You turn left here. When you reach the crossroads you turn left again, and follow the road for about one and a half miles. Then when you reach the next crossroads you go straight on past some houses and some pine trees, and then you turn right. Carry straight on until you see the sign.'

It sounded an awfully long way. It was, and by the time I tottered into the yard an hour later, I had reached the end of my endurance.

This being the first *gîte d'étape* I was stopping at, I hadn't known what to expect and was prepared for something spartan and primitive, but La Billebaude was a long low farmhouse of natural stone with rose-framed doorways, snuggled against the side of a hill and giving a magnificent view eastwards across a pine forest. Inside were low-beamed ceilings, cool tiled floors, baskets of dried flowers, communal dining rooms and lounge, a large kitchen, several dormitories with spotless bunk beds, and clean bathrooms with hot showers.

Soaked with perspiration, my clothes stuck to me, and the black T-shirt looked like a tie-dye fabric covered in white fluffy-edged salt stains. The dye had run into the beige shorts, which were also covered with grass stains. Catching sight of myself in a long mirror, I was surprised that the owner had let me in. I looked unsavoury, if not downright dangerous. That was one of the things I so much loved about the French people — no matter where I turned up, and no matter what state I was in, they always reacted as if my appearance was quite normal. I stood under a warm shower, fully clothed, scrubbing at the clothes, and then under an ice-cold jet waiting for my blood to come down from the boil.

La Billebaude is an equestrian farm, where they breed their own horses. The surefootedness, hardiness and endurance of the Arab

Barbs make them ideal for trekking, one of the main activities available at La Billebaude, where holidaymakers can also learn and indulge in rock climbing, mountain biking, archery and walking. During the last three weeks of October, they run courses in identifying and enjoying the plentiful fungi which grow in the area. For the benefit of the very young, there are also tiny Shetland ponies, like animated fluffy toys. A few miles to the north another farm offers holidays with a difference for children aged seven to seventeen, where they can enjoy summer and winter camps spent building tepees and camp fires, learning about the stars, trees and orientation, and caring for their 'own' Samoyed dog for the duration of their stay.

Until 8.30 p.m. I was the only guest, with an entire eight-bed dormitory to myself. Then a couple of students arrived and took possession of one of the vacant rooms, and we joined up for our evening meal. They had a tin of chilli and a large can of pineapple slices. I had a very old onion, which when finely chopped and mixed with a battered tin of tuna and half a tube of mayonnaise formed a very palatable mush, and a packet of biscuits. We shared the pineapple and biscuits and a large bottle of Coca-Cola. They were both at university, she studying law, and he media and advertising. I envied them. On limited funds they had to keep their holiday expenditure to a minimum, but by staying in *gîtes d'étape* and catering for themselves they could travel around and enjoy themselves for less than two hundred francs a day.

They were so kindly enthusiastic and complimentary about my efforts that when they wanted to know all about it I couldn't bring myself to shatter the illusion they seemed to have developed that they were in the presence of some sort of extraordinary pioneer. They asked how I had known how to equip myself and choose a route, to which I replied, quite untruthfully, that I had used my common sense. What I should have said was that I had employed my total ignorance, because as far as my choice of equipment went it could hardly have been worse. The sleeping bag was picked solely on the basis that it was the lightest I could find, gave no more protection than a paper bag, and was, to boot; extremely uncomfortable. It was shaped like a sarcophagus, so that the part my feet used was about twelve inches wide at most, making movement of my legs impossible. It had a cold metal zip that not only dug icily into whatever part of me it could touch, but also twisted around and tied the bag in knots during the night. All this I could have overlooked if only it had supplied any warmth at all, which it didn't.

The maps were woefully inadequate too, but there was nothing I could do about that, except make sure that the next time I set off on such an adventure I would have learnt a little more about navigation and contours and so be better prepared.

The 65-litre backpack was the cheapest I could find, and I was quite attached to it, because it carried my belongings uncom-plainingly, and couldn't help being too heavy. The boots were a bit of a mystery, because they fitted perfectly, were extremely comfort-able and hadn't given me any problem at all during the months I'd trained for the event. I loved them and couldn't understand why my feet were in such a poor state.

The one thing that I knew I had done brilliantly had been finding Jennifer to look after my animals. Without her, nothing could have happened. I knew that although her mind was often on home, she was looking after my animals with absolute devotion and thoroughly enjoying her stay in France.

But didn't I get very lonely, they asked? The answer was no. It was not the sort of enterprise to undertake if you craved company. I was more than happy enough with the trees, plants and animals, the wind and rain, the sunshine and landscape. I enjoyed company when it came my way, but I didn't suffer without it. It was also a great journey of self-discovery, from which I had learnt much about myself and what I was capable of.

By 10.00 p.m. I was ready for bed, and climbed onto a high bunk next to a window which looked out to the east and Cluny, my next objective. I didn't sleep well. The backs of my legs were scarlet with sunburn, and it was very hot. But it was pleasant to lie on a comfortable bed and listen to the noises of the night, and the horses blowing quietly in the paddock below.

★ ★ ★

You ordered breakfast, if you wanted it, the previous evening, to alert the breakfast maker, but I didn't know that. La Billebaude's owner, Fred, obligingly said he would prepare something for me. While he did so, I went to have a look round the stables.

The horses and their welfare were paramount here. The scrubbed and spotless stables, with their full water buckets, each bore a neat plaque with the name and lineage of the occupier, and on every door there was a board with a meticulous schedule of feeding and foot care. All the feet were well shod or filed, and the horses' manes and tails neat and shiny, like their coats. One of the Barb mares had a two-week-old palomino foal that had been scouring mildly, and it was receiving medication and hourly checks.

Two girl students made up the staff. The senior of the two was very plain with round-rimmed glasses and a pudding-basin hairstyle, but she had a quiet confidence that was very appealing, and I thought one day she might possibly turn out to be a beauty. The other girl, blonde, bespectacled, amiable and tubby, wore a perpetual air of anxiety. They were occupied with a small Shetland foal who was having a lesson in being groomed. The worried girl held its head gently, stroking the little nose, while the other girl very lightly ran a brush over it and picked up its feet one by one. The foal stood poised for flight, but the two girls kept talking softly and stroking it. Fred came out and stood watching them, nodding his approval.

Breakfast was ready, the long dining table set with a packet of cornflakes, a loaf of bread, a large slab of butter, a bowl of jam, a two-litre pot of coffee, a jug of hot milk and a packet of sugar lumps. I worked my way through it, although I wouldn't exactly have chosen to eat cornflakes with hot milk, and rubbing sugar lumps together to sprinkle over them was rather time-consuming, but the careful and obliging preparation that had gone into the meal made up for these minor flaws. The bill for bed and breakfast came to eighty-two francs. Even more frugal than me, the students had only a packet of biscuits for their breakfast, and were appreciative of the coffee I left undrunk.

Suin lies on the dividing line between the basins of the Loire and the Rhône, following a north-south direction. From here, facing north, all the waters that flow to the Atlantic Ocean are to the left, and all those flowing to the Mediterranean to the right. On the summit of the Butte de Suin stands a tall statue of the Virgin Mary, weighing three tons, bought in 1884 from the proceeds of a collection from the parishes surrounding Suin. There was a very pleasant restaurant up there, too. There are numerous large granite rocks with intriguing names around the village, subject of many legends: the Poodle's Head; the Devil's Lair; Caesar's Chair — carved by man, facing east, overlooking the countryside, and believed to be a place from where the Druids observed the stars; the Ring Stone — originally composed of three unequal blocks, beneath which a Gallic ring was discovered, of a very small size which could only have been worn by a young girl. The rocks had been blasted with dynamite to see whether other artefacts existed, but nothing more was found. The Sacrifice Stone was carved by man and possibly used by the Druids as a place of religious ceremonies. The Deaf Fountain is a collection of rocks tumbling down the hillside, resembling a petrified waterfall. Once a trickle of water flowed down the rocks, and pilgrims collected it to wash their ears in the belief that the water cured any problems connected with them.

From La Billebaude's remote location there was no other building in sight. During the winter, Fred said, even the slightest snowfall could trap you here for days. It sounded like an attractive prospect.

Laden with 'au revoirs' and 'bon courages' and armed with directions from Fred, I set off through the forest to look for the GR76c. For once I got it right. It was deliciously cool and quiet in the dark forest, amongst the symmetrically planted pines, and the floor, soft and springy and comforting to sore feet, glistened with enormous black slugs, eight inches long and shining as if cut from jet. There were others, too, slightly smaller and richly amber. In the incredible humidity I was soon dripping with perspiration, and the cool wind was my friend. Delicate fragrant strawberries grew in abundance in sunlit spots, and birds sang unseen from the shadowy depths of the woods. On the pathway a perfect slow worm, shining copper and bronze, slid away into thick leaves where ants worked busily and surprisingly noisily. In places where the forest had been cleared foxgloves had taken over, lakes of spotted purple blooms and velvety leaves. The sun blasted down fiercely, and walking back into the shade of the forest was like stepping under a cool silky shower. On the paths richly coloured flies, dragonflies and butterflies fluttered and soared, and exotically beautiful beetles trundled about their secret business.

Cluny was yet another destination I thought I was never going to reach. There seemed to be a never-ending row of steep hills, and I was tired and thirsty, with a new crop of blisters fighting amongst themselves for sovereignty over my feet. Each corner revealed a new view of the town, and led into another corner, which offered a different view. It was like being caught in a nightmare. Eventually I reached a small bar on the outskirts, and collapsed in a heap in a chair. Once I had sufficient breath, I ordered a lemonade, then another and another.

The proprietor and his wife were not

talking to each other. The tension was breathable and most unpleasant. Madame volunteered her silent husband to drive me through town to the campsite, as he was going there anyway. He didn't exactly exude delight, but he did take me there, and in the campsite's smart office a Monty Python sketch unfolded.

It was a young girl's first day on the reception desk. She produced a smile that was more of a rictus, and chanted: 'Welcome to Cluny! How may I help you?'

I asked for an *emplacement*[1] for a tent for one person, for two nights.

How many people, she asked.

Just one.

She keyed something into her computer.

How many tents?

Just one.

In the shade, or not?

In the shade, definitely.

Did I want electricity?

No, it was a tent.

How many tents?

Just one.

And only one person?

Yes, just me.

She looked perplexed, but soldiered on.

---

[1] allocated area for tent

Did I require a car parking space?

No, I was on foot.

Just one person, then, one tent, no electricity, no parking. Was that right?

Precisely.

And was I quite sure that I didn't want electricity?

Perfectly.

Once we had exhausted all possible permutations of numbers and requirements, with a triumphant flourish and theatrical smile she produced a map of the site, with an X marking my allocated position, and a long list in faultless English regarding the disposal of waste.

I dragged the backpack to the appointed spot, an excellent situation, particularly convenient for the railway line that ran approximately ten yards from it. I sank down onto the cool grass and lay spread-eagled like a starfish, vibrating slightly as the TGV[1] whooshed its way past.

It was too hot to eat much, even though I hadn't lunched, so I walked into town and bought a small punnet of raspberries, some sour cream and a litre of dry white wine. Next day was for rest and recuperation, to give the pulled back muscle a chance to

---

[1] train à grande vitesse — high-speed train

recover. I could see that Cluny had much to offer, and that I was going to enjoy exploring it.

When I phoned Jennifer that evening, the news from home was a terrible shock. Her father had died the previous day. Coupled with my sympathy for her was a terrible dread that she would want to return home immediately, and that I would have to curtail my journey. I asked her whether I should get myself back home, and held my breath.

'I'm OK,' she replied. 'I got pissed, then I went to church. Then I got pissed again. I'm not going anywhere till you finish your journey. Don't you let me down, now.' Incredibly generous lady.

I was so relieved, and so ashamed of my selfishness, that I drank the whole bottle of wine in the space of less than half an hour. I must have somehow managed to get into the tent, because during the night I woke inside it, feeling very unwell, with a powerful headache and a pressing desire to empty my bladder. This posed a problem, because I was stark naked, didn't know where I was, couldn't find my way out of the tent and its crackly wrapping, and couldn't stand up once I did. The best I could manage was to crawl a few yards on all fours and let nature take its course in full view of the moon. If anybody was watching, I neither knew nor cared. I felt awfully ill and the tent spun and heaved sickeningly. It was well-deserved retribution.

I awoke frail and repentant just after 10.00 a.m., and took an oath never to touch alcohol again. Rain wasn't far off, but for the time being it was hot and dry, so I wandered into Cluny.

Much of the beautiful old twelfth-century town, including the ramparts, towers and Romanesque houses, remain, as well as fragments of the Benedictine abbey of Saint Peter and Saint Paul, which was the largest church in the Christian world until the construction of Saint Peter's Basilica in Rome in the sixteenth century. It measured 450 feet in length. Following the French Revolution the abbey was sold to a Mâcon merchant who demolished it and used it for building materials. There is something very poignant in the remains of this vanished empire ruled by the mighty Benedictine order, whose influence spread to every corner of medieval Christendom, and was superseded only by the Pope.

It was Saturday morning and in the bustling market beside the abbey ruins stalls displayed fruits and vegetables, varieties of sausages, hams, fresh meat, cheeses, plants and racks of clothes. Cafés, restaurants, mouth-watering *pâtisseries* and gift shops unspoilt by tasteless souvenirs lined the main street, which sits in a slight valley, with wide alleys sloping upwards to either side. I decided to climb up the tall, narrow eleventh-century Cheese Tower, which was quite a stupid idea for a claustrophobic with a fear of heights. Since so many places of interest on the way so far had been either closed or impossible to visit for other reasons, I felt I really should make an effort. Access to the tower is through the Tourist Office, which was just about to close for lunch. The receptionist showed me the fire exit, through which I would have to let myself out when I descended, as the office would be locked. I started up the steps, lots of them, about 120, crossing bouncy and swaying wooden floors to the next steep flight, until I finally reached the top. It was rather dark, and I was the only person in there. I didn't like to think about the coming down. From the top, the views of the surrounding countryside were spectacular, the mountains of the Mâconnais to the east, to the west the Charolais; below, the straggling roofs and busy streets. It was unnerving to discover that the windows had no protection over them — they were just large holes in the walls. It would have been a simple matter to climb out of them and

311

plummet to the ground. The thought made me uncomfortable, and after ten minutes I started a panicky descent. The wooden stairs were particularly steep in places, and difficult to see in the gloomy interior. I kept expecting the floorboards to give way beneath me and send me plunging downwards. I was trapped between rising claustrophobia fuelled by the fear that the emergency exit would not open for me, and mounting vertigo, which forced me to sit down at one point. I was furious with myself for this pitiful behaviour, but unable to conquer it. The cumbersome hiking boots further added to the difficulty of negotiating the narrow treads on the stairs and I made it down by taking five stairs at a time, counting to ten, taking a deep breath and tackling the next five. I was shaking and my heart was thumping, and the relief when the fire door gave way before my assault was indescribable.

The sky was darkening and I went into a small, virtually empty pizza restaurant and sat down at a table for four. Someone came and took my order, and returned five minutes later to report that they were unable to fulfil it. I would have to choose something else. With a great crack the storm broke and the street was transformed into a gurgling stream in a few minutes. Crowds of wet people poured into the restaurant, and seating was suddenly at a premium. The proprietor asked whether I would consider moving to a small table for two, just inside the doors, which I did. The doors were wide open, beneath an awning that allowed the rain to slither down it and plop off the edge in a satisfying torrent. Despite having jammed my chair as close in to the table as possible, nearly cutting off my breathing, a certain amount of rain dripped down the back of my neck and over my shoulders. For the past few days my left eye had been painful and watering, and I had to keep taking off my glasses to mop it. I noticed people at adjoining tables staring at me curiously, and I realized that they thought I was crying. This made me start laughing, and I sat there, wet-backed, streaming-eyed and convulsed. I had to put my hands over my face to control my laughter, and the proprietor came up and in soothing tones asked if it was the thunder which frightened me. This made me laugh even more, and another waiter came up and the two stood looking at me nervously as I gulped and giggled. I was finally able to assure them that I was neither frightened nor unhappy, nor crying, but suffering from a sore eye and an inexplicable sense of humour. They went away unconvinced, and people kept looking at me and murmuring to each other. I had nearly finished my meal when a very wet and smiling person of about forty came and stood by the table, beaming at me. I beamed back, and he clapped his hands. We beamed vacantly at each other for about two minutes, and I wondered what happened next. One of the waitresses came and took him gently by the hand and led him towards the bar, where everyone made a great fuss of him. They were obviously quite used to coping with strange people.

After the storm the air was cooler and it was pleasant to walk around the town enjoying the narrow alleys and lanes, admiring the beautiful houses with their tiny low doorways, fluted pillars and gargoyles, and everywhere coming across remains of ancient fountains and arches. From the kitchens appetizing smells floated through open doors and windows. Many of the interiors were quite unmodernized, with the original uneven flagstones and smoke-stained fireplaces.

There was a large function that evening in the College of Advanced Technology, and traffic was building up. I thought the only thing that could make Cluny even more attractive would be to pedestrianize the entire centre. Walking through the narrow streets was uncomfortable as it was necessary to keep stepping sideways to allow the continual stream of traffic to pass.

Just on the outskirts of the town a large simple stone block bore the inscription 'REMEMBER: Auschwitz, Bergen-Belsen, Buchenwald, Dachau, Ravensbrück', and beside the church in the town centre was a vast monument dedicated to the bravery of the French people who had fought and given their lives to keep their country free from oppression.

⋆ ⋆ ⋆

Napoleon needed horses. If his army was to continue romping successfully around Europe borrowing other people's countries, it needed reliable transport as well as a full stomach, and so in 1806 the Cluny Stud Farm had been established, amongst another thirty similar studs, to supply this need. The imposing buildings were constructed at the end of the eighteenth century from the dismantled fabric of the mighty abbey next door, and sat on the site of its vanished choir.

Among sixty or so stallions based there are English thoroughbreds, Arabs, French saddle horses and trotters, Connemaras, and draught horses including Ardennais, Percherons and Comtois, and the stud includes an artificial insemination laboratory and training schools, lungeing rings and competition grounds, and its own forge. It also acts as a training centre for young horses. Between March and the middle of July the stallions are away 'on assignment', and many of the massive stalls were empty. But there were about twenty mares there, some with foals sleeping away the warmth of the afternoon in deep straw, gangly legs akimbo, while their mothers stood, bottom lips flopping slackly, relaxed beside their offspring. The boxes are vast, each surrounded by thick iron bars, with ceilings about twenty feet high. There was only one stallion in residence, a vast iron-grey draught horse with a two-foot-long wavy black mane. He suggested that he would like to have his gigantic dappled rump scratched, and I obliged for a couple of minutes, as he closed his eyes and tilted back his ears with pleasure.

The stud is open to visitors, and there is no charge for wandering around the impressive buildings. The previous week it had hosted a national horse show, and the ornate show jumping obstacles still stood in the arena. I was very disappointed to have missed it. I should have walked faster.

Back at the campsite, a poster proclaimed the 'Mr Nude France Contest' taking place the following week, a few miles to the south. What a shame; I was going to miss that too.

The site was filling up with the tents and caravans of guests attending the soirée at the college. My crumpled clothes felt more crumpled than usual, and seeing an English-registered caravan a short distance from the tent I trotted over to see whether they could lend me an iron. My request was answered with, 'Good Lord, no, we're on holiday, I never do any ironing on holiday, but how would you like a cup of tea?'

I replied that I would like one very much indeed.

'Would you like ordinary, or Earl Grey?'

Would I like Earl Grey? Oh, boy!

Over the divine cup, I learnt that Janet was in remission from cancer and her husband John was the vicar of a church near Coventry. They were staying in Cluny to visit the ecumenical community at Taizé, a short distance away, where they were going primarily to listen to some new church music, which they might introduce to John's church. Janet was not going to let her illness interfere with her enjoyment of life, and she had recently travelled to Australia to meet distant relatives, backpacked with her daughter in Brazil, and was planning a visit to Sikkim. She laughed when she told of how one member of their congregation referred to her as 'the semi-detached vicar's wife' because she was not always able to attend both morning and evening services. John was an extremely gentle person, tolerant of all religions and beliefs, with a balanced outlook on the causes of fanatical and extreme behaviour. He had only kind words for everyone.

They suggested that as they were driving to Taizé next day, they could either give me a lift to my next stop at nearby Azé, which I declined, or drive my backpack there. That wasn't outside my rules, and I gratefully accepted.

As evening fell I walked back to the town, enjoying its ancient streets and floodlit towers. The glitterati, all dressed up in evening wear, were converging on the college. In my unpressed jeans, boots and baggy jumper I felt conspicuously underdressed. However, obviously I didn't look quite as bad as I thought, because whilst I was gazing in a shop window a man approached and stood beside me. I thought nothing of it until he put his hand in his pocket, pulled out a wallet and asked me how much it would cost for us to get to know each other better in a horizontal position. I'm seldom stuck for words, but so unexpected was this approach that I couldn't think of a fitting reply. I jammed my hands deep into my pockets, hunched my back and marched off with my boots thumping the pavements as hard as they could. I hoped this display of unfeminine behaviour would deter any similar attentions. It seemed to work.

There was more rain in the air, and I blessed the survival blankets for having kept the tent reasonably dry. I settled down again with Jude and soon fell asleep, despite the TGV roaring past. At about midnight the music from the town woke me as the celebrations started in earnest, and I was able to enjoy the firework display, which I could see in the distance, before the music took over again until the early hours.

I dozed on and off. As the sky began to lighten, a couple nearby were obviously awake, too, and practising their conjugal technique to the accompaniment of loud and uninhibited grunts and groans, and muffled laughter from the neighbouring tents.

15

Grotty By Name . . .

After a shared breakfast of coffee, croissants and freshly baked bread generously supplied by Janet and John, we temporarily went our separate ways. They left for Taizé to be in time for the morning service. Janet had looked askance at my ineffectual red poncho and insisted that I take hers, a far more substantial affair. She also equipped me with her smaller backpack so that I had somewhere for food, water and maps.

It was a heavenly walk, despite the dismal, drizzly weather. From Cluny the GR76c continued towards Azé through Cluny Forest. From out of the damp greenness came eerie noises like raindrops on tin, or temple bells or wind chimes, signalling the possibility of some religious gathering there in the woods — maybe a pagan cult? I walked very quietly

— didn't want to end up as a human sacrifice — until through a gap in the trees I spotted a herd of cattle grazing in a meadow, their bells clanging a ghostly melody. The forest was cool and wet, and the heavy poncho adopted the qualities of a sauna as I started warming up. Soon steam was emanating from me like ectoplasm. Whoever had painted the *balises* here must have been running low on paint, because the dashes became thin in places, and suddenly ran out at a crucial junction. I followed the left fork and climbed a mini-mountain to the back garden of an isolated house and had to retrace my steps for several hundred yards, but the unaccustomed light weight of the backpack made all the difference. It wasn't walking that was the problem, it was the weight I normally carried. With no more than ten pounds on my back, I was almost airborne.

I arrived at the high point known as les Quatre Vents[1] following the GR upwards to where the path narrowed to a steep track slithery with loose stones, and led to a summit at the top of the world. The views in every direction were stunning. Far below to the south-west Cluny sat in a grey haze, but up here the sun had come out. The path

---

[1] the four winds

continued through meadows sprinkled with scabious, edged by ancient dry-stone walls in soft mellow colours, and laced with trees stunted by the wind, and emerged just outside Donzy-le-Pertuis, where a French cyclist was relieving himself against a hedge in that particularly French way they have. He was startled by the apparition from nowhere, but smiled. I smiled back. It seemed the correct thing to do, as shaking hands at that moment was not politely feasible. His eyes lit up at the sight of my map, and being able to help a native with directions was a rare privilege indeed. He was part of a group of six, and once they had decided on their route they pushed on up the steep hill which I had just descended, their colourful Lycra buttocks rocking violently from side to side as they strained on their pedals.

This was the country of the Mâconnais. The first tiny vineyard appeared on the outskirts of Azé, where I planned to stay at the campsite adjacent to the pre-historic caves. Called 'les Grottes' in reference to the subterranean caverns, the site couldn't have been more aptly named if it had tried. It was gloomy, unprepared and ill-kempt; the swimming pool was empty, the sanitary blocks were dirty, and the shower room had a cunningly disguised low step which almost gave me a slipped disc. It was also very expensive and bore no resemblance at all to the photographs in the glossy brochure which had encouraged me to visit it. Maybe it was because it was still early in the season, but I felt that sites should be either open or not open, and if they were open, they should be properly prepared.

On the upside, there was a cosy little restaurant on the site, where you could buy an ocean of *moules* and *frites* for fifty francs. With Friday evening's unfortunate incident and my teetotalling oath already forgotten, I had a glass of wine. Three young men at an adjacent table were enjoying a bottle of rosé, and kept throwing sidelong glances at me. After a couple of minutes of whispers, laughs, and elbow-digging, one of them came over with the bottle, and very gallantly enquired whether I would please them by sharing a glass.

The other diners were an American lady and her two hyperactive but reasonably pleasant children. I asked her where she came from, and learned that she lived in San Antonio, Texas, not far from Jennifer. As they say, it's a small world. She encouraged both children, a boy of about eight and a four-year-old girl, to eat the garlicky mussels and a good ripe Camembert, which they thoroughly enjoyed. The mother had spent two years living in Paris and wanted to introduce her children to the wonders of France and its cuisine. It was a delight to see a foreign family enjoying good French food. In preparation for the World Cup, a huge television sat in the restaurant and an apologetic-looking weather forecaster predicted heavy rain in this area; the skies glowered accordingly. After lunch, Janet and John arrived with my backpack and Janet insisted I keep her poncho for the rest of the journey.

'You can post it back to me when you've finished with it,' she said. I was sorry to see those kindly people leave.

★　★　★

I walked around Azé, a pretty village nestling in a valley surrounded by vineyards, and had my first sight of the Jura in the far distance. The houses of exposed stone with wooden balconies were smothered in roses of every imaginable colour — pink, white, yellow, crimson, mauve, orange. I tried hard to pluck up courage to visit the caves, which house the skeletons of cave bears, lions, rhinoceros, hyenas, bison, aurochs and mammoths dating back 400,000 years, and evidence of human occupation 100,000 years ago. I really wanted to see it all, but the visit entailed a boat ride along a subterranean river to view the caves, and I knew that no matter how I tried I would end up panicking and screaming and probably overturning the boat and drowning all the other sightseers. So I decided to watch the Canadian Formula One Grand Prix motor racing instead, and that was exciting enough, with multiple pile-ups, cars catapulting through the air, and great wedges of turf being strewn over the track. Outside the locals played *pétanque*[1] in the long evening, and the threatened storm passed by, leaving Azé untouched that night.

There was a choice of two routes to Mâcon, and I opted for the lesser D85, a comfortably level road twisting gently through hills of vineyards. At the small village of Martoret a simple stone stood as a poignant memorial to four young men, aged between seventeen and twenty-five, and an unknown person from Camp Gambetta in the Jura, all killed by the Germans on Christmas Eve, 1943. No matter where you are in France, there are reminders of the Second World War on every corner. Town squares are named after local people

---

[1] French version of bowls

deported to die in concentration camps; streets are named after Allied victories; houses bear plaques with the names of former occupants killed in the war. It is often said of the French that they are xenophobic; considering their history of invasion by Romans, Huns, Vikings, Saracens, Magyars, English and Germans amongst others, it would be little wonder if they were. Nevertheless in the four years I had lived in France I had found few of the French people to be other than generous and kind. Unfriendly people were very much the exception.

At Verzé I cut through towards Chevagny-les-Chevrières, reaching the right-hand side of map No. 5. Over the field a kestrel keened sadly on the wind. Chevagny was a pretty hilltop village where I sat on the steps in the *lavoir*[1] and sorted out the latest blisters, prize-winning specimens, before continuing on to Mâcon which I reached at 2.00 p.m. The gardening gentleman whom I asked for directions to the campsite was not very encouraging, and shook his head sadly at the distance still to be covered. The campsite was three miles north of Mâcon town, most unattractively sited in an industrial area, and

---

[1] communal wash house

put paid to my plans for an interesting evening sight-seeing and a good Burgundian dinner in the capital of the Beaujolais.

At the campsite reception office, an impressive modern building, a male person sat with his feet up on a desk, reading a magazine. I waited for him to finish his page, but when he had done so he turned to the next one, and I thought I had been politely patient for long enough. I tapped on the counter. Glancing up he swallowed a sigh as he addressed his computer and allocated me a position before returning to his reading.

Although less humid than the previous day it had still been a hot walk, and I was looking forward to shedding my load and relaxing. As I unstrapped the pack, a voice called out in French: 'Would you like a nice cold drink?'

A couple waved from a nearby Dutch caravan and beckoned me over. A jug of iced fruit juice appeared, and a plate of biscuits. I told them how kind I found the Dutch people, and how many I had met along the way. They laughed, and said: 'Yes, it is what we call the grey circuit — retired people taking their holidays before the schools break up. We Dutch like peace and quiet and nature, and France is our favourite destination, offering all those things right on our doorstep.'

A small group of bold sparrows came over to the table to share the biscuits, and when they had hoovered up all the crumbs they flew onto a nearby tree and started digging beneath the bark which they prised up with their beaks, climbing up and down the trunk very much like nuthatches or treecreepers. We were all intrigued at this behaviour which none of us had seen previously.

I stocked up on supplies at the nearest supermarket, including a small pack of smoked salmon to compensate for missing a proper meal in Mâcon that evening, and wandered round to the marina, which was not very exciting. The park beside it was entirely taken over by travellers, with glistening BMWs, Porsches, Mercedes and Land Rovers, and a great number of very beautiful dogs of varying breeds, all well fed and cared for. On the way back I called on the literary *gardien*. He looked up from his magazine reluctantly and asked uninterestedly what I wanted. I volunteered to pay for my site, and was charged a swingeing fifty-eight francs.

'That seems very expensive,' I said.

He shrugged. 'It's the tariff,' he announced, his eyes returning to the current page as if attached to it with strings.

'Why is it so much?' I asked.

'It's the tariff for a tent and two people,' he explained.

'But I am only one person.'

'That's not my fault. There is no tariff for a single person and a tent. You have to pay for two people.' His tacit implication was that if I was having to travel alone, then I deserved all I got.

It seemed most unreasonable to have to pay for a non-existent person, but there was nothing I could do, except pay up with a poor grace and promise not to come back here again. As a campsite, Mâcon was a disappointment. It was too far from town and too expensive, the showers were cold, and the *gardien* could generously be described as surly. Maybe I was too used to living in the countryside, where people still had time to be courteous. The smoked salmon was quite inedible, stringy, gristly and slimy, but the dog belonging to my neighbours wolfed it down without complaint.

*   *   *

Next morning the crows and magpies were busy cleaning up after the campers, who were all leaving. It seemed that this was a site used as a stopover, and not somewhere to stay, despite a restaurant, shop and swimming pool. Heavily laden with food, a tent wet with condensation, and a one-litre bottle of Coke, I walked along a lovely path beside the river Saône into Mâcon town, where I bought some postcards from a small shop. The person 'serving' was as friendly as the *gardien* at the campsite, and unable to summon up even an insincere smile. Outside, the dreaded parking wardens were triumphantly sticking parked cars. Traffic was heavy, noisy and impatient and I was very glad that visits to towns like this were few and far between. So enthusiastic was I to leave the place, I didn't even bother going hunting for replacement insoles.

Crossing the St Laurent bridge takes you out of Burgundy and into the Rhône-Alps region, and the département of Ain. On the bridge an engraved stone proclaimed that from it, on 19 August 1944, a Resistance member had thrown himself into the river rather than be taken by the Germans. I sat outside a riverside café and waited hopefully to be served. Staff peered suspiciously from the interior. Maybe they thought I was German, because I sat for nearly twenty-five minutes before anyone came out. I was going to sit there all day if necessary; I was in that kind of a mood. I remembered Ine and Martin's advice, but my passport was in a folder at the very bottom of the backpack, so I tried to look as English as I could. Reluctantly and ungraciously a plump girl eventually arrived and asked what I wanted. I asked for a *grand crème* in my most English accent. She nodded and disappeared. Two minutes later, another waitress appeared, and asked what I had ordered from the previous one. I said in English: 'A large white coffee, please.'

'OK,' she grunted, and a few minutes later it arrived. Holding firmly on to the tray she demanded sixteen francs and waited for me to pay before she put down the cup and accompanying jug of thick cream.

It was worth the aggravation and the hefty price, because it was undoubtedly the best coffee I had ever tasted, smooth, rich, velvety and dark chocolate-coloured. Across the lovely bridge Mâcon looked exciting and inviting, and I regretted that I hadn't been able to enjoy this lively town, but one day, I promised myself, I would come back sensibly by car. On the smooth river two swans glided regally, ignoring a rude low-flying heron which buzzed between them. This was the flatlands, and a pleasant change from the hills I had been climbing for the last thirty days and 350 miles. The road signs were slightly sparse, but I turned onto what I hoped was the D51b, towards Villeneuve, and followed the little river Veyle, shaded by willows and water lilies, whose surface reflected the white elegance of two dozen swans. Beside the road grew rich patches of different fungi, and a small grove of young poplars heavily festooned in mistletoe. An elderly man wearing a black beret and bright blue trousers and smock pedalled slowly past on a rattling bicycle, raising a hand in greeting and calling out, 'Bon courage.'

Wrapped in this peaceful reverie, I was unprepared for the attack. They came in great numbers, swiftly and silently until the moment of contact, darting around me in a merciless circle, diving in and stabbing, squealing their mosquito triumph. I beat at them wildly, my arms and legs black with the hateful things, trying not to breathe because they were all over my face. Their numbers were overwhelming, and I had to run fifty yards to be free of them. Numerous red and black smudges on my limbs testified that the whining swine hadn't had it all their own way.

I still wasn't sure whether I was on the right track, and wouldn't be until I reached a small village called Gions, according to the map. When I reached it, the signboard said 'Jonc'. The pronunciation of the two was identical, and I assumed it was one and the same place, but confirmed it with the postman just to make sure. That was typical of the navigational difficulties encountered from time to time. I followed the road through to Faty, where in the elegant garden of the local plumber, who advertised his services via a board on the roadside, a very large pond was covered with outsize waterlilies and teeming with enormous frogs. It seemed that every lily pad sagged beneath the weight of the burly amphibians. It looked like an up-market frogs' holiday village.

The ancient fortified town of Pont-de-Veyle, with its many bridges over the river Veyle, was where I very nearly got killed. I just couldn't find the right road out, despite walking a complete circuit of it four times. Eventually in frustration I took the first road I came to and decided to walk along it until I found a sign, which would give a clue. Traffic was very heavy in this part, and I ended up on the D2. Caught in the turbulence of a lorry that passed by leaving about six inches between it and myself, I lost my balance and reeled sideways into the path of a car travelling at tremendous speed. It scraped my backpack and sent me spinning again, this time into a tree that painfully brought me to an abrupt but grateful halt. I turned off this death track at the first opportunity, making my way through a series of back roads and lanes until I found somewhere named on the map. Even on these minor routes there was a continual flow of traffic.

The villages here were a mixture of old timbered buildings, many in a sad state, and expensive new houses. There was a slightly suburban air about it. Passing through Biziat, for a mile and a half I walked next to a schoolboy of about eight or nine who was trudging home beneath the weight of a heavy backpack. He said courteously: *'Bonjour, madame.'* With his bowed head and his toes scraping wearily up the long hill, he looked totally dejected. I offered him a sweet, which he took politely, and left dangling unopened from his dangling fingers, which dangled from his dangly arm. As he reached his house, he called out, *'Au revoir, madame.'* That was the limit of our conversation. He was a really dangly little kid.

Vonnas, where the next campsite was, is a small but notable town. It houses one of France's finest restaurants, the Georges Blanc, a temple to gastronomy known by foodies all over the world, and is also home to the great man himself. In fact most of Vonnas is influenced by M. Blanc — beside his hotel/restaurant, which started life as a simple family restaurant run by Granny Blanc, there is also a boutique selling his produce, a bistro, and a museum dedicated to carriages and harnesses, the major industry of Vonnas in the late nineteenth century. The masses of flowers that decorate the town's streets are also largely due to M. Blanc's desire to make Vonnas as attractive a small town as possible. He also owns a vineyard at Azé and another restaurant at St Laurent where I had enjoyed the reluctantly served coffee.

The campsite beside the Veyle was crowded with empty caravans and looked as if it was somewhere people regularly came for the weekend. It was situated a hundred yards away from the statuary and helipad adorning the restaurant's smooth green lawns. On my way to find something for an evening meal, I passed the doors of the restaurant and read the mouth-watering menus, which were, by my humble standards, astronomically priced. Now, if this was a work of fiction, M. Blanc would have seen me standing there, tired and hungry and wistfully reading menus I could not afford, and invited me in for a meal as his guest. After listening with rapture to my extraordinary adventures, he would insist I spent the night in one of the hotel's sumptuous rooms. However, this was real life, and if I walked in in my crumpled clothes and dusty boots and asked if they could prepare me a simple and very inexpensive meal, he would probably burn his sauce. So I carried on to the supermarket where I bought a baguette and a tin of tuna mayonnaise, which I ate whilst trying not to think what more privileged diners were enjoying in M. Blanc's gastronomic temple a hundred yards down the road.

There were posters warning of possible floods at the campsite, and all around were signs showing the action to take in such an event. An Olympic athlete of Linford Christie calibre sprinted ahead of a giant rolling wave towards the arrowed emergency exit. It didn't look as if there would be much chance for ordinary mortals. Totally alone on the campsite, I listened to some enthusiasts playing football on the sports ground behind. Tomorrow the World Cup would kick off. The shouts and thuds of boot on ball continued for several hours.

Once darkness had fallen the footballers left, and I was dropping off to sleep when the tent suddenly became illuminated as if by a searchlight. Unnerved, I reached for the knife and whistle beside my sleeping bag and quietly unzipped the netting and tugged the nylon flap upwards to see who was shining the light, thinking that they must be able to hear the rapid beating of my frightened heart.

But it was only the moon rising, throwing out a brilliant beam which blazed in the night sky. It was very hot in the tent, and I left the flap open, lying for many hours watching the gradual build-up of clouds scudding overhead. Whether it was the brightness of the moonlight, or the strength of the excellent coffee that morning, I didn't sleep all night. Just before 6.00 a.m. the storm broke.

The rain fell with furious, uncontrolled rage for nearly four hours. It poured through the gaps between the survival blankets and through the seams and fabric of the tent, which sagged to within six inches of my prone person. Everything was saturated, and I paddled backwards and forwards to a convenient patio belonging to a vacant caravan, where I draped the wet piles over chairs and tables to drip. Two hours later everything was still dripping, and I packed it away wet as I wanted to be on my way to the farm campsite at Viriat, where my friend Carole and the third member of our party were due the next day.

Carole had said many months ago that she would like to walk with me for a few days, and had subsequently suggested bringing along a third person, a new friend of hers.

'She's a super lady. You'll really like her. She has four daughters, is a real housewife and mother, and has never done anything like this in her life. But she'd love to come with us.'

It was difficult to refuse, although I was reluctant to share my adventure with a stranger. Over the course of a few more telephone conversations, I learnt that our third party was anxious that she shouldn't slow me down. I emphasized that I was maintaining a very modest pace and not looking to set records, but was unable to convince Carole that her friend had nothing to worry about. So I had replanned the itinerary for this part of the journey which I had been most looking forward to, shortening the route and keeping as far as possible to the minimum of climbing. I was going to have to slow down my already leisurely pace, and as I felt it only fair to Jennifer that I should finish the journey and get home as soon as possible, so that she could return to America, it would mean foregoing some of the places I had planned to visit. I also knew that Carole would, despite all her fervent assurances, arrive totally unprepared and unfit. Still, I had had six delightful weeks doing things my own way; I shouldn't begrudge making a few concessions. I hoped the weather would brighten up before their arrival.

It was still raining tenaciously as I set off, squelching and drooping under the wet weight.

With the rain spotting the outside, and the steam generated by my hooded head misting them up from within, my glasses acted like a blindfold and I had to stop frequently to wipe them. Walking with my head bent to prevent the rain getting inside the poncho's hood, I noticed two very large orange slugs eating a worm. They had somehow managed to munch their way through it, leaving just a hollow skin. At a barbecue once we had fed the embellishments from a glass of Pimms to a slug and watched in astonishment as it had rapidly worked its way through slices of cucumber, apple and orange, sprigs of mint, and a strawberry. They obviously had very wide-ranging appetites, and the fact that they didn't appear to have teeth didn't seem to be a disadvantage. Actually, slugs do have teeth, I learnt later. They can have as many as 27,000 and renew them just by thinking about it. They are also frequently hermaphrodites, and can even, if the mood takes them, mate with themselves. None of this has anything to do with walking from la Rochelle to Geneva, but I just put it in because I thought you might like to know. As a matter of fact, slugs are altogether far more interesting creatures than you might think.

By mid-afternoon the sun had won the day's battle, and when I reached Viriat I was very hot and red-faced. Panting and thirsty I walked into a bar, where a dozen people sat noisily playing cards. They stopped and gaped at me in silent astonishment, and I felt uncomfortably conscious of my muddy appearance. The friendly barman smiled and a customer patted the seat next to him at the bar and helped me shed the backpack. I asked if they knew where the campsite was. Yes, indeed, just another three and a half miles away. The barman drew a little map. By now I was getting used to having to walk much further than expected, and it no longer made me depressed, angry or exasperated. It was simply a matter of taking it easy and not worrying about it. I'd get there eventually. I'd also learnt that if you walk with your mouth open, you ate insects, and that insects didn't taste nice. I tried hard to walk with my mouth closed.

★　★　★

The farm, named Bon Repos[1], nestled in a tranquil triangle between two busy motorways and the mainline railway, which ran directly through the farm twenty yards from the camping area in a small orchard. With unimpeded views across to the mountains, it

---

[1] good rest

must have been an idyllic situation before the road builders and railway engineers decided to invade it. The farmer's wife said apologetically that she hoped the noise from the trains wouldn't disturb me too much. Many people arrived, she said, and left as soon as they saw the proximity of the rail track. I assured her that I wouldn't be going anywhere, and that the noise wouldn't bother me. Many municipal campsites by virtue of being in towns suffered from traffic noise, and at Cluny the TGV regularly whooshed past. She seemed relieved. Ironically, I had chosen the farm site as opposed to the Bourgen-Bresse municipal site, as I thought it would be more peaceful.

The farm's main produce was chicken, the famous *poulet de Bresse*. With their red crests, snowy white plumage, blue legs and little golden toenails, they resemble a miniature French flag turned sideways. Here there were ten thousand of them scratching around contentedly in the grass. In the guide book sent by one of the tourist offices in the area, the English translation of the French article declared that their diet makes these chickens 'raving and petulant'. There was no sign of such rude behaviour here, where the fowl seemed placid and well mannered. Raised under strict control, each bird had unhindered access to rich pastureland where they find the insects and dietary ingredients that, unfortunately from their point of view, make them so characteristically tasty. Costing up to twice as much as an 'ordinary' chicken, and sold with a ring on their claw to guarantee their origin, when served in the best restaurants *poulet de Bresse* are accompanied by a portion of their blue legs to prove their authenticity. They certainly had a very pleasant life, here by the foothills of the mountains, free to roam over large fields during the day and then putting themselves to bed as night fell, when the farmer went round and locked them safely in until dawn.

The campsite's sanitary block was extremely primitive but adequate and there was plenty of hot water.

Carole and her friend were due to arrive the following morning, and the weather didn't show any signs of improving. It was drizzling again, and I had already started to feel slightly guilty about it.

The chickens made their way homewards as dusk fell, and small white flashes of rabbits' tails bounced around the fields. Despite the frequent trains and the bell at the level crossing which signalled their arrival, I slept well.

16

Hello, and Goodbye

It was still raining the next morning, and as I was hanging up the tent and contents to dry the two ladies came yomping in. Carole's friend Liz didn't look at all like the motherly lady that had been described to me. On the contrary, she looked extremely fit. Carole's face was glowing with pleasure, which was a delight to see, because during the previous year she had been faced with a succession of problems that would have crushed most people. She owned a small fleet of trucks and ran her own business transporting mobile homes throughout France and Spain. Tall and slim, with silky copper-blond hair, huge grey eyes, perfect skin and a gentle voice, she did not epitomize a driver of heavy goods vehicles, and the expression on the face of any male observer when she climbed into the cab of a sixty-foot truck and trailer and reversed it out of a car park or manoeuvred it through narrow busy streets was something well worth seeing.

When I had arrived to live in France she was one of the first people I'd met, and I had a great deal to thank her for. Despite our age difference, she adopted a protective motherly role, and thanks to her I soon knew the best places to shop and the best people to avoid. Bold, ambitious and female, she was the target of a great deal of jealousy and resentment, although many local English people could thank her for giving them employment. At least half a dozen people owed their lunch to her every day. She and her partner were invariably willing to help anyone in need, providing free transport back and forwards to England, lending machinery and tools and giving generously of their time and experience.

Eighteen months previously she had followed some extremely poor business advice, and as a result had found herself entangled in an impenetrable net of French bureaucracy. I had been employed by her during that time, and watched her struggle through mountains of incomprehensible paperwork to mounting financial problems. As her situation had worsened, the people

344

who had enjoyed her assistance and generosity began to relish her difficulties and openly delight in her misfortune. Fighting to keep her business alive, she paid her employees at the expense of her own mortgage, and I knew that her house was in the course of being repossessed. Some of the people she had helped started helping themselves, by stealing her goods and machinery. Maybe they had misunderstood 'The Lord helps those . . .'

Many mornings she would be transparent with exhaustion, beset on every side, but still smiling and fighting on. As if that wasn't bad enough, she had the two fiendish small boys to contend with. Finally she'd had to leave the area, and we didn't see each other often any more, so I was very much looking forward to her company.

Never one for advance planning, she had bought her tent en route to the railway station the night before. It took all three of us two hours of strenuous physical and mental effort to fit an assortment of poles of varying lengths into the channels on the mounds of fabric and to make the whole resemble something similar to a tent. Once it was finally up, an enormous size in comparison with mine, it was decided that all three of us would sleep in it, whilst my loathsome little dome was relegated to storage space.

Liz and Carole showered and changed their clothes, and we started walking to Bourg-en-Bresse, where I hoped to buy some new insoles to replace the uncomfortable chopped-off pair. I couldn't go much further with the sharp edges continually cutting welts into the undersides of my feet. Not far down the road my two companions began sticking their hands out at passing cars, and it was not too long before someone drew up, I suspect his kind heart overcoming his better judgement, and we all piled in. He looked slightly apprehensive, and when we told him that we were going to walk to Lake Geneva his suspicions that he had filled his car with three lunatics were confirmed, and he seemed heartily relieved when he had deposited us in the town centre.

We wandered around the bustling town rather aimlessly until we finally managed to locate some insoles. Carole and Liz were very hungry as they had not eaten en route, and we trundled round trying to find an open restaurant. As it was only 5.30 p.m., this wasn't easy, and nowhere was going to be open until 7.00 p.m. They were rapidly becoming dispirited by the cold wet weather, hunger and tiredness, so it was with great relief that we arrived at the railway station where the restaurant served an unexpectedly

346

good and inexpensive meal. The great flamboyant Gothic abbey at Brou which is Bourg-en-Bresse's jewel and main attraction did not fall into our orbit, and we never got to see it. On the way back to the campsite we flagged down another lift from a friendly hippy girl with an elderly English sheepdog in an old van. She drove us right to the farm, and as we turned off the main road down the farm path two deer bounced across the field.

Back in the palatial tent, Liz studied our thousands of chickeny neighbours for a few moments, and asked: 'Why are their legs painted blue?'

'Just for appearance,' I told her. 'Their owners are very proud of them.'

'But how do they do it?'

'Oh, they have a sort of artist's palette with two holes in it. One person pops the legs through the holes and the other paints them with blue paint. Then they usually paint their toenails gold as well.'

She gave me a funny look. 'How odd.'

They went off for a shower and washed their hair, a forty-minute operation, then we settled down for the night. The other two massaged creams from little plastic pots into necks and faces and under their eyes. I had recommended they bring just one change of clothes, but they had each brought a small wardrobe, and a great number of facial and body treatments, and I wondered if they quite realized what they had got themselves into. Even with the three of us in the tent, it was still cold. Liz had a lightweight sleeping bag similar to mine, but Carole had a good thick one and a thermal lining. We all went out like lights.

When we collectively awoke, it was cold and raining and the skies didn't offer any visible hope of improvement. It was a little disappointing as it was 12 June and we could have reasonably expected summer to have arrived by now. From the depths of her fleecy-lined sleeping bag, Carole exposed one eye, and moaned softly: 'Coffee I — must — have — coffee. Lots — and — lots — with — lots — and — lots — of — hot — milk.' She retracted into her cocoon.

As we had no means of making it, I went to ask the farmer's wife if she could oblige, while Liz showered and washed her hair again. I splashed across to the farm-house, a long, typically Burgundian two-storey building with a fine wooden balcony running the entire length of the first floor. At either end was a very large barn, in each of which delirious dogs on chains jumped up and down and wagged their tails, demanding attention. I found the farmer's wife in a rather sinister modern building wherein a lot of freshly dead chickens were undergoing cosmetic surgery at her hands. I tried not to look. She would be delighted, she said, to make coffee for us, and would make sure that there was a plentiful supply of hot milk to go with it.

Revived by this news, Carole was able to leave her bed and perform her ablutions, and fifteen minutes later we were sitting in the spacious farmhouse kitchen, steaming from the heat of a large wood-fired oven and diving into fresh bread, butter, apricot jam and a giant pot of coffee and jug of steaming milk. Madame took down from the kitchen walls photographs showing the farmhouse in summer, brilliant masses of geraniums tumbling from the balcony, climbing the steps, smothering the yard, and indicated the framed certificates that she had won over many years for these splendid displays.

I asked whether I could leave some odds and ends with her for a couple of weeks — redundant maps, brochures, receipts, anything that I could manage without, to lighten the load. A small pile of papers could add considerably to the weight of my pack.

The princely breakfasts cost ten francs each. Before leaving we held a committee meeting and agreed that we would regulate our pace to the slowest person. It wasn't going to be any fun for someone who had to struggle to keep up. When anyone felt tired, or footsore, they would say so immediately, and we would all rest until they had recovered. This was unanimously agreed. Without ponchos, Carole and Liz's backpacks were going to get very wet and heavy, so we wrapped each in a survival blanket, which made them look like two large mobile Christmas presents, and I was in Quasimodo mode in Janet's big green poncho. In high spirits, singing discordantly, we set off towards a campsite at Treffort-Cuisiat, in the district known as the Revermont, once part of the kingdom of Savoy.

Our joint navigation efforts successfully led through a small village where two fat young horses, delighted to have such exotic company, trotted along the fence whinnying for attention. We followed a mushy path through the Bois de Teyssonge to the village of Meillonnas, where there was an excellent bakery, and laden with gastronomic treats — including a vegetarian onion tart which I stowed away for an emergency — we adjourned to the local café/bar where they obligingly agreed we could eat our purchases, accompanied by hot chocolate and coffee.

It took us a complete circuit of Meillonnas,

searching for an exit, before we found the route out and over the 1,200-foot-high Col de France, from where we picked up the GR59. Liz and I had a mild contretemps regarding the word *col* — she said it meant a hill, which it doesn't, I said it meant a mountain pass, which it does. We climbed to 1,400 feet and Liz seemed to be coping well with the walking and climbing. She was already setting off a little alarm bell in my head. Carrying the large tent, Carole was tiring beneath the weight, and as usual I was finding it a struggle to which I was resigned. At 6.00 p.m. we congratulated ourselves as we passed the sign saying 'Treffort', although privately another little bell tinkled and I wondered what had happened to the 'Cuisiat' part. Just inside the village we passed a *cave* where we stopped to buy a couple of bottles to go with our evening meal to celebrate our first successful day. We bought one bottle of bubbly and a bottle of rosé which they opened for us, as we didn't have a corkscrew. A prominent notice behind the counter stated: 'This is not a bar. We do not serve wine by the glass.' At the counter were three men, all drinking glasses of wine. I asked if they knew the whereabouts of the campsite, and held my breath, because I already had a bad feeling.

While it appeared on the map as Treffort-Cuisiat, and the campsite was listed as being there, Cuisiat was a completely separate place nearly four miles further north. So was the campsite. Carole's silent despair was tangible. Even with her limited French, she'd got the idea. It would take at least another hour and a half of walking to reach Cuisiat. There didn't seem to be much we could do except push on and see what happened. When we reached the northern end of the village we passed a restaurant, and decided to console ourselves with a drink. We walked in, two giant Christmas presents and Quasimodo. A small man with a head of thick black curls and a matching beard glanced up from behind the bar, and with a dead-pan expression said: 'Good evening. You must be the fancy dress party.'

A couple of large kirs apiece relaxed us to the point where we decided to stay for a meal and worry about where we were going to spend the night later. As Christophe, the proprietor, took our orders, Liz went to work on him.

'Do you have a garden here?' she asked innocently.

'Yes.'

'Then could we camp in it tonight?'

'Why not?' replied Christophe, with a Gallic shrug.

While he disappeared into the kitchen, we manhandled the tent into position in the small back garden.

We settled down to a fine meal, warmed by a roaring log fire close to the bar. The only other customers were a smug man in tight white trousers and a loud shirt and a lady of a certain age, extremely well developed all over, in a black, short, very full skirt, tightened round her voluptuous waist by a thick belt, black spotted stockings, very high-heeled black patent leather shoes, and a low-necked black top revealing the major part of her vast pink bosom. With her blond hair piled up over a circular, good-natured face adorned with two vivid blobs of blusher, a lot of shiny blue eye-shadow and enormous false eyelashes, she had the startled appearance of one of those doll's faces painted on the back of a wooden spoon. She gazed with unwavering adoration at White Trousers, her superlong eyelashes fluttering like an army of spiders in close combat.

Treffort, nestling amongst the foothills of the Jura, had been settled since the eighth century. Its development as a wine-growing area burgeoned until by the fourteenth century the population exceeded that of

Bourg-en-Bresse. Then, to protect its trade during the fifteenth century, the sale of neighbouring Burgundy wines in the Bresse was banned, and the prohibition had lasted until the Revolution. In 1601 the Revermont passed from Savoy to France, and during the Thirty Years War Treffort was burnt by the French-Comtois.

Phylloxera attacked the vines in 1880, and the area turned to the manufacture of the dairy products for which it is now famous. When the Germans left the region in 1944, they spared Treffort from burning, unlike the villages further north. For a very small village it had a big history, but that was something found everywhere in France. There doesn't seem to be a single nook or cranny which hasn't seen centuries of turbulence and warfare.

Warm, well fed, and tired, we retired unwashed to the tent. Carole and Liz carefully removed their make-up and dabbed on the stuff out of the little pots, and then it was lights out. We had managed to pitch the tent at an interesting angle, tilting from left to right and top to bottom, so most of the night was spent hanging on with tooth and nail to avoid rolling downhill.

★ ★ ★

Our next destination was Thoirette, and happily the day dawned beneath a clear blue sky. Christophe supplied the essential gallon of coffee and hot milk and breakfast, served by his charming twelve-year-old son. Carole and Liz made good use of the bathroom to prepare for the day, and I managed with a brief wash. With our wine purchases from the previous day undrunk, and agreeing that it was too early in the day to start, Liz volunteered to carry the opened bottle of rosé, and I inherited the much heavier bottle of bubbly. We set off at a brisk march, stopping briefly along the way to watch with horrible fascination a family of one adult and five juvenile slugs in perfect line abreast, enjoying a wormfest.

Up we trotted to Rosy, altitude 2,000 feet, occasionally snatching handfuls of wild strawberries and cherries which were thoughtfully within reach. Liz showed no signs of being tired or having difficulty keeping up. In fact she travelled at racing pace, matched by Carole, their long legs swinging effortlessly and leaving me five hundred yards behind and already weary. Finally they came to a halt in a shady clearing beneath tall, dark green pine trees, where they were able to catch a five-minute rest before I arrived. We sprawled on the soft cool forest floor, and under the terms of our agreement I called for a slower pace, as we had a long way to go, increasingly uphill. Apart from that, moving so quickly had left no time to enjoy the sights and scenery. They agreed to reduce their speed, and then, glutted with wild fruit and cooled by the shade, we set off again with no noticeable slowing down. Very soon they were out of sight once more, as the path kept climbing steeply and became increasingly inhospitable. We were cantering along on top of a high ridge, along a track overgrown with scratchy shrubs on each side, and a sheer drop to the left. There was no sign of human passage, but frequent piles of equine droppings. The surface was made up of flat, round-edged stones embedded at an angle of about 45 degrees into the ground, parallel to each other, creating a slippery and uneven surface which resembled a mule track more than a footpath. The two racehorses sprinted ahead, while I brought up the rear like a Shetland pony, catching a glimpse every so often of their red jackets in the distance. I was so preoccupied with trying not to fall over, or roll down to the plains below, and to keep breathing as the path climbed higher still, that it was quite a long time before I realized we were going the wrong way. My two companions were too far ahead to call to, and there was no way I could catch them up, so I stopped where I was and hoped that eventually they would notice my absence and come back. Looking at the map I could see we had been tracking north for one and a half hours, and climbed to 2,500 feet, all for nothing. We were no closer to Thoirette than when we set out this morning. In Liz's great haste, we had followed the wrong GR from Rosy, and continued north instead of eastwards.

Liz was very cross when I broke the bad news. All that effort for nothing. I couldn't help feeling just a little bit pleased. None of us wanted to risk the perilous downhill run on the treacherous path, but there were a few tracks leading off to the east, none offering any indication of where they debouched, if indeed they went anywhere. I happily passed the navigation over to Carole, who negotiated us into a pretty grassy valley where we were allowed to rest for a while as we considered our next move. Two parascenders appeared, hauling their chutes back to their next launch, and set us on our way. Great clouds of pollen swirled around us, and Liz was soon in the grips of a terrible hay-fever attack, her eyes swollen almost shut. Despite a growing longing on my part that she would vanish in a puff of smoke, or twist her ankle, I couldn't help feeling sorry for her. She was in a bad way, sneezing, coughing and hardly able to see where she was.

Once we knew where we were going, everyone's spirits rose again and when we found a shady stretch of cool grass on the outskirts of a quiet village we sat there for half an hour to recoup our energy for the final six miles to Chavannes, the nearest campsite. The extra weight of the bottle of champagne was more than I could manage, and I wasn't going to carry it any further, so I popped the cork. We took it in turns to drink from the bottle, becoming increasingly giggly before setting off to our next nocturnal haven and, we hoped, a good meal.

It was nearly 8.00 p.m. when we arrived. Even from a distance the village had that 'all closed up for the night' look about it, but I didn't want to be the bearer of any more bad news that day. We managed to get the tents up exactly two minutes before the rain came. The two more hygiene-conscious members of our party went for their evening shower and hair wash, while I walked round the village to assess the chances of getting a meal. Absolutely none at all. There was not a spark of life or light to be seen anywhere.

I still had the small onion tart bought in Meillonnas the day before, and we had the bottle of rosé wine. It wasn't a lot for a three-person meal, and anyway I wanted it all for myself. The village hall behind the campsite was crowded and something was obviously going on, so Carole and Liz went to investigate in case there was any chance of finding food there. We agreed that if they hadn't returned in fifteen minutes, I was to eat the tart. I crossed my fingers very firmly for them and watched the hands of my watch, willing them to move on quickly. I was famished. The assembly in the village hall turned out to be the annual fishermen's dinner, and although somewhat surprised by the appearance of two strange Englishwomen, the organizers welcomed them warmly. Driven by an aching hunger they were soon tucking into frogs' legs and other things they would normally not have considered eating. They danced into the early hours and thoroughly enjoyed themselves. So did I, alone in the tent, with the onion tart, which had not suffered at all from being squashed in the backpack, and a glass of wine. I was fast asleep when they returned noisily at 2.00 a.m.

For the past week my left eye had been increasingly uncomfortable, especially late at night and first thing in the morning. It felt as if there was something sharp in it which I couldn't remove, and it leaked copiously all day. Tonight it had been particularly painful and I couldn't get back to sleep again due to the discomfort, and the fact that I had Liz's elbow in my head for the rest of the night.

Lying awake watching the sky lighten, I thought back over the last two days. I wasn't enjoying myself. Accustomed to pleasing myself, travelling at my own pace and stopping where and when I wanted, now I was being unwillingly rushed along by someone I hardly knew and hadn't invited and was beginning to have evil thoughts towards. I am sure she was an excellent and caring wife and mother, a great cook, an upright citizen, a solid friend, in fact a paragon of all virtues, but none of that justified her right, I felt, to mess up my party. I had covered six regions and eleven départements, and now that my target was only a few days away I didn't want the whole thing spoilt. The Jura was my treat, the reward for having walked across the entire country. Having sacrificed the route I had most wished to follow specifically to make allowances for Liz, I was being frogmarched at a speed and in a direction not at all of my choice. Nothing would make me fall out with Carole, but if I had to spend much more time under Liz's command, blood was going to flow, and I decided then that at the first opportunity I would make a break for freedom.

★ ★ ★

It was a pretty morning, with shreds of mist floating in the valleys, and a patchy blue sky. As I returned to the tent from taking a shower, I overheard Liz saying: 'We must speed up so that we can get to Geneva and start enjoying ourselves. Yesterday was a complete waste of time. We lost a whole day.' That crystallized the situation: while to me it was the journey that was important, for Liz only the arrival mattered, and Carole was caught uncomfortably somewhere in the middle. 'Two's company, three's a crowd' was certainly the case. I no longer felt guilty about my decision.

We were late leaving, because Carole, after the revelries of the previous night, and with no possibility of finding a cup of coffee, wouldn't get up. By the time she had been forced from her nest and the two girls had showered and washed their hair, it was after 11.00 a.m. A friendly English couple called Ron and Anne, who were touring the area on bicycles, stopped to chat for a few minutes, and then under darkening skies we went looking for the GR which would lead to the banks of the river Ain which we would follow up to Thoirette. We never found the footpath. It didn't exist, although it was clearly marked on the map. It was another navigational failure, and we had to settle for marching along the tarmac roads that wound up and down eastwards through the hills. As they had threatened, the skies opened, just as we were passing a large barn full of agricultural machinery, where we took shelter. Once the celestial taps had been turned off we tried to outrun a great purple sky-wave racing up from behind us for two miles, and we beat it by seconds into another barn.

Carole had an ambition to make a camp fire, and she carried her little matchbox hopefully with her. With nothing else to do, and the raw materials at hand, this was her opportunity. Concerned about the legalities and safety aspect of lighting a fire in someone else's barn, Liz and I turned our backs while Carole built a small wigwam of tiny twigs, surrounded by some large stones. She struck a match, and the kindling caught instantly. Although it was only a miniature fire, it produced copious clouds of suffocating smoke and a surprising amount of welcome heat. Carole studied her handiwork, and piled a few more fragments of wood on the pyre. She was absolutely delighted with her success, and her eyes glistened with enjoyment and woodsmoke. We stood around choking until the skies cleared and then kicked out the fire and resumed our tramp towards Thoirette, on the border between the Ain and the Jura, Liz stomping ahead like a bull with attitude. Thoirette was the birthplace of Marie-Xavier Bichat, a celebrated doctor regarded as the father of histology. A Paris hospital is named after him, and when he died at the tragically young age of thirty-one, in 1802, someone wrote to Napoleon: 'Nobody has ever done so many things so well in so short a time.'

The campsite sat in a valley surrounded by small mountains, where the river widened into a small lake. Despite its pretty setting the site itself was disappointing, unkempt and occupied mostly by empty vans in an advanced state of decay. After we had set up the tent and all indulged in the showering/hair washing/little pot ritual, we walked to the nearest restaurant. It was Sunday evening, and it was closed. So was the next one, and we had had no opportunity to buy any food to bring with us. Panic took hold. The responsibility pointed directly at me for having brought us to this place where we were all going to starve in a dreary campsite, but finally we found an open hotel by the bridge and settled down for a good meal. The bar was packed with local people watching football on the outsize television. The World

Cup was in its fourth day. Even the copious amounts of wine we enjoyed couldn't disguise the undercurrent of tension between Liz and myself.

I spoke to Jennifer, who assured me all was well at home. I told her that I would reach Lake Geneva a week from today, and get back home as soon as possible. She asked me if I was enjoying myself, and I said no, and explained that I was missing too much because of the pressure to move quickly and that I had decided to continue alone on Tuesday.

She was sympathetic and supportive. 'Don't forget,' she said, 'the other two are twenty years younger than you. No wonder they can walk quicker.'

It was a damp evening, but fairly mild. Back in the tent, the maps came out. When we had first met up, I had pointed out the route I had chosen as the least demanding for Liz's benefit, but said that I would democratically follow any itinerary that the others chose. The next leg of the journey gave us a choice of three campsites for the following night, all within a couple of miles of each other. If we took the western edge of Lake Coiselet, following a GR through wooded hills, we would be able to have a look at each campsite, and choose the nicest. It would make little difference which we stayed in from the point of view of the distance we covered. We could walk a few miles less one day and make it up the next, or vice versa. However, Liz decided that we would keep to the eastern side and head for the furthest site regardless, in order to make the maximum possible progress. It wasn't quite what I had meant by democracy, but having made up my mind that on Tuesday I was going to escape, I bit my tongue.

Carole was depressed. An Olympic gold medallist in the shopping stakes, she had forgotten her money and credit cards, and was having to depend on Liz's generosity until she could make some arrangements via her home. Although there was absolutely nothing at all to spend on in this area, she missed the feeling of a full wallet.

Sleep came that night as a blessed relief.

Our priority the following morning, once Carole and Liz had showered and washed their hair, was to sort out Carole's financial problem, which despite many gloomy predictions about having to take a taxi to a large town was easily resolved at the local post office. Next stop was to fuel up on coffee, so we headed for the hotel where we had eaten the previous evening. En route, Liz phoned her husband, and we entered a new crisis because for some reason her husband wasn't speaking to her. She was distressed and angry, and in the pervading atmosphere I wished tomorrow would hurry up. An air of doom descended again.

Over coffee and warm croissants with butter and jam, and watched by an old man nursing an empty glass and already looking the worse for wear, Liz took control of the maps, determined to abbreviate the route to Geneva. The problem was that it lay inconsiderately on the other side of numerous mountains of varying heights, along roads that wound and twisted like balls of knitting wool. In a straight level line it was only thirty miles away, but whichever route they took would be at least seventy miles. Furthermore, Carole had a badly swollen knee. She could walk uphill comfortably, but downhill was causing her a lot of pain, and even level ground was uncomfortable. The previous two days had been relatively easy going, but with at least four days of walking ahead, and a great deal of climbing, I couldn't see how she was going to manage. I suggested they should think about abandoning the walk and getting on a train to Geneva, but they were both determined to continue.

We were to walk on the main road, to avoid any navigational errors and risk of delay. We were to travel quickly, Liz hoping we might be able to eliminate tonight's campsite and make the following one. Her legs worked like pistons as she sped ahead, stressed and miserable over the argument with her husband. She was soon little more than a rapidly bobbing blob in the distance. Marching on the tarmac and dodging the traffic, I was aiming invisible arrows between her shoulders, while Carole struggled heroically to maintain the link between us by hobbling gamely backwards and forwards. Wild strawberries at their luscious best carpeted the roadsides; we could have filled a wheelbarrow with them, had we had the time. As it was I contented myself with a few snatched handfuls every so often. It was an uneventful and uninteresting march, peppered with occasional showers, along the road past the lake, with a brief look at the dam and hydroelectric installation at Coiselet. Tiny waterfalls trickled down the steep mountainsides, and amongst the grass pale scabious and giant marguerites, columbines and buttercups passed in a colourful blur as we thundered relentlessly onwards, until even Liz had to stop to rest. In a cove beside the lake an upturned dinghy made a perfect table for our picnic lunch.

After lunch we continued our joyless trek.

Across the lake the first campsite sat enticingly on a sandy beach, and I suggested that as it looked so attractive we might stay there after all, but Liz wouldn't be side-tracked, so we ploughed on to her chosen location at Dortan, where we gazed in united dismay at our destination. It was gloomy in the extreme, and set in a strange semi-industrial area, amongst a collection of very small and depressing prefabricated houses which looked as if they had been intended as temporary homes fifty years ago, and been forgotten about.

'Crikey, we've found a real dump here,' said Carole.

'We certainly have,' I replied, feeling perversely satisfied.

The site was crowded with tinkers and travellers who had no Porsches or BMWs, but instead battered vans and collapsing cars. Ducklings padded around tethered by their legs, chickens scratched in the grass and grubby, runny-nosed and strident children were all over the place. However, the sanitary block was clean and heated with giant radiators. Mysteriously, although the building itself was tropically warm, the water in the showers was tepid. When I went to wash I discovered that the water in the washbasins was steaming, unlike the showers. There were a number of small private rooms equipped with basins, and I had a good wash. When I returned to the tent fifteen minutes later, Liz looked up and remarked: 'That was quick!'

'Yes.' I managed to smile, resisting the urge to poke her in the eye and pull her hair.

Liz went to wash her hair and shower; Carole was exhausted and fell asleep; I walked up to the town to find some chocolate for Carole, who was suffering from withdrawal symptoms, and see what the chances were of finding a meal that evening.

Dortan is a *cité martyre*[1], so-named after the events that took place there on 21 July 1944, when the Germans destroyed 175 buildings and killed 35 people in reprisals against the local Resistance. A large memorial commemorating this event, and aerial photographs showing the carnage, stand in the town centre beside the river Bienne where it hurtles pell-mell beneath the bridge straddling the main road. For a small town of only 1,600 inhabitants there were a surprising number of restaurants. The smartest was closed for the day, one seemed to have closed down permanently, and one was decrepit and dingy beyond description. The fourth was perfect and I booked a table for us that

---

[1] martyred town

evening. Armed with biscuits, chocolate, wine and the good news that we would eat well that night, and with the prospect of regaining my liberty the next day, I trotted back to the site.

In the tent, Liz was in control of the maps. It seemed to have become an obsession with her now, an endless scouring of map after map, as if she was certain that hidden somewhere within them would be a short cut to Geneva if she kept looking hard enough. Tomorrow, she ordained, ignoring Carole's inflated knee, we would, no matter what, reach Saint-Claude twenty-five miles away, and Geneva the day after. Then we would all be able to start enjoying ourselves. Carole's knee was enormous, like a rugby ball, and she could barely walk. With a lot of nursing, if she could take her time, I thought she could make the journey, but I couldn't see how she was going to manage on hard tarmac under Liz's brutal regime.

Once next day's arrangements met with Liz's satisfaction, I announced that it was time for us to go our separate ways. I couldn't possibly keep up with their pace, and didn't want to hold them back. I insisted that they continue without me. They expressed concern that they were abandoning me, but solemnly I assured them that having come so far alone, I felt confident of being able to continue in the same manner. I gave them my best map of the area, and wished them good luck in Geneva. We walked up to town for dinner, five excellent courses, and the other two generously insisted on treating me. After dinner, Carole chewed her lip for a moment, opened and closed her mouth a few times, and suddenly took a deep breath.

'Look, I can't believe I'm saying this,' she gulped, 'but would you like to take my thermal lining?'

It was a very poignant moment, like the ending of *Gone With the Wind*, and I don't know who among us was the most surprised. Carole was offering an immeasurable sacrifice. I would indeed have loved to take the lining, because reduced to the little nylon tent again, alone with the emaciated sleeping bag, I wasn't looking forward to the cold nights higher in the mountains. I remembered the jolly lady in Jenzat who had so cheerfully forecast my possible demise from hypothermia. I was almost tempted to accept.

17

Free

It was another very wet night, but the last time it would rain for the rest of my journey. We walked up to town for breakfast, and then to the local pharmacy to buy a hideous and horribly expensive brace for Carole's knee. Despite its dire condition, she still intended to reach Geneva.

'I'll be fine as long as we keep to the main road,' she said. 'That will be the most level and easiest place for walking. We'll stick to that.'

It was also, as we all knew, the best place to 'faire du stop'.

We set off amicably, and for about a mile followed the D4, until the turn-off to Rhien, where we said our farewells, and I peeled off onto the footpath known as the Tour de Haut Jura en route to Vaux-lès-Saint-Claude. I was as sad to see Carole hobbling away so painfully as I was glad to see the back of Liz, and I watched the two red-coated figures tramping along the road, looking over their shoulders in the hope of stopping a friendly motorist. In my way, I suppose I was just as ruthless as Liz — we were both determined to have our own way.

With a very light heart, I was back to my exquisitely solitary and hygienically question-able odyssey. It was hot and cloudy as I ambled through the little village of Rhien, tracking north across a bridge over the lively river Bienne, and continued along the remains of what had once been the main road, but was now disused. It wound through woods, just a few feet from the river, where the shade was welcoming and cool, and crystal waterfalls tumbled down the rockface. There was absolutely no sign that anyone had been or would be passing this way. One waterfall gushed into a shallow and inviting aquamarine pool in a deep rock basin, an unbeatable backdrop for a picnic, but if I couldn't get back out up the slippery sides no-one would ever find me. With stately swans gliding on the river to my right, lizards scuttling in the rocks and birds singing, in this remote setting of trees and waterfalls, I was truly relaxed and enjoying myself. After a couple of miles the way narrowed into a muddy track, criss-crossed by small rivulets and muddy tree roots. Negotiating the greasy, twisty path involved half an hour of exciting and enjoyable slithering and sliding. The only other signs of life I saw were a few bicycle tyre marks and a vast paw print crossing a small rustic bridge over a frothing stream. From the edge of a deep tractor rut filled with muddy water, a collection of ebullient frogs leapt into the puddle in a slightly guilty way as I approached.

The track widened out again into a flower-dappled meadow surrounded by mountains and skirted by a footpath leading to the campsite at Vaux-lès-Saint-Claude, in a perfect setting by the edge of the fast-flowing river. The friendly *gardienne* hunted round the site to find what she felt was the best location for me, a little closer to the river bank than I would have chosen myself. After pitching the tent and eating a slice of pizza I had discovered in the backpack and had no recollection of buying, I wandered off to have a look round the village, which grew down the sides of the main road from Oyonnax to Saint-Claude.

In a small glass niche at the base of the war memorial was an urn, with a plaque that said it contained soil from Buchenwald, in memory of the mayor and a school teacher who had died there. Many of the names on the memorial were of German and Italian origin, a reminder of the proximity of the Swiss border. There was a smart hotel with a pretty terraced restaurant, and the menu seemed too good and too inexpensive to be true. Now that I had shaken off my bugbear, a celebration was called for; and I asked the *gardienne* at the campsite whether the food could possibly be as good as it sounded.

'It's excellent, *très raffiné*[1]. You will eat very well there.'

It was one of the rare days when I had reached my destination early, and I spent the afternoon sitting by the river with the sun on my shoulders, writing postcards and my journal, which had been rather neglected over the past few days, and looking forward to the evening meal in the chic restaurant.

In the washing block, where there was just one sit-upon loo, with a startling strawberry-red seat and lid, I peered into the mirror to examine my eye, which was causing me considerable embarrassment by making me appear to be continually weeping. It was also becoming excruciatingly painful, but despite a lot of prodding and peering I couldn't see

---

[1] very sophisticated

anything obviously wrong with it.

I stood on my jeans to try to squash the creases out of them, and pulled on a silk shirt. The collar was reasonably flat, and with the designer jumper over the top the effect was clean and fairly tidy. As far as footwear was concerned, it was a choice between the huge leather boots or the cheap rubber sandals bought in Evauxles-Bains. The boots won, and once washed and greased didn't show any signs of having walked over seven hundred miles since I bought them five months previously. I hoped the restaurant would find my appearance worthy of admittance. What a terrible humiliation if they turned me away.

I needn't have worried. Royalty could not have been more warmly greeted, and what luxury it was to sit in such surroundings: thick white linen cloths, sparkling cutlery, crockery and glasses, and discreet music. The menu announced that the chef's sole objective was that every customer should eat quality food faultlessly prepared. It was rare to find a restaurant that would replace the meat course with anything other than an omelette, and consequently I had eaten a great number of omelettes in the last few weeks. Even a perfect omelette is still at best an omelette and hardly a culinary miracle.

The 57-franc menu offered as the main course some sort of meat, and I asked the waitress tentatively whether there was fish, or a meatless alternative, trusting that the chef wouldn't explode into a tantrum and have me hurled onto the pavement; or, even worse, propose an omelette. She returned a moment later. Would grilled bream be acceptable? Or would I prefer to make a suggestion which the chef would try to satisfy? The bream sounded wonderful, and tasted divine, served with a hint of saffron sauce and a portion of wild rice. Followed by a sponge layered with a rich raspberry mousse so light it was a wonder it didn't float off the plate, and washed down with a half-carafe of rosé wine, it was probably the most perfectly prepared meal I had ever eaten, and came to eighty-two francs. I ordered a cognac. When it arrived it measured a good four inches in a large brandy balloon, and even at forty-four francs was a bargain.

With Geneva only three days' walk away, I still hadn't quite worked out how to cross the last ridge of the Jura, so I had taken the maps with me to the restaurant, and studied them while I sniffed and sipped the quarter-pint of cognac. At a facing table sat the prototype of the tall, dark and handsome man. He had ordered one of the house specialities, some sort of meat dish. It was served from a two-foot-tall wrought-iron framework, in the form of a miniature gallows, with a long, thick skewer speared with a number of chunks of grilled or roast meat hanging from the crosspiece. He raised his eyebrows in appreciation and, catching my eye, smiled. He watched me measuring and plotting routes on the maps, and asked if I needed help. I explained that I was looking for a route up to the Crêt de la Neige, the highest point on the Jura range, which I wanted to reach before descending to Lake Geneva.

'I am a colonel in the mountain regiment,' he said, taking the map. 'I know this area very well. Are you very fit, very experienced in the mountains?'

'No, neither.'

'Then you cannot cross at this point alone.'

Of course I couldn't — he would have to come with me. I smiled encouragingly.

'I really don't recommend you going up there. The descent is very steep and treacherous. If you take my advice, you will take this route.' He drew a wiggly line on the map. 'This is your best way. You will be safe on your own.'

Ah well. He knew what he was talking about. Since I had come this far, it would be a shame to fall off a mountain so close to my destination. I strolled back to the campsite under a night sky that was ice-blue and blurred with tiny explosions of wispy pastel pink and lilac clouds. It was the sort of sky that made me want to weep for its brief beauty. All along the river signs warned that the water levels could rise very quickly and unexpectedly, due to the many dams and hydroelectric plants, and I was slightly apprehensive with the tent perched within two feet of the edge of the bank. The current rushed along at a brisk pace, as I stood watching for a change in the level. I didn't fancy struggling out of the little tent whilst white water rafting at the same time. However, the *gardienne* assured me there was no danger.

It was still mild and I left the outer flap open, and lay looking out at the black silhouette of a mountain against the light blue of the fading dusk; the river continued its dash past, and I was certain I could hear the level rising. The warm evening disintegrated into another terribly cold night, and although I wrapped myself in all my clothes and the poncho I couldn't sleep. I consoled myself with the thought that if the river did suddenly flood at least it wouldn't catch me unawares. I hoped that in Saint-Claude there would be somewhere I could buy a thermal lining for the sleeping bag.

18

Paradise Found

Being restricted by the location of campsites had meant that my path led to places I had never heard of, and would probably never have visited. Few places along the way had been what I had expected; some had been disappointing and others had far exceeded my hopes. Here it was all I could have dreamed of. Within a hundred yards of the campsite, the footpath to Saint-Claude opened out of the trees into a sunny meadow where three herons strode long-legged through the grass and wild flowers, overlooked by the Chapelle of Saint-Romain de Roche six hundred feet above. A low murmur from a row of beehives, the birdsong and the chuckling of the river were the only sounds. There was nothing to spoil the beauty of nature. It was perfect.

At Molinges where I stopped to ask for directions, I sat drinking hot chocolate and trying to staunch an endless flow of tears which put my left eye completely out of service. By Chassal it was even worse and the pain was agonizing; I had to pack a thick wad of absorbent paper inside my glasses to stop the tears flooding down my cheeks. I had a glass of wine (for medicinal purposes) and a croissant, and learned from the lady in the café that although unmarked on the map there was a peaceful and little-used footpath which ran parallel to the railway line as far as Lison. After that, the only route to Saint-Claude was along the wide and busy D436 for several miles, through the extensive commercial and industrial outskirts of the town. It continued past high-rise council flats where the entire population seemed to be made up of veiled Arab women and dark-skinned children, giving the area the look and feel of a north African bazaar, until I reached the Grand Pont. A hundred and sixty feet above the ravine hewn by the rivers Bienne and Tacon, the bridge gives splendid views of the town splashed over the hillsides and the valley below, and leads into the town centre.

There had been an interesting collision of two cars near the bridge, with shattered glass all over the road and pavement, and four belligerent-looking policemen shooing onlookers away. One car was embedded well into the front of somebody's house, and a tearful lady was explaining to the stony-faced occupants that the accident hadn't been her fault. One of the policemen waved me past irritably.

Saint-Claude has been a precious stone cutting centre and the world capital of the briar pipe industry for the last hundred and fifty years. It is a sprawling industrialized town with a large immigrant population, and nothing like the quaint village I had anticipated. The people of the Haut Jura have a centuries-old history of skilful carving of wood, stone and metal, which they practise to while away the long winter months. When tobacco arrived in France in 1560 the German-made meerschaum and porcelain pipes were expensive and fragile, so manufacturers experimented with different materials. Pipes made from boxwood, pear, maple and walnut were unsuccessful, the wood burning as quickly as the tobacco, and tasting vile. Even worse were the pipes fashioned from horn. Then in 1854 the first pipes were made using briar roots from Corsica, where they grew in abundance, and by 1914 Saint-Claude was producing five million briar pipes annually, mostly for export. The area is also world famous for the production of toys at Moirans-en-Montagne, the toy capital of France, nine miles from Saint-Claude. At Morez a few miles northeast of Saint-Claude, the first spectacle frames to be supported by the nose and ears were designed in 1796, and today the area is renowned for its production of frames, producing ten million pairs a year.

Two miles away, on the far side of the town, the campsite occupied a picturesque valley setting encircled by mountains. While I was wandering about looking for a good place to pitch the tent, two familiar beaming faces came into sight, the friendly cycling English couple I had met in Chavannes, Ron and Anne. There is something very satisfying about unexpectedly meeting people you know in an unfamiliar place. We shared tales of the trials and tribulations we had enjoyed since we last met.

In the late afternoon I walked back into Saint-Claude, a crowded, bustling town, seething with activity. The main street, la Rue du Pré, is lined with souvenir and gift shops, cafés, restaurants, bakeries, greengrocers and pipe shops. Although there were a couple of sports and outdoor goods shops, they didn't sell, and hadn't even heard of, thermal linings for sleeping bags. A very determined saleslady said that even if they had them they wouldn't keep me warm, and what I needed was a good goose-down sleeping bag. She pulled one from the shelf and shook it so that it expanded until it filled most of the shop. She assured me that it was very light and would, with little persuasion, compact into a sufficiently small mass to put in the backpack. If it didn't, then all I needed to do was to roll it up and tie it to the outside. She stood between the door of the shop and me, cutting off any potential escape route from her forceful sales tactics. I said I couldn't possibly afford seven hundred francs. She took my arm and jammed it inside the bag. I agreed that it was delightfully warm, exactly what I wanted, and offered her two hundred francs for it. Then she let me go.

From the adjacent bookshop I bought a map of the area showing in fine detail all the local footpaths for the final leg, where I was determined not to be lost. For an hour I strolled around, admiring the ornate pipes on display, the superb chocolates in the *pâtisseries*, and the Cathédrale Saint-Pierre, dating back to the fourteenth century and fortified as a place of refuge for the town's inhabitants in case of attack.

At the campsite there was a good, simple restaurant, where I ate a meal I could hardly see as the tears spouted from my left eye and the right eye was exhausted from having done the work of both all day. The pain had become unbearable. Anticipating a cold night, I swathed myself in all my clothing, and then rolled up in the crackly survival blanket and the thick green poncho. I was certainly warm, but lay awake all night. I knew I couldn't go any further without medical attention. It felt as if someone was tapping glass spinters into the eyeball. There was a strange noise — a high-pitched, distant whine. It was me, screaming in my throat. I knelt, twisted, turned, rocked backwards and forwards, and banged my head and cheeks with my fists, but nothing I did alleviated the agony. As soon as daylight lit the tent, I lurched out, my hand over my eye, which would not open. The *gardien* saw me reeling around, told me to stay where I was, and ran for his car and drove me to the casualty department at Saint-Claude hospital.

'You're very lucky,' said the receptionist. 'Dr Joinier, the ophthalmologist, is in the hospital at the moment, and he will see you before he leaves.'

A drop-dead gorgeous young doctor who had far more than his fair share of good looks and charm carried out a preliminary examination. He bent over me tenderly, and crooned: 'I am going to put something in your eye to make it go to sleep.'

He took hold of the upper eyelashes, and tried to open the lid. It stayed doggedly clamped shut. He tugged again, and I felt a few lashes come adrift.

'I am so sorry,' he breathed.

It didn't matter. He could pull them all out if he wanted to. He tried again, and again, until finally, possibly with the last remaining lash, he succeeded in dragging the lid open and applied a drop of liquid, which brought instant, blessed relief to both of us.

Shining a white light into the eye, his face inches from mine, he murmured and purred softly. His aftershave was delicious.

'I cannot find anything wrong,' he announced apologetically.

'It hurts terribly. There has to be something in it,' I insisted.

He took up a blue light, and continued his search. Suddenly he gave a shout of satisfaction. 'Ah, yes, aha, I see it!'

He ran to the door and shouted down the corridor. 'Doctor, come quickly! I've found something!'

The ophthalmologist, who was wearing a Starsky and Hutch sweater and had only called in at the hospital to collect a letter on the way to his office, peered into the eye for a fraction of a second.

'It hurts you very badly,' he told me, 'very badly indeed in the morning, and again in the evening. Normally, during the day, it does not trouble you quite so much, but there is a lot of water. Have you had a severe injury to your eye some time?'

Yes. I had managed to propel fragments of a rusty nail into my eye about ten years previously during a disastrous attempt at upholstery.

'You are going to need an operation. But not straight away. I can give you some medicines to control the pain. When you go back home, you must arrange to see a specialist.' With that, he was gone.

Armed with a prescription and a lasting devotion to the young doctor, I waited in the car park for the *gardien* to return from his shopping expedition.

'I was talking to the shopkeeper about you,' he said as he drove me to the pharmacy. 'I told him you had walked from la Rochelle.' He hesitated. 'He says it is not possible. He says no-one could walk that far, alone.'

I shrugged.

'Of course,' he replied, 'I believe you. But the shopkeeper doesn't.'

Well, there you go.

Anointed with three assorted potions, my

eye improved rapidly, and an hour later I was walking along the magnificent Gorges du Flumen. Beside the clean, beautiful river, the moss-clad beeches and pines exhaled cool, light green oxygen into the air. On the far side of the river the mountainside rose to 3,500 feet, and massive steel electricity pylons surmounting the ridge were a monument to the ingenuity and determination of man. The path ended where four waterfalls spilled down, one gushing ferociously from the rocks high above while three gentler versions poured more sedately down the fern-covered rockface into a sapphire-blue pool. It looked inviting, but not for someone alone — there was no way of telling that a giant serpent was not lurking within the pool, lying in wait for the unwary. Strolling back to the campsite I met Ron and Anne sitting on a peaceful shingle bank, soaking up the sun and contemplating a swim in the clean blue water. They were just about the most smiley people I could ever recall meeting.

The campsite washing facilities were excellent and spotless, and the *gardien* took pride in keeping the grass mowed and the hedges trimmed. It was a very large site for one person to manage, and he worked at it from early morning until dark. If I had to put all the thirty-five campsites I had stayed at so far in order of merit, Saint-Claude would definitely have taken first place, just ahead of la Souterraine. The only thing I found just a little strange here was that in every toilet the toilet brush was chained to the wall.

Next to the site was the *centre nautique*, offering three azure pools of different shapes and depths. Campsite residents were issued with free tickets to the centre, where the pools shimmered under the warm blue skies, and surrounded on all sides by mountains looked most inviting. I had carried a swimming costume optimistically with me since I left, and this was my first opportunity to use it. But first I had to sort out my feet. After the multi-layers of plasters were peeled off, they left myriad sticky grey lines which took a long time and a lot of scrubbing to remove.

The *gardien* had said that the pools were heated. I can't imagine what with — possibly ice. These must be the chilliest swimming pools in the world, and, notwithstanding vigorous thrashing, after ten minutes my limbs were as blue as the waters and rigid with cold. Walking back to the campsite, I met Anne and Ron, off to enjoy themselves in the pools, and I wasn't surprised to see them returning a quarter of an hour later, rubbing their hands together and banging their arms against their bodies to restore circulation.

A brisk walk back to Saint-Claude to renew my Loto ticket warmed me up. On the way I met an elderly lady in psychedelic leggings, stooping along beside the road. I asked what she was doing.

'Looking for four-leafed clover. There is usually some along here.' She combed the grass with her fingers. 'If you find it, you must give it away,' she explained. 'Then you both have good luck.' I hoped she would find some and give it to me, but although we both hunted diligently for a while we didn't find any.

That evening I ate again at the campsite restaurant. The cook made the most wonderful blue cheese tart, and with just a little persuasion parted with the recipe. Ron and Anne arrived just as I'd just finished eating and invited me to join them. We shared a bottle of wine, and laughed at Ron's story of one of their cycling holidays some years earlier, in Brittany. Needing somewhere to stay for the night, they had approached a farmhouse and explained to the owner, in basic and very laborious French, that they were looking for overnight accommodation. The owner replied courteously in French, and then, catching sight of Ron's bicycle, exclaimed in his native English: 'Good Lord, a Coventry Eagle! I haven't seen one of those for years.'

To celebrate having sorted out the eye problem, I had an extremely potent plum liqueur, which was like drinking burning diesel and seemed to make the ground tilt. In the dark I swayed back to the tent, which I decided to turn sideways on to the rising sun, to give the drying process the earliest possible start the following morning, so that I could leave in good time for the climb to Lajoux. Pulling out the pegs by the light of a torch which I dropped, and couldn't find as the light went out, I dragged the whole thing through 90 degrees. Patting round in the dark I could only find four of the pegs, and prodded them back into the ground as well as I could. Then I tumbled inside into the misshapen pile of disordered belongings and fell fast asleep.

What I had forgotten when reorientating the tent was that I had pitched it behind an enormous pine tree, which so effectively screened the tent from the sun that when I woke blearily at 9.15 a.m., the whole thing was still completely sodden, as were all the contents, which lay in damp disarray all over the place. I was absolutely sweltering, wrapped in a strange assortment of clothes, poncho and survival blanket. It took me quite a long time to untangle myself and struggle out into the daylight, where I spread out the poncho in the sun with all my things laid out on it to dry.

In the meantime Ron and Anne hadn't been idle. They had thoughtfully made coffee and some delicious egg sandwiches, and two further boiled eggs for my journey.

My eye had stopped streaming and hurting, which was a good thing because today I faced the challenge of a steep climb up to Septmoncel and on to Lajoux, at 3,840 feet the highest village in the Jura. The *gardien* came and asked where I was heading for. When I told him, he remarked that it was a distance of at least twelve miles, and did I think I would be able to get that far. I hoped so. He didn't look convinced.

I had been warned that the Chemin des Moines[1], the footpath leading up to Septmoncel, was incredibly long and steep. Alongside the river I met the first and only other hikers I would come across in the entire journey, a friendly German couple and their dog, who had just completed a five-day walking tour of the surrounding area. They too said that the footpath was very hard work and that there were other routes to

---

[1] monks' path

Septmoncel which I might like to consider. I thanked them for their advice and carried on.

I crossed the river by a rustic bridge sporting a sign giving the estimated walking time to Montbrilland as thirty-five minutes. Whoever had estimated these times must have had in mind mountain goats at peak fitness, because they always seemed quite unrealistic. The first hundred and fifty yards of the ascent was all but perpendicular, over dry gritty soil scattered with small loose stones. I started up it and slithered backwards. It was too steep for my stick to be of any use. The path traversed an area of scorched grass, and there was absolutely nothing to hold on to. The weight of the backpack threatened to drag me downhill again, and the only way I could progress was by bending almost double, like an African tribeswoman under a load of wood, and putting all my weight on my toes. It was touch and go whether I would make it or be towed back down to the valley. In my backpack was a long length of rope, and I decided that if I couldn't manage the ascent wearing the pack, I would tie the rope to it and try to haul it up behind me. With just another six feet to scale a scrawny little bush was just within reach. With a final toe-pushing scramble I lunged at the startled shrub, which very nearly surrendered its tenuous hold under my assault. It was the forerunner of several more, and with their unwitting but vital assistance I reached a point where the path levelled slightly and led into a shaded area. It still climbed steeply enough, and in the heat, and with the heavy load, I had to stop to drink every fifty paces, sitting down and munching a few dried apricots for energy. Sweat poured down my face, arms and legs, my clothing stuck to me, and the only noise was muted birdsong, the distant hiss of the waterfalls and the jungle drumbeat of my heart.

Eventually I reached the D436 and the Roche Percée, a hundred-yard tunnel blasted through the rock. Water dripped from the roof of the tunnel and I expected the whole thing to cave in on me. I wished I wasn't such a wimp about heights, enclosed spaces, caves, and all the other things that normal people take in their stride. Back once more in the open, and struggling up the incline, I thought about abandoning the tent and as many other things as I could live without for the final two days. I could wrap them in the survival blankets and push them into the under-growth; and if anyone wanted them enough, they were welcome, particularly to the wretched tent. In the meantime I would carry on with the weight as far as I could. The well-signed path was in places wide smooth gravel, and in others earthy forest floor carpeted with the previous autumn's cornflake-crisp leaves. It was very peaceful and mostly shady, and in the very steep parts exposed tree roots made useful footholds. I felt like a human waterfall, with sweat running down my body and legs in a rapid stream. Now at 3,250 feet, I was finding it even harder to breathe. To my right the mountain rose steeply, dropping away hundreds of feet to the left. Looking back down to the valley, I couldn't believe that a few hours ago I had been down there, and that I had somehow managed to haul myself up here.

At 2.50 p.m. I had reached 3,315 feet at the Plateau sur le Replan, and walked into Septmoncel, a small village set against a backdrop of mountains, just as the village clock struck the hour, twice. The sound echoed on the still air, blending with the deep, soft clanging of the cowbells from the cattle who shared the alpine pastures with the bees. Septmoncel is renowned for its acoustic qualities. I stood at the acoustic point with my eyes closed and hands cupped behind my ears, as the notice board suggested, turning my head in different directions and catching the cowbells, the bees, and the drone of a tractor engine. The sound was very pure and extraordinarily amplified by my cupped hands.

An old lady came slowly up the hill. 'Bonjour, monsieur,' she called.

'Bonjour, madame,' I replied.

'Oh! Excuse me, madame.' She laughed. 'Your clothes . . . '

'Yes, I know I don't look very ladylike.'

She recommended that I drink from the fountain in the village. The water there, she said, was the purest and most delicious I would ever find. It was very good. I bought a bag of cherries for lunch, and continued towards Lajoux. The farmers were taking advantage of the hot, dry summer weather to cut their hay: tractors were working the valley floors, and brown-armed men swinging scythes on the steep hillsides.

By now it really was hot, and I had to stop and sit down every twenty paces. My face burnt from the salt of dried sweat, and my heart was pounding alarmingly. I looked in vain for wildlife, but saw nothing except a voracious herd of sheep munching their way across a flowery field. No doubt any creature with a modicum of sense would be sheltering from the searing heat amongst the silent pine trees. The summer weather had brought out the flies, which, attracted to my unladylike rivers of perspiration, added their bites to my woes.

On a plateau a smoky tractor was cutting he hay, and the air was so pure and clean it was like being on top of the world. Carried away by the scenery and euphoria, I marched hotly and happily down a long shady road for about a mile in quite the wrong direction, and then hauled back up the long, shady road — the D436 — towards Lajoux, having lost contact with the footpath. Small brilliant purple flowers sprouted from the bare rockface, and the miles to Lajoux seemed to have an elastic quality, but it didn't really matter in this paradise. Hugo Grotius, the sixteenth/seventeenth-century Dutch politician who laid the foundations of modern international law, said that France is the most beautiful kingdom there is — after the kingdom of heaven. I couldn't comment on the latter, but he must be right on the first count.

A heavily laden donkey on delicate hooves came into sight, led by a thin young man wearing a jungle hat, shorts and boots, and dark glasses with one crazed lens. He had perfect teeth and a beautiful, gentle smile. He told me he had been wandering with his donkey for three years, fulfilling a dream. I asked where he was heading.

'We follow *la bonne étoile*,' he replied.

He carried a very small map of the whole of France measuring no more than ten inches by six in a pouch round his neck, on which the place names could only be read with a magnifying glass, and made no forward plans. Each day was a new adventure, following the lure of the lucky star. Each night he found someone who would allow him room for his tent and grazing for his adored donkey, who was eight years old and came from near the Pyrenees. Her sleek sides supported several robust sacks, a large canvas tent, an umbrella, a cooking pot and a bucket.

I asked if he would write a book about his experiences.

'What for?' he responded. 'What is important is to live, to follow your dreams. That is all that matters.'

He had another dream — to cultivate a huge garden.

Where would this garden be? When did he plan to start? I asked.

That would depend entirely upon *la bonne étoile*. Of course.

He walked slowly down the narrow road out of Lajoux with his patient companion.

It was 6.28 p.m. when I reached the *gîte d'étape*, a large chalet-style building. I was very lucky, said the *gardien*. In another two minutes, he would have been gone. He showed me to a spacious three-person room, with a writing desk, a bathroom including a shower and two washbasins, and a balcony overlooking a scene of pastoral perfection. The *gîte*'s capacity was about eighty people and I was the only guest.

★　★　★

The village of Lajoux is nothing more than a collection of low chalets on a plateau overlooking high valleys. On its gentle slopes graze the brown and white Montbeliard cattle which produce the milk for the region's fine cheeses — Bleu de Gex, Morbier, and the incomparable Comté. The post office houses the ski school. On all sides mountains rise, and the air is deliciously pure. This is the heart of the Jura National Park — a remote and unspoilt region of tranquil mountains and dense forests. Every painful step, every freezing night, every exhausted baking day, was worth it to reach this beautiful, beautiful part of France. I just fell in love with it.

At the elegant restaurant, despite my travel-stained clothing I was greeted just like a normal person and enjoyed a fine meal. The wines of the Jura, amounting to no more than 1 per cent of France's total production and beyond the scope of my pocket, come in five colours — red, white, rosé and, most unusually, straw and yellow. It is the yellow wine, the flavour known as 'the peacock's tail', which is the most celebrated. During the six years that the wine must be aged before bottling, it loses 38 per cent of its volume by evaporation ('the angels' share'), and uniquely it is sold in 62-centilitre bottles instead of the normal 75.

Walking back to the *gîte* as the first stars pierced the darkening blue of the night sky, I passed a man standing beside the road, whistling home some unseen animals. A girl in a dark green tunic and red shoes was hitting a tennis ball rhythmically against a wall, and a couple of dogs strutted importantly along the single-track road. It was a heartwrenchingly beautiful evening, and if I had dropped dead there and then, I would have died happy.

Despite the comfort of the bed, I was restless, and lay for hours watching the stars blinking in the dark blue velvet sky. Only the faint note of the cowbells broke the silence occasionally.

I thought of the *gardien*'s words when I arrived. 'You're lucky.' From the very beginning, luck had been with me. Luck in finding Jennifer, who had made the whole project possible, luck with the weather which could have been so much worse. And most of all, luck with the people who had helped me so much, both friends and strangers. Yes, I was indeed very lucky.

19

The End

Saturday, 20 June 1998 — 51st day

After today, climbing over the Col de la Faucille at 4,425 feet, it would be downhill all the way.

Reluctantly I walked out of Lajoux, past the chalet-style buildings with their signs warning of snowfalls from the roofs above. According to the signpost, Mijoux was fifty minutes away along the Tour de Haut Jura Sud. I don't have the ability to describe the beauty of this place. The path was cool and green, the ground soft and springy, the air very clear, and the hint of a breeze riffled through the beech and pine trees. Beside the path boulders coated in emerald-green moss sat like plump cushions, and wild roses pushed up through the undergrowth, purple splashes against the leafy canvas. From Mijoux in the valley below came the familiar sound of cowbells, and an occasional car. The path curved uphill, and was blocked by a sloping fallen tree. Where the end of the tree lay to the left was a sheer drop, but it was the only possible place to negotiate the obstacle. It was too high to climb over in the middle, and not tall enough to pass beneath. If my foot slipped as I climbed over the log, I wouldn't stop flying for a very long time, so I off-loaded the backpack and dumped it over ahead of me, then cautiously followed it. The path climbed up and up. I was still searching for signs of wildlife, hoping to spot chamois, boar, or squirrel, but even the birds were hidden in these thick woods. The only things to see were the ubiquitous giant slugs. At one point deer tracks crossed the path, but they disappeared as abruptly as they came. Underfoot became wet and slippery, and horses which had recently passed along the track had left four-foot-long skidmarks in the greasy mud.

One and a half hours later there was no sign of Mijoux and I knew I shouldn't be heading south, but it was so enjoyable that I carried on regardless, with no idea of where the path was leading, hurdling several more fallen trees and penetrating deeper and deeper into the forest, feeling like half of Hansel and Gretel. Two hours later I sat in a sunny clearing and studied the map. The path continued to Lélex, and from there turned north to the Col de la Faucille. It was a detour of about twenty-five miles, which would mean arriving in Geneva a day late. I had already arranged for a friend to meet me the following day, so the only option was to backtrack to Mijoux.

The return journey downhill over the muddy track was exhilarating and I slipped and slithered in a spectacular manner, only maintaining my foothold by snatching at branches as I whizzed past. By now I was fairly expert at negotiating fallen trees, and when I reached the first one, which had caused me such a problem on the outbound journey, I was confident enough to vault over, complete with backpack in position.

Today was the first day I had not had any plasters or strapping on my feet, and so far they were holding up well, although the second toe on my right foot was slightly painful and seemed to be growing into a rather funny shape. As I had expected to reach Mijoux no more than an hour after leaving Lajoux, I wasn't carrying anything to drink and would have given a pint of blood for a mouthful of cold water. The more I thought about it, the thirstier and more panicky I became, until I was studying pools of water lying in ruts, which looked clear enough, and wondering whether I could just dip my fingers in them to wet my mouth. The temptation was almost strong enough to overrule common sense. And then Mijoux was just ahead. I had passed within fifty yards of the turning on the way past, but the sign was obscured by undergrowth.

Just beside the path was a large terraced bar, and the door was wide open. On the counter a coffee machine bubbled, and the shelves were tantalizingly lined with bottles, but there was no-one there. I called, and knocked on every door in the building, but failed to find any sign of life. It was like the *Marie Celeste*. After five futile and frustrating minutes I gave up, walked to a hotel in the town centre and ordered a Coke.

I watched in disbelief as the girl behind the bar prepared this desperately needed drink in slow-motion slow-motion, in fact almost freeze-frame. First she found a glass. Then a tray. She took a bottle from the fridge, and put it on the tray. Someone came in from the restaurant and she interrupted herself to prepare a tray of drinks for them. Back at the Coke, she uncapped the bottle, and replaced it on the tray. She tidily dropped the cap into a bin. The glass joined the bottle on the tray. She had just turned her attention to the till when in came a waitress and they spoke for a minute or so. She punched the till. A little roll of paper sprang out. She hunted for a saucer, and carefully placed the little roll of paper on it. Then the saucer went on the tray. Everything was set now. Except for the ice. Delving into a giant bucket, she scooped a ladle of cubes into the glass. With a triumphant smile, she delivered her work of art, and I swiped the glass from the tray before she could put it on the table, downed it noisily in four gulps and ordered another. She probably thought I was a philistine.

The stunning colonel at Vaux-lès-Saint-Claude had plotted a route which led up to the Col de la Faucille and then along the crest of Mont Chanais and down to Crozet. From there it would be a short walk to Lake Geneva the following day. Before leaving Mijoux I phoned the *gîte d'étape* at Crozet, luckily, because it was fully booked, leaving little choice but to go straight over the col and on to the campsite at Gex.

On the way out of Mijoux I bought three large bars of luxury chocolate, which was rather a silly idea in the heat. The footpath signs were clear enough, but I felt there must be some mistake. The first hundred yards of the path was like the aftermath of an avalanche, almost perpendicular and strewn with loose rocks, with no footholds or handholds. I searched for an alternative, found it didn't exist, so once again, in tribeswoman style, dug my toes in and bent my nose to my knees. It was really quite perilous and I hoped it would sort itself out quickly, which it did, opening out into a wide track of glaringly white stone, zigzagging up the side of the mountain under the white heat of the sun. Across the valley the hill I had mistakenly climbed earlier looked like unbroken forest, and gave no hint of its hidden grassy clearings speckled with marguerites, buttercups, and wild orchids.

As ever, the road seemed infinite, and I was reduced to a snail's pace by the heat and the effort. I was used to being exhausted, but this really was the big one. I could hardly lift my feet and was deafened by the sound of my own heartbeat thumping hard and fast in my ears, but I didn't want to reach the top. This was the last day of my journey — tomorrow's few miles to the lake would be just a formality. Today was the sweltering end of a dream born on a January day five months earlier.

And then there it was, the pass through the mountains, altitude 4,300 feet, opened by

Napoleon in 1805. It was crowded with sightseers soaking up the warmth and the views across into Switzerland. I sat for an hour in a restaurant sipping another icy Coke and forking at a *tarte aux myrtilles*[1], putting off the moment when I would begin the descent.

Outside, as I dragged the backpack aboard, I could hear a group of people at a nearby table laughing at me. I turned and smiled at them. I was used to being laughed at. Since leaving la Rochelle fifty-one days earlier, I had been stared at, pointed at, and giggled at. I had laughed at myself many times. It didn't matter at all. I had done what I set out to do, and if the worst thing I had suffered at anyone else's hands was a laugh, I thought myself very fortunate. So I stood and laughed with them before waving and heading downhill.

But first I wanted a photograph, and roamed around until I found the signboard: Col de la Faucille, alt. 1,323 m. Turning away from the sign I had my first sight of snow-capped Mont Blanc in the far distance, and the hazy indigo smudge of Lake Geneva in the foreground. My eyes stung and the mountain dissolved in a misty blur, which

---

[1] blueberry tart

was strange, as my injured eye had stopped watering two days ago. Now both eyes were leaking profusely.

★   ★   ★

The N5 wound its way down to Gex in a series of hairpin bends stretching for six miles, and was teeming with fast Saturday afternoon traffic in both directions. Walking along it was an unappealing idea, so I was delighted to find a footpath called the Sentier du Facteur[1], which avoided the main road for about three miles. Despite the heat of the afternoon, each sight of the lake and Mont Blanc brought me out in shivers, and I couldn't stop tears streaming down my face and stinging my cheeks. Raging stomach cramps, probably due to the freezing Cokes I had drunk, bent me double.

The footpath ran out at a fountain built on the side of the road to commemorate Napoleon's opening of the pass. The cuckoo, which I had heard every day but one since leaving la Rochelle, had gone. It had been with me across the distance of nearly 550 miles I had covered. Now there was an eagle soaring above the lake.

---

[1] postman's path

When I reached the elegant campsite at Gex, the *gardienne* seemed very pleased and quite excited by my arrival.

'Your friends were here,' she said. 'They said you have walked all the way from la Rochelle!'

I nodded.

'Here is where the caravans park,' she indicated a plan of the site, 'and the tents go here, at the back. But you,' she smiled, 'may place your tent anywhere you choose. It is a small privilege for your effort.'

I planted the tent in a place where I could clearly see the Col de la Faucille behind and Mont Blanc ahead, and where the first morning sun would hit it. An elderly gentleman watched as I put the tent up, and once I had finished he came over and passed the time of day for a while, asking where I had come from and where I was going. Then, clearing his throat, he pointed to the rear of the site, and explained apologetically that I would have to take my tent down and move it there. This area was reserved for caravans.

'I know,' I replied, smiling sweetly, 'but my tent is staying here.' Having earned the privilege, I was not going to let it go to waste. Shrugging and shaking his head, he wandered back to his caravan, where he and his wife seemed to be in a permanent state of war.

They argued loudly and continually on everything from the time they should eat, where they should put their shoes, and what time they would go to bed and get up, to what they would watch on their television.

After a shower I went off to get something to eat from the campsite restaurant. It was closed for food, but they served a couple of excellent kirs, which helped to wash down two of the rather bendy chocolate bars. By the time I realized I had left my watch in the shower, it had vanished. Considering how far I had travelled, how many places I had stayed, and how often I had left everything in the tent, losing only my watch wasn't bad.

I rang Jennifer to tell her I had arrived safely and would be home in a few days' time. She had some news, too. Gloria's husband, Bill, had been released on bail.

After writing postcards to my friends and wellwishers, with the discordant conversation of my neighbours spitting into the evening, I tried for an early night. But it was Saturday, and there was some sort of celebration in town, and although it was over a mile away the monotonous sound of techno music thumped loudly until dawn. I was still awake when the sun came up, hitting the tent broadsides.

By 7.00 a.m. all my belongings were spread

out in the sun to dry for the last time. The next-door neighbours were up and squabbling, too.

The *gardienne* came over, and handed me my watch. 'Someone found it in the shower last night.'

Heaving on the backpack, I set off for the rendezvous with my friend at le Creux de Genthod, an unknown place chosen from the map as a convenient point for us to meet. As I marched along, I just had to keep looking behind to the mountain range, where eagles spiralled on thermals. By mountain standards the Jura are not high, but by my standards they were, and I still didn't believe I had crossed them.

Sunday morning cyclists and equestrians rode under the blue sky, and a steady stream of aircraft arrowed in and out of the airport at Ferney-Voltaire, named after the writer/philosopher who, disenchanted with the unappreciative Swiss, bought the land at Ferney in 1758 and was the driving force in transforming the desolate, depopulated village into a thriving town.

The French/Swiss frontier was marked by a simple red and white painted upraised barrier in le Bois de Chaton, which translates prettily into English as Catkin Woods. I passed it at 11.05 a.m. In a Swiss field a pair of thorough-bred horses were galloping for joy.

At 12.20 p.m., on the fifty-second day, and over 550 miles from where I had started, I reached Lake Geneva at le Creux de Genthod, a pretty little bay with yachts bobbing at anchor and children playing on the grass and shingle beach. Peter was waiting there for me. One-time employee and long-time friend, he owned and ran a ski-chalet just outside Chamonix, where he lived with his wife Zoë and daughter Nathalie, who was celebrating her first birthday today. They had invited me to stay with them while I waited for Terry to come and collect me and take me home.

'Sorry I'm late,' I said, being twenty minutes behind our agreed meeting time.

'Never mind. I'll overlook it in the circumstances.' He laughed.

I dropped the backpack and walked into the water. People no doubt thought I was rather odd as I filled the battered green jungle hat with water and tipped it over my head to cover the stupid tears that I could not stop from pouring down my face.

When I had gone to buy my boots five months earlier, I had set a price limit on them. However, I had fallen irredeemably in love with a pair of leather Meindl boots, which cost three times what I had planned, but I knew I had to have them.

I had asked the salesman: 'Are you sure these will last all the way to Geneva?'

He replied, very politely, 'Madame, if you do, they certainly will.'

And we all had.

When we arrived at Peter and Zoë's chalet, Zoë presented me with a soft pair of cotton slippers. 'I thought your feet might want a rest,' she smiled. Yes, they did. And I think they deserved it. Despite my ignorance and miscalculations, they had got us to our destination. I took them to soak in a deep hot bath, and lay there steaming, seeing the faces of all the people along the way: the charming mayor in Saint-Christophe; the black man on the bicycle; the postman and the undertaker; Carol and Norrie; the ladies who gave me water, willingly or otherwise; Dominique and Charles; all the men with hats; all the kind Dutch people; Madame Beaupain; Mowgli; Fred; Ron and Anne; the *gardien* and the doctors at Saint-Claude; the gorgeous colonel; the scruffy couple; all the restaurant staff who had made me feel welcome; Terry, who had financed the mission and supported me all along the way; Jennifer who had made it possible. I mused and puzzled over the often-heard remark that the French are unfriendly and unhelpful to foreigners. I started trying to count just how many people I owed thanks to for getting me here, but then I fell asleep.

THE END

We do hope that you have enjoyed reading this large print book.

Did you know that all of our titles are available for purchase?

We publish a wide range of high quality large print books including:
Romances, Mysteries, Classics
General Fiction
Non Fiction and Westerns

Special interest titles available in large print are:
The Little Oxford Dictionary
Music Book
Song Book
Hymn Book
Service Book

Also available from us courtesy of Oxford University Press:
Young Readers' Dictionary
(large print edition)
Young Readers' Thesaurus
(large print edition)

For further information or a free brochure, please contact us at:
Ulverscroft Large Print Books Ltd.,
The Green, Bradgate Road, Anstey,
Leicester, LE7 7FU, England.
Tel: (00 44) **0116 236 4325**
Fax: (00 44) **0116 234 0205**

Other titles published by
The House of Ulverscroft:

PILGRIM SNAIL

Ben Nimmo

Inspired by the murder of the girl he loved while working for charity in Belize, Ben Nimmo set out to play tribute to her memory and raise money for her memorial fund by walking from Canterbury to Santiago de Compostela in Spain — with a trombone. So began a nine-month, two thousand mile odyssey across Europe. Weighed down by a mammoth rucksack (the Pack From Hell) and his trusty trombone, sleeping in the open, in caves and ruined castles, jamming in smoky French bars and rain-swept Spanish streets, Ben struggled on, supported by old memories, new friends and improbable encounters — and an indomitable sense of humour.

A FREE SPIRIT

Betty Shine

A lifetime of healing has given Betty Shine an insight into the humanity that prevails in today's society. Though many people try to sweep these issues under the carpet, the interaction between every living thing on this planet affects us all. In fact, so many life forms have become extinct, it is only a matter of time before it happens to us. There is a way out, and that is for everyone who cares about our planet to take up the challenges represented in this book. With courage and tenacity you can become a Free Spirit. Whether an animal lover or simply seeking to improve your relationships, here is a simple philosophy that could change your life.

PINK STRIPES AND OBEDIENT SERVANTS

John Ainley

John Ainley was twenty-three when he went out to Tanganyika (Tanzania) as a Government Agricultural Field Officer in 1949, in an age when Britain still had African colonies. Here he writes a fascinating account of those distant times. Whether he is describing Africa's unlimited horizons, its people, or life without telephones, radio or television, he seems to have a special feeling for that immense country.

WUHU DIARY

Emily Prager

In 1994 Emily Prager adopted a seven-month-old baby in China. Almost five years later, she goes back with LuLu, now a little American girl, to spend three months in Wuhu, the town where her daughter was born in Southern China, searching for clues to unlock the mystery of LuLu. Looking beneath the surface of modern China, bringing real people and places vividly to life, this is a gripping and intensely moving account of their experiences, both poignant and funny, as well as the dramatic story of the search for LuLu's roots, and the meaning of family.

PARTNERS FOR LIFE

Jane Bidder

For over ten years, the charity Canine Partners has been making a real difference to disabled people's lives. Established to help people enjoy greater independence, each year the charity trains up to twenty carefully selected puppies and places them with suitable owners. These remarkable dogs are far more than just their masters' eyes or ears; they are among the most highly skilled and specialised dogs in the world. Here is a collection of moving, real-life stories about Canine Partners' dogs. Every one of them has assisted its severely disabled owner to live a richer and happier life.

SNARL FOR THE CAMERA

James Gray

This is a book about animals and the filming of animals. During his many years as a leading wildlife cameraman, James Gray has filmed everything from human lice (which he had to feed on his own blood) to elephants in Thailand, polar bears in the Arctic, anacondas in Venezuela, mountain gorillas in Uganda, and golden monkeys and pandas in China. James describes his (sometimes very scary) experiences filming wild animals — like the time he found he'd parked himself right on top of a polar bear's den — and he reveals the eye-opening truth behind the making of nature programmes.